Praise for *The Gatekeeper*

'Kate Fall was in many ways the heart and soul of the Cameron operation, a genuinely insightful and fascinating account of what it is like to be at the heart of power.' Tom Bradby, *ITV News at Ten*

'Kate Fall has a exquisite eye for telling details and a rare ability to express it.' Anthony Seldon, Historian

'For a decade, Kate Fall was the most influential woman in British politics. This is her fascinating, honest and sometimes hilarious story of life behind the door of No. 10.' Alice Thomson, *The Times*

'Kate Fall was David Cameron's indispensable right-hand woman as he ascended from Leaer of the Opposition to Prime Minister. A highly readable account of the rise and fall of the Cameroons, which historians will scour . . . a touching account of the demands that modern politics makes on people and their families. I read it, gripped, in one sitting,' Niall Ferguson, Milbank Family Senior Fellow, the Hoover Institution, Stanford

'Kate Fall was not just the gatekeeper; she was at the heart of the No. 10 operation.' Camilla Cavendish, *Financial Times*

The Gatekeeper

KATE FALL

ONE PLACE. MANY STORIES

HQ
An imprint of HarperCollins*Publishers* Ltd
1 London Bridge Street
London SE1 9GF

This edition 2020

1

First published in Great Britain by
HQ , an imprint of HarperCollins*Publishers* Ltd 2020

Copyright © Kate Fall 2020

Kate Fall asserts the moral right to be
identified as the author of this work.
A catalogue record for this book is
available from the British Library.

ISBN: 978-0-00-833609-7

Typeset by Palimpsest Book Production Ltd, Falkirk, Stirlingshire

Printed and bound in Great Britain by CPI Group (UK) Ltd, Croydon CR0 4YY

MIX
Paper from
responsible sources
FSC **FSC™ C007454**
www.fsc.org

This book is produced from independently certified FSC™ paper
to ensure responsible forest management.

For more information visit: www.harpercollins.co.uk/green

For Olivia and Guy

CONTENTS

INTRODUCTION

For eleven years, I lived my life as one of David Cameron's closest advisors. In No. 10 I sat right outside the door of the Prime Minister's office, earning myself the title of 'gatekeeper'. David called me his wingman. I wrote this book with the hope that it would shed some light on the world behind the public façade. The 'blood, sweat and tears'. The chaos and camaraderie. The friendships and fall outs. The victories and regrets. I want to share with others what it is like behind that famous door of No. 10, and behind the less famous but more critical one to the Prime Minister's den. And, what it feels like to live your life at the heart of power.

No. 10 is more than just an office for those who work there; it takes up so much of your time that it comes to signify a way of life. The pace is relentless and the work all-consuming. The time I spent working on 'Project Cameron' covered a good part of my daughter's and son's childhood – they were 6 and 3 when I started, and 17 and 14 when it was all over.

At its core, No. 10 is a 24/7, Rolls-Royce operation, whose purpose is to support the prime minister of the day. Ed Llewellyn and I were essentially there to run the show – in other words, to help Prime Minister David Cameron run an effective government: the strategy, the policies, the communication plans, the campaigns. We were involved in making decisions about what David was going to do and say each day, and for what purpose. We brokered relationships with the Cabinet, party, and others. Sometimes we were a shoulder to cry on, sometimes the deliverer of bad news. I sat at the centre of the spider's web, working with some of the brightest and the best people I have known.

I attended nearly every meeting with David. I spoke to him beforehand about what we were trying to achieve, and afterwards about what we wanted actioned. In the end, everything comes down to your judgement. Does the PM want to hear your view, day after day?

As one of David's closest advisors, I wasn't afraid to 'give it to him straight'. Sometimes you have to close the door and battle out the issues in a very small group, trusting that nothing of what is said will leave the room. This is why there is always 'an inner circle' of some sort around a prime minister, even if it forms to the consternation of some of those who do not find themselves in the room when the decisions are being made. As gatekeeper, one of my jobs was to decide who was in that room.

But the gatekeeper doesn't just manage access of people; you also moderate the flow of information. What is the priority today? You are there to manage the PM's time and attention.

The atmosphere of any No. 10 ultimately comes from the boss. Is it an effective, punctual, and decent operation that operates as one team? Or is it leaky, bitchy, and handicapped by rival factions? Can you see the PM if and when you need, or is there a bunker mentality? Here again, the skill of the gatekeeper is knowing when to keep the door shut – and also when to open it.

We were a close team, grounded by strong ties of friendship and political philosophy. We spent over a decade in each other's company, so it is not surprising that we shared so much – not just in our political journey, but also in life. We weathered many highs and lows. Successes and failures. Births and deaths. The absurd and the tragic. We faced difficult decisions to send British troops to fight; we made attempts to hold the peace. There are decisions we are still proud of – and a few of which we are less so.

We were elected in 2010 to fix a problem: to restore economic security amidst the uncertainty caused by the global financial crisis, and the worst recession since the Second World War. From 2010 to 2015, while in coalition with the Liberal Democrats, we were a government prepared to make difficult, unpopular decisions for the long-term good of the country, working to put Britain's finances back on track. We successfully spurred a recovery in jobs, though it was slower in boosting wages than we wanted. We tried to do other things too: reform schools, champion equality with gay marriage, stand by the world's poor, and open up a conversation about what is fair in welfare. Despite our differences, the economic rescue plan was the glue that bound the Coalition over five years.

In the pages that follow, I describe how we grappled with and tried to confront these big questions rather than dodge them. We believed that if you sweep difficult issues under the carpet, they have a way of coming back to bite you.

I try to show how and why, during our time in power, Britain was beginning to face an impasse in Europe. The other countries of the EU were hellbent on going in one direction, propping up the euro, while we were striving to carve out a different relationship. The financial crisis drove the Eurozone countries closer together, and encouraged migrants to come to Britain seeking work when our economy grew stronger. Meanwhile, those who had paid for the financial crisis at home didn't seem to be benefitting from our recovery. And all of this was playing out against the backdrop of a mandate that was fraying.

Our unexpected victory in the general election of 2015 gave us the prospect of five more years in power. We thought we were riding high. Instead, we crashed into a wall at full speed, falling out of Downing Street with all the harshness of abrupt defeat. Our strategy – to call out our relationship in Europe, and resolve it once and for all (by staying in) – failed. The sweetness of the election was short-lived, followed by the sadness, regret, and division surrounding the referendum.

I HAVE WORKED IN politics since I left university. I could have avoided it altogether and instead become a classical musician, which was my earlier trajectory – and might have been a more sensible decision. But I come from a political family (albeit with a small p). My father was a diplomat. His generation were the Cold War warriors, and his last post was as ambassador to Moscow, just after the break-up of the Soviet Union.

If I had to pinpoint the moment when my keen interest in politics began, it would have to be at a so-called 'informal' Sunday lunch at Lord Carrington's house, Bledlow. It was 1981, and I was about 12 years old. We were there because Lord Carrington was the Foreign Secretary and my father's then boss. At one point, Lord Carrington left the table to take a phone call. It was Prime Minister Margaret Thatcher.

When he returned, he turned to me and asked my view on the latest foreign debacle. He was intently interested in my answer – or at least that's how it seemed to me – and that was the beginning of my love affair with politics. When the time came, I chose to read PPE at Oxford instead of going to music school.

In 1996, at the end of the Major years, I started working at the Conservative Research Department as the desk officer for Europe. I was the junior member of the political team around the relevant Cabinet ministers, and I was responsible for briefing MPs on European issues. Apart from one other woman, the desk officers were an army of competitive young men, many of whom were eyeing a career in the House for themselves. But after nearly two decades of Tory rule, the party had begun to feel stale and tired, especially in comparison to the energetic young Tony Blair. The Major years came to an end with the massive Blair victory in 1997 and my situation changed.

With Prime Minister Blair came over a hundred female Labour MPs, who were irritatingly nicknamed 'Blair's babes'. The Conservatives had just thirteen women in Parliament. So, in 2001, with William Hague as our party leader and an election looming, there was a push to encourage more Tory women to be MPs. Some of my friends and direct contemporaries were selected to fight safe seats. I was on the candidates' list. But although I still loved politics, I was not convinced that I wanted to be an MP. Plus, I was pregnant with my second child. I had faced a constituency association while pregnant with my first. The good people of Derbyshire had eyed my stomach and asked my husband if he was the candidate. I decided not to stand.

Not long afterwards, David Cameron, whom I had known since Oxford, offered me a job on his campaign in Witney, Oxfordshire. So, in the early hours of 8 June 2001, heavily pregnant, I sat on an uncomfortable chair in a leisure centre sports hall as the count drew to an end and David was declared Witney's new MP.

That was my first campaign for David Cameron, but there would be many more. When David decided to run for Leader of the Opposition, he approached me again.

Then, five years later, life changed once more. It became normal for me to go home to my children and walk round the park with them, waiting for my phone to ring: 'No. 10 Switch here. Prime Minister on the line.'

THE HOLY GRAIL OF prime ministerial ambitions is to make a dignified exit at the time of their choosing. But more often than not, the exit is abrupt and unexpected. Suddenly the solidarity of purpose disappears. The team you have spent an uncountable amount of time with is disbanded, and everyone goes their separate ways. I imagine that it is always a shock, and the events of June 2016 were shocking indeed. On leaving No. 10, I found myself in a ditch, of sorts, and so I began to write my way out of it.

I wrote in the hope that I could shed some light on the world behind the façade of politics, to share with others what it is like behind that famous door. The blood, sweat, and toil. The chaos and comradery. The victories and regrets. The friendships and fallings-out. I wrote about my own experience of being part of a dedicated, focused team during the Cameron years, as well as more generally about what life is really like at the heart of power. I wrote about why the atmosphere of No. 10 matters, about how it feels to live your life at such a pace under so much pressure, much of it private, yet under the public gaze. Mine is a book which focuses on the political plumbing.

The first part of the story starts with pizza nights around the kitchen table as we planned a leadership campaign. We won control of the party and then tried to change it before the party decided they'd had enough of us. It goes on to fighting the 2010 general election, with all the stress, hilarity, boredom, and terror of being out on the road with the candidate in the full glare of the public eye. This was amplified by it being the year of the first *X Factor*-style TV debates.

The second part looks at life at the heart of No. 10: how it feels on your first day when you realise this is where you work now. Who really runs No. 10 and how do they do it? Why does a circle of trust always form around a prime minister, and how can we make sure the important voices from outside it are still heard? In the final part, the story explores our relationship with Europe, from the creation of the European Union, the Eurosceptics and the Europhiles to the fallout of the 2016 EU referendum.

WE HEAR A LOT about unelected advisors these days, the so-called 'spads'. This is the special political advisor who, for a time, acquires a semi-official status in government. At the most senior level, they form part of a prime minister's inner circle. I was a spad. They may be amongst the most powerful people in the country, yet you might never have never heard of them. (If you have, though, don't muddle power with profile; the two don't necessarily go together.) Their power comes from one source only: their boss. They are unelected and their sole function is to serve their boss. Those who forget this do so at their peril.

Spads are not a new invention. They have always existed in some form and always will, because a prime minister needs a close team of people who they can trust. Kings and queens had similar coteries of advisors or courtiers. Like today's spads, some of them got too powerful, too famous, or fell out of favour. Thomas Cromwell is perhaps the best-known spad in history.

A wider group of spads serves Cabinet ministers. Usually there are two spads for each minister – one to do the press and one to check the policy. They help their boss keep track of the large political operation that runs alongside their governmental role. Good luck telling them that their role is to support the prime minister of the day.

DO POLITICS AND FRIENDSHIP go together? I used to think so, but now I am less sure. Politics tests friendships with its conflicting priorities of loyalty, belief, and personal ambition. Sometimes you have to choose, and it's not always pretty. I examine what happens when, as they say, the shit hits the fan. How does the PM execute a reshuffle and, more importantly, cope with the aftermath, which can morph into revenge?

All premierships are a race against time, where you try to do the things you said you would do while simultaneously sorting out all the other stuff you didn't expect, which hurtles towards you from left field at great speed. The sand flows through the egg timer faster and faster – or so it feels – whilst the electorate eyes you up, wondering if they can bear seeing your face all over their TV for another five years. If you last that long, that is, because your future also depends on the people sitting on the benches behind you, the so-called faithful supporters, who are wondering the same. Over time, the sentiment of goodwill and loyalty towards a leader fades, as the number of those fired, added to the number of those who never got hired, reaches a critical mass. Then, like bees starved of royal jelly, they swarm in hope of better treatment by a new queen.

There have always been powerful, though mostly invisible, women running Downing Street, and in part this book tells how it felt to be one of them, working in what is still a relatively male world. I chose to work behind the scenes, but we still need more female MPs. So, I want to encourage women who set their sights on politics – whether in the front line or as an advisor – to be brave and push back on what can be a latent sense that a man's view carries greater weight in the world of politics. This includes not getting stuck in jobs that pay you to 'do things' rather than 'think things', if that's not what you want. There is still a sense that some topics are for women and others for men, as there is with domestic tasks. Men take out the rubbish and make fiscal policy; women do the dishes and look after 'women's issues'. At the time of writing, we have had two female prime ministers but, I wonder, when will we see a female Chancellor of the Exchequer?

POLITICS IS WAR WITH little peace. You fight for what you believe in and try to do the right thing, often to find your work is then unravelled by those who follow. And it is not just what you do that matters; it is how you do it.

Decency and tolerance in government matters. So does trying to rule for all, not just the majority. I have tried to show that the centre ground that we inhabited with our brand of modern progressive compassionate Conservatism was not a place of political compromise and watered-down policy designed to appease everyone, but rather a place of bold, brave, creative thinking about how to resolve our problems. And for a while, it resonated with the electorate.

Yet, alas, the Brexit fog clouds these months and years after our departure. As with all major political events, there is fury, division, and blame. The chaos and antipathy weigh heavily. Did David get it all right? Of course not. But find me someone else with the temperament and depth of judgement more suited to the leadership of our country. David the decisive leader; George Osborne the creative political intellect – this partnership dominated a decade of politics. Britain will wait a long time for another government that is as decent and effective, one that can achieve so much.

I believe that we were a government with a sense of purpose, a group of people who weren't afraid to do what we believed was right to turn our country around. Some accused our team of being too close, but that seems like a small criticism when set against the deeply divided politics of today. Personally, all I can do is hope I did my best for my boss and the country – and didn't let it go to my head.

It was the greatest privilege of my life to work in David Cameron's No. 10 with some of the best and brightest people I have known. It was certainly life-altering. There will always be regrets; otherwise, you won't have learnt anything. It was a roller-coaster ride, but I would not have missed it for the world.

PART 1

Journey to Power

BLACKPOOL

Blackpool, October 2003. I have not been to a party conference since having had my two children, and I've left my job working at the Conservative Research Department, so I don't strictly need to be here. However, I have decided to make a brief trip up because I am still officially on the parliamentary candidates' list. I feel out of place wandering around the neglected conference hall wearing an old work dress, which is now a little tight-fitting. Why ever did I think I ought to come?

There's no getting away from it: the Conservative Party Conference is a ghost town. Morale is low; the delegates seem quieter than usual. It's no wonder. The Conservatives, stubbornly polling around 32 per cent of the vote, with a historically small number of Tory MPs, have now lost two general elections to New Labour and are well on their way to losing a third. Nobody seems to know what to do about it. Under Iain Duncan Smith, they have begun to look less and less like a party of government and more and more like a political movement. The party is languishing in a vacuum of leadership and of ideas. There is a sense that it has turned in on itself, forgotten how to reach out beyond its base, or even that it wants to.

A party conference is not just an opportunity to cheer up the party faithful. It is supposed to mark the start of the political year, the moment the leadership sets its course. And, especially if you are in opposition, it is a rare moment in the sun. For a few golden days, the spotlight will fall on you as the media gather to hear what you have to say. This is your chance to set out your stall to the party but also to the public at large. Above all, party conference week is show time (accompanied of course by a series of alcohol-infused, gossip-rendering after-parties).

Blackpool, with its strings of lights, amusement arcades, and air of faded grandeur, is a peculiar host. It seems incongruous when hordes of politicians, journalists, lobbyists, and activists, old and young, pour in to this unassuming town, mostly populated by pensioners, filling up every hotel, hostel, and bed and breakfast. But there is something about the freshness of the coastal wind and the kindness of the reception we receive that helps to propel us through an exhausting and totally unhealthy week. I loathe and love conference week in equal measure. Though this year I feel a particularly deep sense of relief when, exhausted, I get on the train to leave.

IDS lasts barely another month. Without a contest, the Tory MPs rally around to crown Michael Howard as the new party leader in November. Michael manages to take control of the party and draw it back, for which he deserves great credit. But while he saves the party from political oblivion, he does not transform it into something new and electable. That is to be another man's job.

Michael announces he is standing down the day after he is defeated in the 2005 election, calling a leadership election for early autumn. There is a growing movement, especially amongst the 1992 and 1997 intakes of MPs, to avoid a full-blown competition. They want a coronation rather than a contest. And they want someone of their own political persuasion; the focus falls on David Davis. But there is pushback from those who think the party should be given a real choice. After all, they didn't get to choose Michael Howard. There are also some who actively don't want DD. He is not without talent, but he is the sort of old-school Tory – reciting a mantra of tax cuts, tough on crime, and Europe – that the electorate has rejected three times already. There is a mounting view that something more innovative and radical is needed if the

Conservatives are ever going to be a party of government again.

Under pressure, Michael moves the date for the leadership election back to December. This gives an outsider a chance.

I HAVE BEEN WORKING as part of Michael Howard's team, juggling a role in his office covering foreign affairs and business liaison with a job working as the director of Atlantic Partnership, a bipartisan think-tank that Michael himself set up. I run the think-tank from my attic, which has the advantage of allowing me to see my young children. On his return from nursery, my son makes his way upstairs and hovers at the bottom of the loft ladder. 'Are you there, Mummy?' He waits patiently for me to climb down and keep him company while he eats his lunch. I often return to my attic after tucking him and his sister up in bed. I feel a bit stretched, between the two roles and, most importantly, being a mum. But at least I am busy doing what I love.

All this is about to change.

One day in June, I am getting my lunch at the canteen in Portcullis House. I am not overly fond of the place, which serves large quantities of 'school food' and has yet to encounter the lettuce leaf, but I like the atmosphere. Everyone eats here – MPs, researchers (many barely out of university), parliamentary assistants. It is a place of chance meetings and political gossip.

In the canteen, I spot David Cameron. He is in his first term as MP for Witney and a friend since we both read PPE at Oxford, a year apart. And I had helped him win the seat in 2001.

'What are you up to?' David asks.

I tell him we are winding down Michael's office in preparation for his departure, which is sad. The leadership election has just been announced and I have heard that David is considering stepping forward to offer a more centrist, modern agenda. This seems as good a time as any to offer my twopence worth, so I do. 'Oh, and by the way, I think you should run for leader,' I say. I then add – with possibly not enough consideration – 'I'll help you if you do.'

I am not the only person urging him to run. David has a natural gravitas and authority about him that seems to be lacking elsewhere in the party. In this respect, he looks like a potential winner. But he is unsure. It does seem like a tall order that someone who has only been an MP for one term, who has not yet reached their fortieth birthday, should seek to be party leader. Audacious even. But who else is there? If the party really do want a game changer, then it's not going to be DD.

David takes his time. While he ponders whether or not to run, he accepts a job as Shadow Education Secretary in Michael's post-election Shadow Cabinet. George Osborne, who also became an MP in 2001, in the same intake as David, becomes Shadow Chancellor, and asks me to come and work for him. With over four years in age between them, David and George did not overlap at university in Oxford, or even in their previous jobs at the Conservative Research Department, but they have become close as new MPs. They live near each other in west London, bicycling in together most mornings.

I've known George a long time – since my first job in the Conservative Research Department, in fact. The dream of every desk officer was to be a special advisor to a Cabinet minister. I asked around about how this could be done. You need to nurture a friendship with an MP 'going up', I was told. Otherwise, just send in your CV when there's a reshuffle and hope for the best.

When William Waldegrave was replaced by Douglas Hogg at the Ministry of Agriculture, Fisheries and Food in 1995, I wondered if it might be my opportunity. Admittedly, having grown up in cities, I didn't know much about farming. But, as the desk officer covering the brief for Europe, my remit included agriculture and animals, so I was certainly learning, and I reckoned I should be in with a chance.

I had decided to try the idea out on the boy in the office next to mine. George was highly regarded in CRD as the prestigious head of 'political section', a job which had until recently been inhabited by another talented young man called David Cameron.

'I am thinking about applying to be a special advisor to Douglas Hogg,' I said. 'Do you think it is a crazy idea, given that, you know, farming is not exactly my thing?'

'No – it's a very good idea,' he said. 'There's just one hitch.'

'What's that?' I asked.

'I've already got the job.'

A WEEK AFTER I accept the job with George, David rings. 'I've decided to stand – will you come and help me run the campaign?'

'What sort of timing?' I ask.

'Tomorrow,' he says.

I speak to George, who agrees I should help David, and then come and work for him afterwards.

It has been an honour to work for Michael Howard, and I feel disloyal as I pack up my things. And there is awkwardness too, as I know that I would not have been David's first choice. Rachel Whetstone had been Michael's political secretary, and she and David were firm political friends from their time together in the CRD. Had they not fallen out, it would most certainly be her, not me, running his campaign.

I move into David's office and the leadership campaign begins. On my first day, there is only me and David, with George next door and Steve Hilton texting random thoughts. I feel pleased to still be working in Westminster but I have no idea what running a leadership election entails. Perhaps that's why I have no premonition that it is about to take over my life – and not just for a summer, but for the next decade. I sit in blissful naivety, innocent of the looming storm.

2

'COME WITH ME'

Most leadership campaigns are set up around an individual. An idea or two. And a few loyal friends. David's was set up around building a new brand of Conservatism. He and a group of key allies have been busy crafting it for a while. So, I am initiated into this Sunday night group, to eat pizza and chart a new course for the party.

The Camerons' home in west London is modern and chic, with black and white pictures of their glamorous wedding guests lining the walls. Sitting round the kitchen table are David, George, and a few other faces, some familiar. There's the Diet Coke-swilling Daniel Finkelstein, who has finally given up on trying to be an MP after a few attempts in favour of a career in journalism. Danny hones his humour into a highly targeted weapon, waiting for lulls in the conversation to launch his witty one-liners. Oliver Letwin looks permanently confused by finding himself in politics at all – as if he has fallen unexpectedly out of a Tolstoy novel and is trying to find his way back as a matter of urgency. Then there is Steve Hilton, one of David's closest friends – a radical blue-sky thinker cum March hare whose mood swings can confuse everyone, including himself. And sometimes we have Michael Gove, a courteous and brilliant Scottish journalist who is shyly considering a political career for himself. He always speaks like he is presenting a bouquet of the sweetest smelling flowers.

David is the natural head boy to George's more bumptious, 'rock the boat' style. Both are clever and talented but in different ways. This partnership, which seems almost brotherly, is to remain at the heart of our operation: George, the creative intellectual, and David, the intuitive decision taker. Although their politics are not entirely aligned – David comes from more traditional conservative stock, whereas George embraces all that is modern, sophisticated, and liberal – they mostly see eye-to-eye. They are fiscal conservatives and passionate social liberals. And perhaps because I know them both well, I play my part in keeping them close, especially when we later come into government, when convention conspires to divide them.

These two men are the 'creative intellectuals' of Team Cameron. They are progressive Conservatives, whose beliefs are anchored in sound finance. The aim is to move the party back towards the centre ground that has for too long been occupied by Labour under Tony Blair. They call themselves 'Modern Compassionate Conservatives'.

Alongside these 'ideas' people is a small but faithful band of MPs, many of them ex-Army: Hugo Swire, Hugh Robertson, Andrew Robathan, and Greg Barker, who are busy drumming up support for David amongst the parliamentary party. David's old friend, and mine, Andrew Feldman, joins our operation as fundraiser-in-chief. His role is important not only for the campaign itself, but for showing that David has support from the wider Conservative family and the business community. Andrew takes to the task with the enthusiasm of a pit pony released into pasture.

Our select group meet in David's Commons office most days. There are lots of ideas and lots of action points, but only me to do the action. (I find that most MPs prefer to 'advise' rather than 'do'.)

I am swamped with work, at the centre of a tiny tornado. I am trying to manage David, manage the campaign, and organise a growing team. As the campaign builds momentum, we are inundated with offers of help. My phone doesn't stop ringing. I set up a makeshift office in David's rooms in Portcullis House, where I sit with my laptop balanced on my knees. Steve, now sitting beside me, sketches out a plan of articles and speeches for the weeks ahead. He calls this 'the Grid'. We persuade George Eustice, a talented young press officer from Conservative Campaign Headquarters to join us. And now we are three. Between us, we are drafting articles, writing speeches, arranging media interviews, meeting with MPs, hunting for endorsements, and thinking about our strategy.

A LEADERSHIP CAMPAIGN IS like a mini general election. You need to stand for something. Be someone. Plot your interventions carefully, think about what you are saying, and how it will resonate in the media and beyond. To build up momentum you need endorsements from MPs, councillors, and other party grandees, as well as businessmen saying they would trust you with the country's finances. Having a bit of money behind you helps as well. At the same time, you must not lose sight of who your electorate is. In a leadership election, this is first and foremost 'the colleagues', meaning the MPs. Beyond them are the party membership more generally.

There is a norm in politics that in order to win Tory leadership elections you need to tack right to pick up support in the party and then move towards the centre afterwards to appeal to the country. Early on, we reject this in favour of saying something about what we want to achieve. David boldly sets out his Conservative 'modernising' stall knowing that he will put off some of his colleagues but hoping the wider public will like what they see. If we can show that David Cameron is a 'winner', then the MPs might begin to take notice – especially those in marginal seats. It is a high-risk strategy.

Perhaps it was at this moment that David's rather contractual relationship with his parliamentary party was forged. He never wooed them and in turn they never fell in love with him. But they recognised and respected him as someone who could lead them back into power. The consequence of this would be that when they thought he was not delivering, there was no love lost. Support melted away like ice cream on a summer's day.

We march on. David gives a series of speeches, interviews, and articles, talking about the ills in society and the importance of social responsibility – issues which have been, until now, largely marginalised. He asks the party to think more about these problems and less about Europe. His focus does seem to resonate, bringing a breath of fresh air to a stale political environment. The papers like what they hear. People are listening.

Then we hit choppy waters. A two-week 'trial by tabloid' ensues over whether or not David took drugs in his youth. The story runs and runs, until we think we will never put it behind us. But then they finally peter out, and we're at last able talk about something else.

Back on track, summer approaches and with it comes the 'big beasts', with Ken Clarke, Malcolm Rifkind, Liam Fox, and others joining the race, and suddenly David looks young and a bit out of his depth. There is a low moment when he is convinced he is going to fail. As we walk across the lobby of Portcullis House, David says to me, 'At some point we need to discuss how I pull out, in a dignified way.'

'Pull out of what?' I ask, confused.

'You know, admit defeat.'

'But we're going to win,' I reply.

Over the next weeks, even I have to admit we are not winning – in fact, we are not gaining any ground at all. It is all DD versus Clarke and Fox, with DD remaining the firm favourite. And it is time to head off for our various family summer holidays. Struggling to find internet coverage in a friend's villa in Spain, I take to standing on a chair to send emails in the hours when my children are resting. Steve and I prearrange times to speak, so he in turn can walk to the end of a field to get a signal. It is a relief when we all are back in London.

In early September, the tide shifts suddenly again, as it does so often in politics, and just for a moment we are given another chance. DD gives his formal leadership launch, surrounded by mostly white, mostly middle-aged men in what looks like a club room in the Commons. His speech is more select committee hearing than rousing oration. The whole things feels a bit out of date.

Although DD has a strong political foundation – son of a single mother, brought up on a council estate – he has no vision. He's all backstory, no forward movement. We seem to have the opposite problem: David has so much he wants to do for his country, but his happy, privileged childhood is hard to build a political narrative around.

Steve and I meet to discuss our next move. We have run out of money. We decide to go ahead with a formal launch of David's leadership bid anyway. Andrew Feldman rises to the occasion and finds the cash. Our launch is fresh and modern, and the audience is a far cry from a men's club, as Samantha fills the room with young mothers, some of whom are breastfeeding. David's speech captures the imagination. Suddenly he is the coming man again.

THE LAST WEEK OF September leading into party conference is pandemonium. I wake up on Friday relieved to think I have a day to play with, and then I remember David wants to meet at a tapas restaurant on Golborne Road he is fond of. He bills it as a 'take stock' lunch before we all head up to Blackpool. I am uncomfortably aware that time is ticking, plus I have promised to pick my daughter up from school and take her out for tea. We are only a third of the way down our checklist (speech, press, visits, ties . . .) when Danny Finkelstein drops by. I know what's missing, he says. American-style mementos to hand out – bells and whistles. Great idea, everyone says, nodding away, only it's clearly me who is going to have to magically conjure up these items at the eleventh hour. Right now, I wish Danny would just stop having great ideas, or any ideas at all.

We head up to Blackpool with 'the mo', as the Americans are fond of saying. But although we have the momentum, we have a long, long way to go. We have the backing of just fourteen MPs – the 'early Cameroons', as David later dubs them.

At conference, there is a growing sense of excitement around

David. We are hounded by camera crews and enthusiastic supporters. Our team roams the halls wearing 'I love DC' T-shirts and handing out badges. DD has a group of women decked out in T-shirts saying 'DD for me'; most of them are large-breasted, which hits a sexist note. Steve is too edgy to sleep. Rachel Whetstone (his future wife) has booked him in to the main conference hotel to help with Michael Howard's valedictory speech. From his room, he pens a conference newsletter, 'DC News', which he prints from a mobile printer overnight. Our supporters put copies under people's doors in the early hours of the morning. Broadcasters are clutching their sheets as they begin their morning rounds. There is a sense that we are fighting for it, and people – on the whole – like to be fought for, in a robust democracy.

However, by this point, the conference has morphed into a beauty parade. Expectation around the candidates' speeches is growing. David and I sneak onto the balcony to watch DD. His speech feels flat and workmanlike to us. 'Don't smile,' says David. 'People are watching us.'

David is up shortly. We sit in the green room at the back, still feeling very much the outsiders. David has been practising his speech for days. A few minutes before he goes on, Steve, Samantha, and I are taken to our seats. I feel a bit sick. Steve is wriggling in his chair. I am amazed: Samantha is all pregnant calm.

'Come with me,' says this audacious one-term MP as he lays out his vision for the Conservative Party's future of aspiration and social responsibility.

He electrifies the audience, not least the party grassroots, who are tired of being in opposition and served up a diet of thin political gruel. At this moment, they have no idea where this young man is heading exactly, but it's clear they want to be going somewhere new. We just have to hope that – when it comes time to cast their vote for leader – they are in the mood to take a bit of a risk.

Tom Bradby declares on the *ITV Evening News* that David won the hall.

We leave Blackpool with the support of forty-two MPs and the resounding enthusiasm of party activists. It is interesting that this group, who are often parodied for their affection of the status quo, have so fully supported the candidate of change.

It remains a crowded field, however, and Ken Clarke, Liam Fox, and DD himself are still very much in the running. Yet, it feels as if we are now on our way. At the very least, we will have shifted the conversation in the party.

The official leadership election begins with a series of ballots amongst the MPs, who whittle the candidates down to two. The final choice from these two is put in the hands of the wider party membership. Michael Spicer, as head of the 1922 Committee of Conservative backbenchers, adjudicates the rules of engagement as if supervising a duel.

Whilst it may be the case that no man is an island, it is soon evident to me that every MP is a planet, many in a rather unfamiliar orbit. Each potential leader is vying for their support, so this is the moment of maximum power for the backbench MP, and they exercise it to the full. In practice, this means hours of one-to-one meetings. They each arrive with a mysterious cocktail of asks, personal and political, some driven by ambition, others by friendships or dislikes, even revenge. They seem to want their leader to be of them but also above them. Most of all, they want to back a winner and then, down the line, to be promoted by them.

David does not find this bit easy. Many MPs are not sure about him. For some this is because they fear he is too centrist for their taste, but for others, it's more personal. They think he has had a golden life – private money, a good-looking wife (who works!). His family is in London, while theirs live miles away. Some feel he has arrived in Parliament already the coming man, while they have struggled for recognition. And then there is the irritation that he does not always catch their eye when he passes them in the corridor. He does not mean to do this, but he does. This has given him a reputation amongst his colleagues of being a little aloof. I spend a lot of time with David talking about eye contact.

We also have to talk to him about his suits. We wean him off his double-breasted baggy jackets, which make him look a bit like a jolly farmer. A new, smart 'David the candidate' emerges, with single-breasted jackets and a firmer 'look'. He is also beginning to acquire a certain homegrown charisma.

We are nervous going into the first ballot of MPs. David Davis remains the mainstream candidate, but Liam Fox seems to be gaining momentum on the right. It's quite possible we may crash and burn in the middle. But David comes second in the first ballot of MPs, with fifty-six votes to DD's sixty-two. And then he comes first in the second ballot, with a strong ninety MPs (and DD down to fifty-seven).

Wind in our sails, we move on to the next battle: convincing the party membership. The final ballot is fixed for 6 December. It is weeks of regional tours and hustings against DD. And it is not all plain sailing. DD knows how to press the buttons of the Tory heartland. But David Cameron seems to appeal to Middle England, possibly because he shares their values. (This is a man who would cook a full Sunday lunch to eat on his own.) And David is giving them hope.

In the middle of the leadership campaign, we hit a glitch. David, now the favourite to win, gets incredibly nervous ahead of a special *Question Time* debate. It is a surprise because until now he has been so natural on television. Relaxed and accessible, he usually impresses by actually trying to answer the audience's questions. Yet this time he seizes up, his hand reaching up constantly to wipe away the sweat forming on his top lip. I find it hard to watch. This is the first time this happens to David but not the last. There is something in the intense pressure of these moments that can be too much to bear, especially once you have become the frontrunner.

The final hustings is in Exeter, and we return to Hugo Swire's Devon home for a feast to celebrate his birthday. The meal comes courtesy of Hugo's wife, Sasha Swire, who is an extraordinary cook and a sharp critic of all things political. Sasha has a camera, and – *Snap* – a picture is taken of Team Cameron, comprised at this moment of David, Hugo, Liz Sugg, Sophie Pym, James Cecil, and me, sitting on the sofa. We've had a couple of glasses of wine, and we're relaxed, nearing the end of the campaign, with nothing much left to do but wait and see if we have convinced the party membership that this one-term MP should be their leader.

WE ARRIVE AT THE Royal Academy for the announcement of who will be the next leader of the Conservative Party. David is getting miked up when Michael Spicer comes in and whispers in his ear. He has won. When we have finished with the speeches and fanfare, we find Terry, Michael Howard's former driver, waiting for us in the courtyard. David is the Leader of the Opposition now, and as such, he gets a car and driver.

'Where do you want to go?' Terry asks.

I look at David, the victory beginning to sink in, and wonder what we have got ourselves into. We had better go to Norman Shaw South – to Michael Howard's old offices, tucked away at the far side of the parliamentary estate.

I wander through the abandoned rooms, looking out over the beautiful view of the Thames and the London Eye beyond. It has been a tough journey back to my old desk. Now I am to be deputy chief of staff to the Leader of the Opposition. We have persuaded Ed Llewellyn, another old colleague from the Conservative Research Department and former political advisor to Chris Patten and Paddy Ashdown, to return from Bosnia to be David's chief of staff. Despite being only a few years older than me, Ed already has the air of an experienced public servant and brings a stamp of credibility and professionalism to the team. He is not one to throw his weight around (in any sense; he is a not a large man), having instead a quiet but firm authority and soft charm. Ed will sit in the desk opposite to me for the next eleven years. We are a team from day one.

I join David in his office. We have PMQs the next morning, and he needs to prepare.

3

THE CLUNKING FIST

We are, we realise, in a mess.

Gordon Brown is basking in a prolonged honeymoon, having replaced Tony Blair as prime minister a few months previously, whereas we have just gone through a series of disasters. There is talk of a snap election. Labour are ahead in the polls, so if this happens they are most likely to win. Things do not look promising. I feel we may be in danger of morphing into a one-party state, with Labour entrenched in power while we remain side-lined and in exile.

'He was the future once,' said a cocky David to Blair during their first PMQs exchange, to roars from the Tory benches. When Blair left the Commons for the last time and the Labour benches got to their feet, so too did David and George, gathering the rest behind them. Then Brown – the 'clunking fist' as Blair described him – arrived in No. 10 in 2007, and the polls surged to Labour.

Despite the hesitancy of some on the more traditional wing of the party, the Conservatives had been starting to look to be electable again under David's leadership. But in light of Brown's recent success in the polls, the chorus of discontent from parts of our own party is growing louder.

However, Brown lacks a mandate of his own from the electorate, and it makes sense for him to go to the country quickly while he looks strong and new. We fully expect an election announcement any minute.

In addition to our woes in light of the appeal of fresh-and-serious Brown (we still cannot believe this), our own party is in a bad mood with us. When David asked them to 'Come with me' to change first the party and then the country, he really meant it. But some have found the realities harder to bear. We are focused on social responsibility: fixing our 'broken society' and 'hugging hoodies' (as the press put it; David never actually says this). We also advocate doing our bit for the world's poor and set about trying to get more women into Tory seats. None of these are traditional party issues, to put it mildly.

As we move the party towards the centre, it is not surprising that we annoy the 'core'. Their aggravation grows with the daily drip, drip, drip of criticism from some of the Tory press. We're still recovering from a row about grammar schools in May 2007, which brought things to boiling point. Since then, there have been demands to add more mentions of 'tax cuts' and 'Europe' to David's repertoire.

We have continued to try to be fresh and modern, not just in what we have to say but in how we say it. At town hall meetings up and down the country, David likes to surprise people by answering their questions directly. We call these 'Cameron Directs'. We video David and post them online. We call these 'webCameron'. We have set up chances for David to work as a teacher in Hull and live with a Muslim family in Balsall Heath, Birmingham, a genuine effort to engage with people's lives outside the SW1 bubble.

David is also the first leader of a major political party to embrace 'green' issues. He launches our local government campaign with the slogan 'Vote Blue, Go Green', and our first foreign trip was not to Washington but to the Arctic, to highlight climate change. It's brave – and it's brilliant politically, as it's helping to remould the party, which has become stuck in a certain mindset, including with regards to the environment. It has been a conscious rebranding exercise in which Steve Hilton has played a crucial part.

Years later, Tom Bradby, then political editor of ITV News, tells me over lunch that he feels responsible for David's political success on two accounts. One, because he called his speech at Blackpool in 2005. Tom was clear: David Davis flopped and David Cameron blew them away. Two, because he never reported what a 'total dick' David looked when he fell off his dog sled on our Arctic trip. We have been friends ever since.

Yet despite all our new ideas and thinking, the truth is that in opposition you only have the promise of change. You have no country to run, no real power. At most you have the power to influence. You are only as good as your last sound bite, at the mercy of events you largely have no control of, working against a machine of government that is much bigger and stronger than you. You have to be agile and make the most of opportunities as they arise. Government doesn't like working on weekends, so you can make a speech on Saturday, and it will take them a week to agree a policy.

Our greatest challenge has been trying to keep momentum going, keeping the feeling alive that David encapsulates the potential for realising long-awaited change. We operate as a small, tightly knit group on permanent standby, 24/7. We must be able to react to a moving situation in real time.

So, it has been a busy time for all of us, but especially for David. For most of the pressure falls on the leader in opposition, because they are the only figure the public really knows. David has grown into the role. He is more focused, more assured, and more professional, and he looks more polished. And all this despite the fact that he is now a father of three, with the arrival of his second son on Valentine's Day 2006.

'You cannot call your child Elwen,' says his bossy press secretary, Gabby Bertin. The boy is duly named Arthur, a good English name. But Arthur is quickly discarded at home and for evermore, in favour of Elwen.

Now that my own children are at school, working full-time seems more achievable. Even so, Project Cameron is less a job and more total immersion. Each of us is able to manage our family lives because David is careful to make time for his, but we are always on call. Always working, from the playground or the park.

Can we try to keep the mewling and puking down, David asks, as we grapple with our young children on evening and weekend calls.

IN SUMMER 2007, WE have planned a trip to Rwanda and Pakistan. The African leg is to visit a new social project that is the brainchild of Shadow International Development Secretary Andrew Mitchell. But then the rain starts to come down in buckets and the UK is covered in floods. Witney, David's constituency, is hit especially badly. We argue amongst ourselves about whether or not David should go ahead with the trip. There is a team call to make a final decision over the weekend. I am in Devon perched on a sea wall, surrounded by water, so naturally I lean towards staying (though I am not scheduled to join them on this occasion). Others, like George Eustice, think pulling out looks panicky. We plough ahead with the trip. The result is disastrous: classic 'leader abroad while Blighty sinks' stuff. Then there is a power cut as David addresses the Rwandan parliament, which just about sums it all up.

George Eustice rings me regularly from the trip. 'Things aren't so bad,' he says cheerily.

'Well don't be fooled,' I say. 'It's a complete disaster back here.'

This begins a tradition, which stays with us throughout our time, of the 'away team' being out of sync with the 'home team' during foreign trips. The 'away team', utterly satisfied by their diet of red carpets and banquets, seems oblivious to the press coverage and always thinks the trip is going swimmingly. The 'home team' – which is normally me, as I try to avoid being away from my children too often – is surrounded by *Daily Mail* headlines that don't make for happy reading. On the countless occasions, I try to explain this to David he says, 'Don't read the bloody *Mail*.'

The floods seem to symbolise a summer of falling polls and fading prospects. So, faced with mounting pressure from our own party and the prospect of an early election being called by a seemingly confident Brown, we start to prepare a lifesaving party conference and manifesto. Just in case.

Over the years, we will finesse our approach to party conference, building it around a strong, clear message and trying to deliver ten good announcements that fit with our big-picture narrative. It is a simple strategy: keep the predators from writing about things we don't want them to, by giving them lots of things to write about that we do.

We need some nice, softer stories for this weekend's interviews. A hospital visit for the Saturday. Something strong for *The Andrew Marr Show*.

Monday is George's day, and he wants at least one story to brief into the morning papers as well as one for the conference hall. Tuesday is our weakest day, when things can blow off course. (In later years, it will become Boris day, and we will never have a clue what he is going to say, though we are pretty sure it will overshadow everything else.) Wednesday is David's big speech.

We spend the week before conference in a manic series of policy meetings and speech prep while standing by on 'election alert'. We reach Friday without Brown having called an election, to sighs of relief all around the office. We have a strong programme of policy announcements and a media plan ready to roll out. We are as ready as we are ever going to be.

Most secret of all is George's plan to announce the abolition of inheritance tax for homes worth less than £1 million. We think this is the right thing to do, and it is also about time to throw a bit of red meat at our unhappy supporters who are tired of their menu of soya beans. This new policy is known only to David's and George's teams, and we trust each other completely.

Then I look up to see George's chief of staff, Matt Hancock, approaching my desk. He has bad news: the entire conference policy package, which was due to be sent to him, has in fact been emailed by mistake to Mike Hancock, the Liberal Democrat MP whose email address is HancockM rather than Matt's HancockMJ.

'Fuck,' says Andy Coulson, who has recently joined the team as. the new head of communications and must now be wondering what he's got himself into. It is what we are all thinking. We break the news to David. Over the years I learn that he always takes very bad and very good news in exactly the same way: with a calm acceptance of fate. There is a long discussion about whether we should phone this guy called Mike Hancock and beg him to be merciful. Some think a call might simply alert him to the email. We decide to leave it. We will know soon enough. After a week of waiting for an election to be called, we are now anxiously expecting the Lib Dems to reveal all our policies on the eve of the conference. We may as well pack up and go home. Which is precisely what we do. There is nothing to do but wait and hope.

By the time we arrive in Blackpool we are all nervous wrecks, watching the television anxiously. We discuss whether to bring forward any of the announcements, but decide against. It is heads down, let's get on with the plan.

By Sunday night it's clear there is a god – he is called Mike Hancock! – who clearly does not check his emails on a Friday afternoon. At least not on this occasion.

The week progresses as well as can be. I stand at the back of the hall with Ed to listen to George make his big announcement on inheritance tax. No one is expecting it, and there is a roar of approval from the audience. He looks so surprised and pleased with himself, we are worried he is going to burst out laughing. David joins him on the stage and pats him on the back. A gesture of pride in his friend and political ally, and also of relief. Something is going to plan.

After he won the leadership, many had urged David to move George and make way for a more experienced Shadow Chancellor, someone who might complement David's own youth. But he did not. Instead, when the pressure mounted, he chose to appoint Ken Clarke as Shadow Business Secretary to add a bit of grey hair to the economy team. Right from the start, David embraced George as his political partner and equal.

As we approach the end of conference week, there is a growing excitement around David's speech. This year, however, there is a twist. We'd been well into our twentieth draft when Steve had taken David aside and persuaded him he must make the speech from memory, his argument being that this was one of those moments when you need to stun the audience, and an ordinary scripted speech would not cut through. It started as their secret – David and Steve's. Steve loves to do things secretly, which is ironic for someone who is so keen on transparency.

'God, this is high-risk,' said Ed, nervously, when we found out. 'Just don't mess up,' George added, helpfully. Andy remained silent, probably wondering once more why he had joined this mad house.

At the Imperial, I watch David pace up and down his suite while he tries to memorise pages and pages of text.

Then Andy has a sort of 'surrogate' meltdown about Samantha's outfit for the next day (he is actually anxious about David delivering his speech from memory). She is not yet in the habit of finding a 'conference dress'. We show Andy the options, which, in his eyes, fall short. Always with an eye to the photos, he wants bright colours, and Samantha has chosen elegant black. He charges furiously down the hotel corridor and demands to see my wardrobe. I am about five inches shorter than her, but Andy is undeterred. Flicking through my dresses he turns and says: 'That's the one.' And in that horrible moment I realise that he is referring to the dress I am wearing. A favourite, it is black and white with angels and hearts all over it. Apparently, I have no say in the matter. Dress duly handed over, Samantha takes to the stage, looking much better in it than me.

I wait with David in the wings for Liz Sugg to give the go-ahead. Soundtrack: The Killers. David walks onto the stage to deliver what we hope will be another career-altering speech. It is. A full fifty minutes without a single false note. He takes the conference patiently through his aspirations for the country and, hearing him addressing them so directly, his audience responds.

David leaves Blackpool with the goodwill of his party behind him. We are all so exhausted that we can hardly speak. But I am not so tired I cannot make it to my own birthday party, which my husband has arranged with my twin sister. The celebration soon evolves into a 'We saved the day' party, as, straight off the train from Blackpool, Team Cameron join us.

But we have not quite saved the day. The mood about us may be more positive, but there is still talk of Brown calling an early election. And everything depends on whether our conference has had any effect on the polls. Walking back from CCHQ with George and Oliver Letwin on the Friday morning after the conference, we hear rumours that the election is going ahead. We are full of despair. Oliver quickens his pace. He has a manifesto to write! It turns out to be a false alarm. A key poll comes through: we have drawn level with Labour.

In the end, Prime Minister Brown, who has waited over a decade for the crown, cannot bear to take the risk of losing it after just a few months. Gordon bottles it and we are back in business. We'll have another chance to convince the country that we have something to say – that there is another way but Labour.

4

PLAN A

B y the time we face the Tory faithful the following year, it is not our political future we are battling for, but the entire global financial system, which is in meltdown. On 15 September 2008, Lehman Brothers files for bankruptcy, and there are rumours that the whole financial system is about to collapse. The US Congress is trying to vote through a rescue package, which it first rejects on 29 September – the eve of our party conference. Things feel extremely precarious. While Brown's honeymoon period had looked to be well over, now he has been granted a second lease of life, heading off to New York to save the world while we sit in Birmingham looking like an irrelevance.

Ed Llewellyn, Andy Coulson, Matt Hancock, and I join George, David, and Samantha for our customary dinner to take stock on the eve of conference and prep David for his appearance on *The Andrew Marr Show*. We ponder our predicament over steak (for the boys) and Caesar salad (for Samantha and me) in David's smart new suite, complete with a baby grand, on the twenty-first floor of the Birmingham Hyatt. After much discussion, we decide that David must address the developing financial situation at the conference the very next day. We abandon work on the main conference speech and get drafting.

David promises to work with the Labour government to ensure financial stability. George jumps on a train to London with Rupert Harrison, his economic advisor, to meet with Alistair Darling and as many other serious people as they can conjure up. The conference itself is subdued while the drama plays out elsewhere. And we are missing our usual brief moment in the sun.

Back in London, Brown continues to dominate the airwaves. 'This is no time for a novice,' he says pointedly. In the office, Oliver, who probably should have been a don, is giving us all seminars on economics: how to avoid a recession becoming a depression. I wipe the dust off my old economic textbooks, wishing I had listened more to my university tutors.

In early October, Brown announces a £500 billion bank bailout package, which comes on the heels of the Americans' own package worth $700 billion. Labour's answer to everything is to throw money at the problem. Their foot firmly on the gas, they seem unconcerned that the economy is heading off the cliff as our deficit spirals out of control, on its way to being the highest in our peacetime history. In late November, Labour launch a massive fiscal stimulus of £20 billion on top of the bank bailout.

Britain feels like it is hurtling towards economic catastrophe. And we are stuck, increasingly uncomfortable but unable to comment because, just over a year ago, we agreed to match Labour's spending plans, a move we thought clever at the time, in order to neutralise an argument over public spending, just as Blair had done in 1997, but for opposing reasons. Our aim had been to stop Labour accusing us of being the party of cuts. Blair had been hoping to stop the Tories warning voters off a Labour spending binge.

We discuss our predicament for hours, and then decide. Enough is enough. We cannot go on like this. We oppose the stimulus. Now we have set out our own path. We will not spend our way out of the recession and risk a disastrous spiral of low or no growth, an ever-growing deficit and debt, and high interest rates, like those we're witnessing in Greece. This is the end of our initial Team Cameron strategy and the start of 'Plan A'.

We had begun with a political narrative largely focused on our broken society and social responsibility, only to find the landscape had radically changed. We were now grappling with a broken economy, which required a different focus. It would be this shift that created much of the disharmony in the team in the lead-up to the 2010 general election.

Steve Hilton – back from a year living with his wife, Rachel, in Palo Alto, California – is uncomfortable when he learns the economy is now taking centre stage in our messaging. It wasn't that he had been totally off our radar whilst he was in California; when he first left, we tried to fix strategy meetings so he could Skype in. Most of us hadn't yet heard of Skype, so the vision of Steve sipping his morning juice while wearing shorts and a T-shirt that appeared on the computer which we placed in the centre of our meeting table was a bit of a shock. We soon decided that Skyping Steve didn't really work. We are worlds apart – literally.

Now Steve wants us to return to the emphasis on society that so dominated our earlier years. He's worried that the messaging around the economy is too negative and that we must signal a sense of hope, not just of efficiency and sacrifice. David is sympathetic to his point of view, especially on the tone. But he is an intuitive leader and knows things have changed. We cannot ignore the central issue of the day: people are worried about their future and their jobs. Most of us feel that social policy must now take a back seat. Especially George and Andy.

Over the course of the past year, spent under the ever-expanding shadow of a mounting financial crisis, and with growing prospects for an election, there has been pressure on us to reveal more substance around our economic policies. George is very focused on the dilemma. Saying too little undermines our credibility; saying more is likely to scare the horses. In the end, George decides to lean into the 'c' word ('cuts'), which we are all a little afraid of. And with good reason. After still more discussion, we decide again, and announce a programme of £23 billion of cuts, with the aim of eliminating the deficit over the lifetime of the next Parliament. Then George decides to go even further in his 2009 conference speech, promising immediate ('in-year') cuts if we win the 2010 election.

In his suite on the twelfth floor of the Midland Hotel, George gathers his team to comb through his speech line by line, as he always does, carefully placing policy announcements like bunnies into the hat ready for their 'reveal' the next day. He likes to entertain, does George, understanding that politics – amongst many things – is a show. But this year it is a deadly serious one.

I check in to see how things are going. They are hard at it – and hungry. The hotel, full to bursting, is late with room service. Poppy Mitchell-Rose, George's right-hand woman – who is usually calm and smiley, a rock of support – looks anxious. I am due a feast from M&S courtesy of my old university friend Simone Finn, which we intend to eat together in front of *Downton Abbey* in my room. Always generous of spirit, she arrives with enough food for an entire army – or certainly the Shadow Treasury team. After a few mouthfuls of hummus, we repack the food guiltily and take it next door to share.

After David's speech, we gather in a room at the back of the conference centre to celebrate and have some lunch. The week has gone as well as we could have hoped for. Both George's and David's speeches were well received. But it still all feels a bit risky.

We are now going into an election as the self-confessed 'party of cuts', giving Labour the opportunity to accuse us of undermining virtually every programme in government. We feel we need to be straight with the electorate, however. If we win, David will be handed the keys to Downing Street and expected to sort the mess out. Things will be difficult, so we need to have a mandate. We have little inkling just how defining these decisions are to be.

And then there is the wild rush for the train. Everyone is dying to get home. We charge across the station platform clutching our tickets like a rabble of unruly school children – only Steve has lost his. He rushes past the barrier anyway and is stopped by a policeman. Steve explains that he is with our party; he has a ticket but just can't find it. The policeman won't let him through. Steve has always had a problem with authority and I can see he is about to lose the plot. When the policeman tries to calm him down by touching him on the arm, Steve explodes. The next thing we know, Steve is being led away in handcuffs. Andy volunteers to go with him to help sort things out.

I find David and Samantha on the train. 'By the way, Steve's just been arrested,' I tell them. Not exactly the headline we were looking for.

5

THE GIANT DUE DATE

All elections ultimately come down to the same questions: 'Is it time for change?' (essentially the argument of all challengers) vs. 'Can you afford to change?' (the central message of all incumbents). In 2010, we have to sell a message of change. So our first task is to explain, A change to what?

Ever since Brown bottled a general election in 2007, we have been on election footing, which looms like a giant due date. According to parliamentary rules, the last possible date that Brown can hold the general election is 3 June. There is no way out, only the certainty of sleepless nights and the prospect of success or failure lie ahead.

The first rule of planning a campaign is to decide what you are trying to say. What is your central message? This needs to be entrenched in your values. In politics, if you have no values, then you have no roots – you will sway in the wind and ultimately fail.

We know what we are about and, although sometimes we disagree with each other, we are mostly aligned. This is David's brand of progressive Conservativism – socially liberal, fiscally conservative, tolerant, internationalist.

Strategy is drawn from your values and gives your direction of travel. From it comes your policies – or, in other words, spelling out the precise things you want to do – which are then revealed to the public through a series of announcements.

If you want people to know what you are doing and saying

beyond the Westminster village, you need to get on television. The easiest way to do this is with a speech, visit, or TV interview – and preferably all three. A good, strong picture of your boss on the evening news hammering home your message is basically 'bingo'. But bingo is not as easy as it sounds. Think of all the times you have seen a politician standing in a faded room behind a podium looking dull and sounding duller and you have gone to bed not remembering a thing he or she said.

What is required to deliver bingo is careful planning. First, an announcement that encapsulates the overall message and is bullet-proof – or, in other words, a message that stands up under scrutiny. Then you also want a picture that reinforces that message, say, David smiling with school children, visiting a hospital or standing in front of a tank. All the better if this can occur on a day which does not become hijacked by a completely different story emerging from left field.

Out on the road with a pack of journalists, you are at the mercy of the weather – literal, metaphysical, and political – not to mention the hazards inherent in being 'on tour'. The road is navigated by the ops team, ours run by the legendary and fiercely loyal Liz Sugg. Their duty is to deliver the candidate, ideally with dignity intact, to their next appearance, and the appearance after that. Missed trains, cancelled helicopters, broken-down cars, and harassment from angry members of the public are pretty commonplace delays. In our case, this list soon includes angry chickens (sent by the *Mirror*) and butlers carrying silver platters.

It is our job, as the core team, to pull the various strands together. The strategy, the policies, the comms plan, the ops schedule. Write the manifesto. Decide what David is going to do and say each day, and for what purpose.

This won't be my first general election campaign by any means. That was Major in 1997, when my role was to write rebuttals to news stories about Europe at 5 a.m., ahead of the daily press conference. Next, driving around the beautiful Cotswold villages, pregnant with my second child, I helped David win his Witney seat for the first time in the summer of 2001. By 2005 I was back in CCHQ supporting Michael Howard. But I have never been at the heart of a campaign.

This is new.

WE GO INTO FULL election-planning mode before Christmas 2009. Every Sunday night, David, George, Steve, Ed, Andy, and I sit in David's study in North Kensington, with its sharp ochre velvet chairs and reindeer carpets moulting onto our clothes, working through the detailed plans for the week ahead and discussing strategy. We complement each other as a group and like each other a lot as people. And although we dive into all of the elements of strategy, policy, planning, and comms, each of us know what particular 'value' it is we bring. Steve is the blue-sky thinker, Andy is the comms whiz. George is the strategist, propelling us forward with new ideas and challenging us. Ed and I keep everything moving in tandem. And David is the decision taker, and our leader.

We are not without our differences. Steve's liberal, radical conservatism doesn't always gel with Andy's more traditional variant. Andy comes to politics from the sharp end. He deliberates like a tabloid editor: *What would his readers think?* He is not keen on lofty ideas dreamt up in Westminster. He worked as a journalist since leaving school and rose under the Murdochs as one of their golden children. When later we decide to include Michael Gove, whose brilliant, creative political mind we hope will add to the proceedings, the meetings begin to appear in *The Spectator*, which is unfortunate.

The aim is to start the year with a bang. Articles are being written, videos recorded, and – despite some opposition – a poster campaign is in preparation. George is especially keen on this, as he believes posters speak of confidence. If done right, a poster presents a memorable image that conveys a message clearly and succinctly to the electorate.

However, no one can agree what the images should be, and we

are running out of time. We cover the office floor with drafts, burning through image after image. Of course, everyone has their own pet idea – even though we have been told categorically *not* to try to be amateur creatives ourselves and leave this to the professionals, it's too irresistible. Even my dad is emailing ideas.

David heads down to his home in Dean, in Oxfordshire, for the beginning of his winter break. Realising we still have a lot to sort, he calls us down to the country for a meeting. It is a few days before Christmas and the weather has changed for the worse. I wake up to see inches of snow outside my window in London. I ring our ops genius, Liz, and suggest we move the meeting to Oxford. This is an easy place for those of us in London to get to and it's only forty minutes from David's constituency home. But David is resolute. He will cook us lunch in Dean.

I set off with George in Andy's rather flash three-door convertible. We speed down the motorway talking ten to the dozen and before we know it we have passed Oxford into the Cotswolds, which is covered by mountains of snow. Just after the turn off to Dean there is a steep hill. Andy slows down, carefully steering away from what looks like ice at the side of the road. But halfway down we seem to be in a slide. 'Watch out!' shouts George, and before we know it, we have crashed over a wall and into a tree.

There is silence in the car while we take in the situation and establish that no one has been hurt. 'Fuckin' hell!' screams Andy, jumping out to check if his pride and joy has sustained any damage. The situation seems to be: Cotswold wall, 2–Andy's car, 0.

I call David. 'Um, hi . . . Just to say we've crashed.' David doesn't believe me at first, thinking it is a joke to make him feel bad about dragging us down to Dean. 'No, we really have.'

David appears minutes later in a four-wheel drive and thick winter boots to help. We stand at the top of the hill, redirecting other members of the team away from the ice to avoid a Cameroon pile-up.

Despite Andy's preoccupation with his car, we manage to get a lot done. The discussions revolve around the 'air' war – which means how we communicate what we propose to do once we're in government, through speeches, interviews, and visits – and the 'ground' war, which is about the party's operation – knocking on doors, telephone canvassing, handing out leaflets, finding out where our vote is, and, ultimately, on polling day, getting people out to vote. Finally, over a cup of tea, we return to the poster and give the go-ahead to an image of David looking reassuring with the caption: 'We can't go on like this. I'll cut the deficit not the NHS.'

The poster is launched with great fanfare but falls flat. Seeing it on the motorway a few weeks later, I can see the problem straight away. David looks smug and spruced up rather than how we wanted him to look – fresh and trustworthy. We then discover the ad agency has airbrushed the picture. When word of this gets out, we are caught in a frenzy of press criticism. David is accused of being a PR man and a vacuous show pony. This is not how we had wanted to start the year.

THE ARGUMENT ABOUT WHETHER to lead on the economy or social issues remains unresolved. But we must progress with the manifesto.

A manifesto is a tricky thing to get right. It needs to be substantial enough to set out a path for government, but not so long it bores everyone to death. It should say something about what you really plan to do for the country – setting out your direction of travel and main policy offer. It needs to include some big-ticket items, but it also needs to cover all of the main areas, so that no one can accuse you of not caring about their pet subject. Most importantly, the manifesto should aim to appeal to voters – which is not as obvious a point as you may think.

Your manifesto is critical because it's your mandate for government. And if you are lucky enough to win an election, it will stay with you as a blueprint for your first Queen's speech, and the one after that, and after that one too. If you have a group of MPs in your party who do not like you, they will be hard-pressed to vote against something that is in this document, because people have voted for them on the basis of it. So, it is worth all the hard work, in the end.

Oliver Letwin oversees our manifesto process, which is a pains-taking and at times painful task. It's really hard to successfully include the wider party in the process while avoiding a free-for-all. The series of policy groups Oliver sets up are popular – in that they are deemed 'inclusive' – but ultimately lead to pandemonium. Some of the less desirable policy recommendations leak into the pages of the tabloids. Members become increasingly disenchanted as their proposals are rejected left, right, and centre. All in all, this year's exercise cannot be deemed a success.

And yet slowly and surely, the manifesto comes together, including a commitment to cut the deficit, boost business, and reform schools and welfare, as well as an ambition to be the greenest government ever. We launch it in Battersea Power Station, hoping the iconic backdrop will speak to reconstruction and a 'can do' attitude. The Shadow Cabinet is there in full force. Samantha is there too, heavily pregnant with Florence.

I hold my copy of the manifesto, 'An Invitation to Join the Government', and listen to David's speech. It has been written by Steve and is all about 'Big Society' – encouraging people to get involved in their communities. In reality it confuses just about everyone.

IT IS AN EARLY Easter in 2010. I roam round the garden of my sister's house in the country, hiding eggs ahead of the traditional hunt. I feel strangely detached, like I am simply going through the motions of family life. I know that in just a few hours, this normality will be suspended for a while. On Tuesday, Gordon Brown will go to Buckingham Palace to ask the Queen to dissolve Parliament, and thereby officially fire the starting gun. We will then move onto full election footing, with its gruelling schedule of early morning starts, long days, and late nights.

We have already left our offices in Norman Shaw to join the rest of the party team in CCHQ at Millbank, where we are packed

into the open-plan office like sardines. The place smells of takeaway pizza and unshowered bodies. I feel excited and a bit
apprehensive. We have been anticipating this moment for years,
and now that it has come, win or lose, the end of *our* years in
opposition is in sight.

My last night with the family will be Sunday night. From
Monday, the core team will decamp to a hotel in London for the
duration of the campaign, so that we will able to conduct our
punishing schedule with no distractions from family or friends
(although on weekends we will be allowed home). It is a terrible
wrench to part from my children, but I know I would be up too
early and back too late to see them anyway.

This is a long-standing but rather hushed-up election tradition.
Michael Howard and his team stayed at the luxurious Mandarin
Oriental in Knightsbridge for the 2005 campaign. We know
anything like that is completely out of the question now. How can
you fight an election on austerity from the Mandarin Oriental?
Andrew Feldman books us in to the Park Plaza, a monolithic
building of darkness that dominates the roundabout across
Westminster Bridge. The place is a labyrinth of orange carpets,
dark hallways, and tiny rooms, many of which face onto an internal
well seemingly designed to house the entire pigeon population of
London. I discover this depressing view of the pigeon sanctuary is
not something I share with my more illustrious colleagues, who
have palatial, river-facing rooms. They seem more positive about
the hotel, strangely enough. I cannot get away from the sensation
that someone has died somewhere along my corridor.

We are used to working together as a tightly-knit team, but you
can't run an election campaign by committee, especially if the
members don't always agree. And David cannot lead the campaign
himself: he's our front man. So, the idea is that George does it,
though in reality he was never going to manage the day-to-day
work. We need him out campaigning too. So, there is a gap – a
large gap. We will learn our lesson and fill this in 2015 with Lynton
Crosby. But in 2010 we go ahead with Andy and Steve as co-

managers. Despite their differences in style and politics, they put themselves in a small office in the centre of CCHQ in a show of joint decision-taking. It is less an office and more a 'pod', really, which quickly earns it the ironic nickname 'the love pod'. It is from this loveless pod that our 2010 election campaign is orchestrated. There is neither window, nor air, nor anything healthy at all in the pod – just two very tired men surviving on adrenaline.

Soon the routine is set. The media team gather at 5.30 a.m., ahead of the 6 a.m. broadcasts. My first meeting of the day with key members of the team – David, George, Steve, Andy and Ed – is at 6.30 at CCHQ. Also joining us are Liz, Stephen Gilbert, who oversees the campaign on the ground, and Rupert Harrison, who has taken over from Matt Hancock as George's chief of staff now that Matt is himself standing for Parliament. We go through the main points, which have emerged from earlier meetings: which story we want to fly, which story we want to kill, what Labour are up to.

By 8 a.m. at the latest we set off on the campaign trail. Most days we try to get back to London for the evening, so we can discuss the day's events and the state of play over dinner in the hotel and watch the news. Occasionally, we stay out on the road and spend the night in a hotel.

Each day involves a series of visits to target seats, with a speech and interviews planned at each stop. Getting to them requires one form of transport or another, sometimes of the winged variety. We have a plane in the 2010 and 2015 election campaigns, which David calls 'Con Air'. The team and I sit up at the front with David. Sometimes journalists are at the back, filing their stories as we go, but mostly the press is taken round the country on a large bus.

The election bus is home to teams from each of the main national broadcasters: BBC, ITV, and Sky, as well as a representative from the Press Association and sometimes Bloomberg. A random selection of journalists from other outlets are out on the road with us for each day too. This needs careful handling by our press and ops teams. You are dealing with the most high-maintenance, low-pain-threshold, easily bored, unsympathetic, and ever hungry group of people in the world. There's a lot of ringing their mate on the Labour bus to compare who's getting the best pictures and, god forbid, better food. The scary thing is that your fate is largely in these people's hands. How they interpret your day will be how the public sees it. It feels a lot like a one-way relationship: all give from us, all take from them. But ultimately, we have something they need – access to the campaign – and they have something we need – press attention.

When David and I join the bus, we sit in a private part at the back. A black leather seat forms a semicircle, and all the windows in this part of the bus are tinted. I assume it is designed for the use of a boy band on tour. Only instead of being thrown beers and girls, we get the occasional journalist sent back to do the daily interview. We spend hours at a time in the back of the bus, being jolted around, the British countryside speeding by, driven from event to event and stopping at market towns, factories, supermarkets, and new-build housing developments, our progress tracked by twenty-four-hour news. Mornings and lunchtime, Liz throws some food at us, usually of a healthy nature. By late afternoon we are at the chocolate and crisps.

Being out on the road is a risky business at the best of times, and even more so during an election campaign, when the potential for a high-profile disaster is high. A member of the public harassing a politician live on television can define an entire election campaign. Remember a furious Sharon Storer confronting Blair outside a Birmingham hospital in 2001 for failing to give enough support to the NHS? Only worse is the appearance of a member of the public being prevented from harassing a politician – or the politician complaining about it afterwards.

The considered view is that a politician is fair game and should take criticism on the chin. Fortunately, we have already learnt this lesson the hard way. In summer 2008, David did a series of interviews in Newlyn, Cornwall. In the middle of a question a man approached him, gesticulating. 'Be quiet, we're doing an interview', pleaded Gabby Bertin, David's press secretary, who is a half French, half Croydon girl, and takes no prisoners with her notepad and bright lipstick. The man began yelling even louder. The cameras swivelled round to take in the angry man. 'I won't be silenced,' he yelled. 'Effing Tory!' David walked towards the man and shook his hand. 'Tell me what the problem is, sir,' he said, calmly. And the man began to regale him with accounts of his inadequate local Tory MP, live on national television.

Even without the gaffes, there is simply the hard graft of travel, which takes its toll – not just the trains, planes, and automobiles themselves, but the difficulty in getting your work done on them. Answering emails, reading your briefs, and making your calls is not easy as the car swerves in and out of the fast lane following the convoy.

Somehow I seem to attract more than my fair share of fiascos on the road, like losing my shoe under an intercity train. I have chosen a well-worn, comfortable pair for the day, but they come loose when I walk, so much so that my right shoe flies off my foot and lands in the gap between the platform and the train. Perched on one leg, I peer down the crack to see it nestled between the rails. I notice at this point that David has moved quite some way up the platform. 'No, I don't wish the train to be delayed while the guard fishes it out, thank you very much,' I say. A delayed train (and lots of angry passengers blaming David) is a far worse fate than a single-shoed aide. After this incident, I never leave home without an extra pair of flats in my handbag.

There are other, more serious encounters. Helicopters seem to be a major culprit. They are beguiling creatures: they can land anywhere and halve your travel time. But they are also extremely dangerous. Returning from a visit, the pilot tells us the wheels are stuck and we cannot land. This, he says, is not really a problem but we cannot go to the heliport at Battersea. We head off instead to Biggin Hill Airport. There is a small runway there. As we approach, we spot a fire engine and ambulance on standby. This is not reassuring. The pilot brings the helicopter down to hover near (but not too near) to the ground. All we have to do is jump out, he explains. There is another pilot waiting to catch us. David makes a respectable exit. Gabby and I – all summer dresses, no tights, and bags galore – fare less well. Our poor pilot now has to fly around to get rid of the fuel before attempting an emergency landing. The firemen hand him a helmet and get the hoses ready. We are told the helicopter will flip round on landing. Thankfully, he manages it.

On another visit, we are due to land in a field. We are nearing the ground when suddenly the pilot pulls back and up at great speed. Hovering above the field, the pilot hammers on the window, shouting at the people down below, though of course they cannot hear. The sight of the hysterical pilot has reduced me to a nervous wreck. I am of little use, busy saying my Hail Marys, so David takes charge. He puts on his earphones and asks the pilot what is the matter. The pilot explains that he had to abort the landing because the farmer has put down a carpet in the field so that David will not get wet feet when he gets out of the helicopter – only the carpet flew up and very nearly got tangled in the propellers. We have barely avoided a blow-up. 'Wait a moment,' says David who then rings the team on the ground. The carpet is removed, and we land safely.

6

THE WORM

Grappling with the challenges of the campaign trail is par for the course in a general election. However, the run-up to the 2010 election featured something totally new, at least to us in Britain. It was the first to import the American tradition of the presidential TV debate. The drumbeat calling for a live head-to-head had been going for some time. It was hard to ignore. No one wants to say they won't face their public. Even if privately we're wishing the other side would back out, publicly we are saying, 'Bring it on.'

So, we know a TV debate is coming, but the question is – in what form? The broadcasters think this is up to them to decide; we think otherwise. Which is why we start meeting in secret with Peter Mandelson, to work out what is in both our best interests. I am perhaps overly excited by the covert nature of the operation, involving the infamous Mandelson. Andy tells me to calm down. We creep in the back door of some office block to find Mandy and his team waiting for us. He begins, 'The broadcasters may think they can tell us what to do . . .'

In the end, it's decided that there will be three debates with the three party leaders – Gordon Brown, Nick Clegg, and David Cameron – over three weeks in the final weeks of the campaign. In theory, the first debate will concentrate on domestic affairs, the second on foreign affairs, and the third on the economy, but in practice they will be wide-ranging.

Had we known how much the debates were going to detract

from the traditional style of campaign, we might have thought twice before agreeing. Because in 2010, the debates cut a huge hole out of the centre of the short campaign. Where old-style campaigns had been constructed around a daily message deployed at the morning press conference, these new debates made it all about one man's performance on a weekly show: potential prime ministers, meet *The X Factor*. The first half of the week was taken up with the rev up, the second half with the come down. A once-steady poll lead could go into freefall based on a single night's performance; all the years of effort put into building the trust and support of a nation could be lost in a moment. Plus, all the weight of the campaign came to rest on David's shoulders. This, we quickly realised, was the curse of reality TV.

We set aside time for rehearsals but it isn't nearly enough. We should have doubled it. At least we had the sense to know we lacked the expertise amongst ourselves to prepare for the debates. We reach across the Atlantic for help from people who do, and are lucky enough to find Bill Knapp and Anita Dunn, who had helped Obama into office in 2008. With their guidance, we get to work.

We start by preparing for what we think of as a slightly more complex – and longer – version of PMQs. Which it is, in a way, but a *lot* more complicated. It is like deploying an army over a vast landscape. Above all, there is the overall strategy for the battle ahead. The first step is to identify key topics – the ones you know will come up. Because the broadcasters only have time for a few questions, it is not so difficult to work these out.

We imagine the first debate, on domestic affairs, is likely to cover welfare, health, immigration, and maybe education. So, we pick one area, health, to start with. We work out what our strongest points are – the positive story that David has to tell. Next, we address our vulnerabilities – and this needs to be a very honest appraisal, the Americans tell us. What are the most difficult questions that could come up on this topic? What are the best answers? After that, we dig up everything the other side have said about health. What are their strengths and weaknesses? We are building trenches, from which David can mount an offensive but also retreat to safety.

However, while all this is good groundwork, it's not what wins you the debate. Your key message is the thing you want the 'folks' back at home to remember. (We don't have 'folks' in Britain, we tell our American friends. You do now, they say.) To land the key messages you need some good strong lines, which Bill Knapp calls 'the zingers'. A zinger should speak to your point with absolute clarity. It should be short and focused. Think tweet rather than prose. 'Senator, you're no Jack Kennedy' goes down in history as the ultimate debate put-down. In those words, Democratic senator Lloyd Bentsen showed Republican senator Dan Quayle (who had dared invoke President Kennedy) to be arrogant, naive, inexperienced, and out of his depth, having made a bad judgement call in trying to identify himself with Kennedy in the first place. Opponent crushed. Enemy in retreat. That's a zinger. (Even if George H. W. Bush still went on to win the actual presidential election.)

BUT WHAT HAPPENS IF you don't get the chance to deploy your zinger because no one has asked you the right question, we ask? Not a problem, says Bill. This is when he teaches us some fancy debate footwork called 'the pivot'. You pivot from your answer on subject A (undesirable topic) onto subject B (desirable one), and then glide into your zinger.

David has to practise his moves. Offensive hit, defensive back down in the trench, then pivot, glide, and zinger.

Once we have prepared the scripts, Bill and Anita say it's time to turn to the show itself. They insist that David rehearse properly – meaning a real, live practice, with people playing the parts of the other party leaders.

We gather for the rehearsal in the press conference room. Michael Gove is acting as compere. He bowls a few questions. A few answers in, it becomes apparent that Jeremy Hunt (aka Nick Clegg) is hogging the limelight and getting on our nerves. We can't make up our minds whether it's Jeremy being annoying per se, or Jeremy doing a superb job of being Nick. We need a Nick strategy, say Bill and Anita.

Until now we have had a Lib Dem strategy – which is to ignore Nick and 'love bomb' his supporters. We spend some time discussing what to do – but again, not enough. We really just want Jeremy Hunt to stop talking so we can focus on our main opponent, which is Gordon Brown.

We don't spot the fact that the real problem is Nick. He is about to launch himself as the change candidate.

THE FIRST DEBATE IS in Manchester. By the time we arrive at Granada Studios, the place is heaving ahead of the big fight. The city is divided by colours – reds, blues, yellows. The candidates are clipped on the lunchtime news. Clegg looks the most relaxed and says he has gone for a long walk to clear his head.

That afternoon we look round the set. It is always good to see it in advance. The stage is all laid out: three podiums, with one extra for the compere, the audience seats stretched in a semicircle around it. Though it looks huge on television, it is a tiny set. The reality of the evening's show hits home. We talk lights and camera positions. David is getting nervous.

Back at the hotel, David takes a nap and I join the rest of the team. George has arrived. He's not here just to support David; he is also our chief 'spinner' for the night, representing David's performance to the press. He will call the debate a win for David, whether it is or not.

My son calls. He has been away for a week in Venice visiting his grandfather. I miss him terribly. There has been a last-minute change of plans – he is to fly home on his own. He is only 8 and I am uneasy. My father-in-law gets on the phone to reassure me. Guy's bag is all packed and he is dying to see his mum. He's very excited about the flight; it is a big adventure. Then Guy's small voice is back on the phone. 'I'll see you tomorrow, Mummy.'

I rejoin the team hovering by the TV. There is a story about a volcano erupting. I watch the dust emerging from its angry mouth. Liz comes in to tell us we can't use the helicopter, or Con Air, to get back on the road tomorrow. In fact, all flights are grounded because of the volcano. It takes me a few minutes to put the two things together: the dust cloud and my son's flight home. I try to put it out of my mind. It is bound to be fine by tomorrow.

We leave in a chaos of cars. David is with Samantha; I am with the rest of the team. There are protestors outside the studio and cameras everywhere. Journalists shout at us as we drive past. Our group divides. We are all given special wristbands that determine where we are allowed to go. Andy and George are directed to a special 'spin room' where others, including Theresa May, will talk to the press after the debate. Samantha and Ed head to the Cameron green room – a tiny back office set up with a large TV.

I go with David to make-up. We have to wait our turn; the Prime Minister is ahead of us, we are told. Minutes later, Gordon Brown emerges looking wild and covered in white powder. 'HELLO, DAVID!' he barks. (He speaks in capitals. He is not usually interactive in conversation, preferring statements to dialogue.)

'Whatever you do, don't let the make-up woman put all that powder on you,' I say to David once he has passed us.

After make-up, David is led off by the production team. I feel sick to my stomach. I find Samantha and the others in our 'green room' broom cupboard. We have only Fanta and peanuts for sustenance. I make a mental note to remember to bring some wine next time.

The debate begins shortly after 8 p.m. It quickly devolves into a slow-motion, live TV torture of David Cameron. He is answering the questions well enough but lacking the warmth that normally comes naturally to him. He is clearly nervous – we all are – and doesn't look into the camera. I am glad he cannot see the line at the bottom of the TV screen representing what a group of undecided voters are thinking of the answers in real time. They indicate this using hand-held dials, creating this worrying infectious line, which is called 'the worm'. The worm does not seem to have taken to David Cameron. It doesn't seem to like Gordon Brown very much either. But the worm likes Nick Clegg – a lot. Fresh-faced Nick is coming across as Mr Honest and Reasonable Nice Guy. The antipolitics person. He is looking straight down the barrel of the camera as he answers each question – straight at the 'folks' at home.

Nick is winning this, Samantha says every two seconds. It's fine, I reply, David is doing really well. But I know she is right. After the gruelling hour is up, David returns and sinks into a chair. We head back to his suite at the hotel and open a bottle of wine. The general agreement is that it was not David's best performance, but it was adequate. Gordon was much worse. So what? One down, two to go. He will do better in the next debate.

Half an hour or so later, George and Andy reappear, exhausted from their copious spinning. They have done their best, but it has not been as easy to sell as a win. 'Give me the hard stuff,' Andy says, reaching for the spirits. George has been picked on by his old bête noire, Peter Mandelson. His briefing to a gathering of journalists was interrupted. 'Look who's over there,' George imitates Mandy. 'It's my little friend Georgie – poor Georgie . . . spinning his little web, but he has nothing to spin with, 'cos his old pal Dave didn't do very well.'

The next morning, we awake to a wall of failure streaming from every orifice of the media. Nick is the hero of the day – the man the nation has been waiting for. David is yesterday's man. No one cares about Brown anymore. A lightning poll puts the Lib Dems ahead. Suddenly Nick stands as a potential prime minister. The political landscape has been completely altered. We are no longer sure what sort of election we are fighting. Is it against Labour and Gordon, or against Nick and the Lib Dems? We seem to be neither the incumbent nor the change candidate – and we're heading fast, too fast, into political oblivion.

An exhausted and disheartened David heads down to Dean for the weekend with Samantha. The rest of the team regroup in

London. Bill Knapp is still here, unable to fly back to the States, courtesy of that volcanic dust cloud. Andrew Feldman takes him home for Friday night Shabbat. My son is still stuck in Italy, thanks to the same cloud.

I speak to him every day, his voice getting quieter and quieter. 'When will the volcano stop?' he asks.

IT FEELS LIKE ONLY a second has gone by and the next debate, like the dust cloud, is looming ominously. I can feel the pressure mounting on David. This debate is being filmed in Bristol, and we have set aside a night and a morning for prep in Exeter. We all agree we should not fixate on Nick too much. We simply need David to relax and be more himself – to think about what he is trying to say. Look down the barrel of the camera, David repeats again and again. 'To the folks at home,' he adds, to reassure Bill.

The carnival arrives in Bristol. The normally cosy and calm West Country city is throbbing with camera crews and journalists. We find what looks like a quiet café and sit down to have a cup of tea. Within seconds a cameraman appears out of nowhere and starts filming us. More and more emerge from the back of the café like wasps. We sip our tea live on TV.

Back at the studio, Liz hands out the wristbands again and we head off to our different posts. David gets off to a good start. He is more relaxed and remembers to look directly into the camera lens. Nick sticks with his fresh-faced routine. Anyone who is tired of old politics, I'm your man, he is arguing, and almost everyone is tired of politics. Gordon is Gordon. The worm wavers between Nick and David. It is a draw.

The weekend polls are all over the place. We are not losing the election, but neither are we winning it. We have one more debate and then just over a week of campaigning left.

The dust cloud continues to hover, grounding planes everywhere. The summer term is about to begin but half of my son's class are still stuck in a foreign destination unable to get home. The school's website is offering car shares from the far corners of Europe. One friend rings me from a luxury resort halfway round the world. 'I'm dying here in paradise,' she says. I half feel sorry for her, then think better of it. My son is still in Venice, and he's stopped coming to the phone. Something must be done.

A few days later, my son, accompanied by his noble grandfather, sets off on the long journey home by train. They carry food, books, and a deck of cards – anything they can think of to amuse them-selves. My husband fights his way onto a ferry, rents a car, then drives to Paris, where the three generations are reunited over steak-frites. The weekend before the third debate, my son is finally home.

I talk to David about how he wants to approach the preparations. He is tired of rehearsing and wants some space. Too many people, too many points of view. He needs time to collect himself.

I phone my friend, the highly respected comms coach Anthony Gordon Lennox, who helped us in the early days of the leadership election. He has an extraordinary ability to bring out the natural strength and confidence in people, shutting out the external noise so that the person is able to concentrate on what they are trying to say. I ask him to come and have a quiet session with just David and me.

We will not rehearse ahead of the final debate.

THIS TIME WE ARE in Birmingham. The lead-up has been totally overshadowed by Gordon Brown being caught ranting in his car about a woman called Gillian Duffy whom he has called 'bigoted', unaware that he was still wearing his microphone from a previous interview. The clip is played nonstop on all the media outlets. Gordon has blamed the gaffe on Sue Nye, his long-time aide. It feels like a career-ending moment.

David has been mimicking Brown all day – 'How could you let this happen, Sue?!' – and telling Liz and me how lucky we are to have such an easy-going boss. We don't engage. Later in the day, Brown is photographed, head in hands, as he is forced to listen to the clip live on Radio 2. I actually cannot bear to watch the footage.

It seems almost cruel – Brown, the wounded animal being hunted by the pack.

Backstage at the debate, I experience a sudden desire to leave, to head back to the hotel and sleep through the whole thing. I can't face the tension of the worm. But I stay. After a few minutes or so, David gets into his stride. The audience is warming to him and he is visibly relaxing. Some of the freshness around Nick seems to have worn off. Gordon is looking out to space, presumably in the hope that someone will come and take him away to a less hostile environment.

The worm is with David. It is a win. We collapse back at the suite, for once enjoying the post-debate commentary on the television. A mass of pizzas arrive that no one will admit to ordering, but it doesn't stop them being eaten. It is late when we finally get some sleep. There is one week left until polling day.

In the short time left, Labour mount a massive attack against our economic policy. It is all about 'Tory cuts', and bit by bit, we see our poll lead nibbled away. In the end, Nick's huge success during the debates is not borne out in the final poll. He loses ground: his breakthrough was just a blip – testimony to the fact that the 'X Factor' can put people on a pedestal, and then bring them down to earth again, even more quickly.

So, did the debates make a difference to the election? Not to the Lib Dems. And to us? We lost ground and then recovered it. But David has a different take: without the distraction of the TV debates, he thinks Labour's campaign might have gained more ground. After all, we had bravely gone into the general election being honest about our plans for austerity, and we might well have paid a price for it at the ballot box.

7

THE ELECTION BUS

It was George's idea for us to do the all-nighter into polling day. (Notably, though, 'for us' did not include him.) Coverage of our election bus stopping every hour or so during the night would be new to British politics. Hopefully, it would show real energy and our will to win.

I pack a small bag for the trip and then repack, choosing a slightly bigger bag that will fit a pillow. The plan is for me to meet up with the team who are already in Scotland, where we will begin our descent, zigzagging the length and breadth of the nation. We are all in good spirits when we stop off at a local chippy in Longtown, near Carlisle, to get supper. An hour or so later we stop to meet some firemen, and a few hours after that, to visit a smelting factory.

Towards midnight we try to get a bit of sleep in the back of the bus, and I sneak my pillow out of the bag hoping David won't notice. 'I can't believe you've actually brought a pillow,' he says, beady-eyed, before admitting he'd thought about bringing one himself.

I lay my head on what feels like a million pounds' worth of down. I am not able to enjoy the luxury for long. It is like having a newborn. Every hour and a half, Liz comes to wake us for the next visit, and we smarten up and get out of the bus. David chats away to people, does a few interviews, and on we go. By 3 a.m. I am paralysed with exhaustion. I cannot think how David is managing to be so awake and 'on it'. Then a photographer from *The Sun* arrives. David sits up looking all bright-eyed and bushy-tailed, but I cannot actually move. I lie there, just by him, with a blanket over me, hoping that I am invisible, a bit like a small child playing hide-and-seek who thinks if they shut their eyes, no one will see them. Arthur Edwards, who I learn is something of a legend in the trade, takes a number of photographs of David that appear to feature a small ear protruding from his left elbow. This is me.

At dawn we arrive at the fish market in Grimsby. The place is a hive of activity, and the sea air feels refreshing after the sleepless night. Back on the bus we continue to drive south. All I want is a shower and a large cup of coffee, but neither is on the agenda. We are on a mission to pick off as many target seats as we can, and we do not have time for comfort breaks. The bus smells of unwashed bodies and fish.

By lunchtime there is rebellion brewing amongst the journalists in the front of the bus, which – given that they are representing us to the nation on the eve of the poll – feels more than a little perilous. Joey Jones, deputy political editor for Sky News, saves the day by buying a large hunk of steak and switching on the bus's yet-to-be-used oven. By the time we have finished listening to a children's choir in Wales, Joey is handing out steak sandwiches. Morale is recovering. The smell is now of unwashed bodies, fish, and Sunday roast.

In the back, we are tired but in good spirits. We have had our ups and downs but we are now slightly ahead in the polls. Is it by enough? We are far from complacent, but nor are we downcast. Labour has dominated politics for well over a decade, winning three elections and seeing off as many Tory leaders. Driving through the final day of the campaign, our destiny approaching, we feel we are on the cusp of something historic, a winning team in one way or another. And as we arrive in Bristol for the final rally, there is a palpable sense of excitement, not least because we can just about reach out and touch the finishing line.

We check into a hotel in the centre of the city. We have time for a cup of tea and a bit of speech prep. David looks at his dishevelled hair in the mirror and I suggest we try a little of the dry shampoo that Isabel Spearman, Samantha's fashionable and determined right-hand woman, has given us in the event of a 'bad hair day'. I am nervous with the can. David grabs it off me, spraying it generously over his head at close range. I look at him aghast. 'What's the matter?' he asks. 'You've gone completely grey,' I say.

Liz comes in. 'Five minutes,' she announces. I point at the grey-headed David. We clearly need more than five minutes. He rushes into the shower while Liz holds up the rally. I have another cup of tea.

And that is our work done for the 2010 campaign. Tomorrow the country will go to the polls. David will vote in Dean, and I make my way back to London to vote in the morning. I arrive home happy to see the faces of my children before it is time to put them to bed.

They are old enough to know that tomorrow is a big day, but too young to really understand. 'We want the blue team to win, don't we Mummy?' We settle with that.

AFTER ALL OF THE strategy meetings, planning sessions, conference calls, interviews, speeches, TV appearances, visits, and debates, all of the hours spent in cars, trains, helicopters, and planes – plus, the all-nighter on the bus – everything comes to an abrupt standstill on election day, as there are strict rules about what the media can report while the polls are open. And there is only one sort of picture the media want on election day – that of each of the party leaders voting for themselves.

Instead, this is primarily GOTV Day – 'Get Out the Vote' – the busiest day of the election for the party machine. This is what all the canvassing is for: to find out who your supporters are so you can mobilise them on the day. By late afternoon, anyone you were counting on who hasn't turned up to vote should be getting a call.

By late evening, the team should be literally offering to drive any 'no shows' to the polling stations. In a rural seat they might even pass through the villages with a loud hailer.

Every election day we face a choice: add an extra couple of people to the GOTV effort, or hunker down and start planning for what will happen if we win. Both times, we have gone with the latter, for the simple reason that if you win, there is a great deal to plan. You need to form a government for a start. And then you need to start announcing things – big, strong things which speak to your values and your agenda. First impressions stick, and you've got about a hundred days to form them.

THURSDAY, 6 MAY. I am one of the first at my local polling station. Clutching a large cup of coffee, I then join my colleagues and we set off to the country. The plan is to spend the day at Steve Hilton's house in Oxfordshire, out of the sight of the media who are gathering a few miles down the road at David's house in Dean.

David, George, Oliver, Ed, Andy, and I, along with our Chief Whip, Patrick McLoughlin, converge on the farmhouse that Steve has quite recently bought with his wife, Rachel. Steve is buzzing round the kitchen when we arrive – extremely house-proud. We settle down to work around the kitchen table. And although none of us are sure of victory, we plan for a win, running through our initial plans for the first three days, first week, first month. There are key events to schedule, like the first meeting of the Cabinet and of the newly formed National Security Council. If we win, we have a Queen's speech to prepare. We have also promised to hold an emergency budget this side of the summer break, since we have 'in year' cuts that we plan to announce. And of course, we have a government to form.

We talk over the make-up of the Cabinet. Some of it is straight-forward: William Hague will go to the Foreign Office, George to the Treasury. Some of it isn't. We are mulling over George's idea of putting Theresa May in the Home Office. Then there is the question of whether we reach out to Iain Duncan Smith – possibly for the Welfare job. IDS has made a name for himself over the past few years campaigning on social justice issues. David wants to build broad church if he gets the chance to form a government.

More sensitive than all of this is our discussion around the Lib Dems. In the event we don't quite pull it off – that is, if we win the most seats but fall short of a majority – the question will then be whether to reach out to the Lib Dems, and if so, on what basis? The 'what basis' part is what we have asked Oliver to think about very, very privately over the last week. He has read and reread the Lib Dem manifesto, churned through their past statements, and met privately at George's house with William Hague and Ed to mull over the issues. Oliver already has a handle on how to form part of a common agenda for some sort of coalition agreement, formal or otherwise.

After lunch, like nursery school children, we all go for quiet time – wandering round the house to find a bed or a sofa to lie down on. Most of us are far too anxious to rest, but it is a good idea, in theory. We will be up all night.

We re-gather in Steve and Rachel's kitchen a few hours later with cups of tea and work in hand. Soon George has a date in the field next door with a helicopter, which will take him up to his count in Tatton. Oliver too will disappear, to Dorset. The rest of us will go with David to his home at Dean. We do a sweepstake of how many seats we think we will win. Ominously, we all choose numbers that suggest we will not win an outright majority. Then we say our goodbyes. When we next meet we will know the outcome of the election (or at least we think we will).

Samantha is at the house with Isabel Spearman when we arrive. There is a mounting tension. David strides round the garden. We offer to help Samantha with the supper. Chopping is therapeutic. There is nothing really to do until the ten o'clock news. Isabel pulls me aside: 'You need some make-up,' she says, looking at me critically. Half an hour later I join the others, made up to the nines, feeling rather self-conscious. We sit down for dinner. Texts are flying in from friends, family, political colleagues, which we share with each other. Some good news, some less. It is difficult to tell what is going on.

The chimes of the news bring with them the exit polls, which forecast a hung parliament with the Tories as the largest party. We are neither surprised nor disheartened, considering the news as a final forecast rather than the definitive result. The difference between being the largest party and the overall winner is so slight it is in fact difficult to call. We feel cautiously optimistic. At least we are somewhere near a win of some sort. David looks set to be prime minister.

But the evening does not feel like a victory. Even though the results are coming in strong for us, they are also fairly consistent for Labour. We are neck and neck when, in the early hours of the morning, it is time for us to head off to David's Witney count. There is not room for us all to attend the count, which is a sought-after ticket for local members, so Ed and I remain in the car, listening to the radio in a sort of wakeful sleepiness. When David finally emerges from the count, we start back to London, a convoy of cars. BBC and ITV helicopters are above us, filming our journey. Some random results are coming in, keeping us away from definitive victory. It feels like we are driving into limbo land.

It must be after 5 a.m. when we finally arrive at CCHQ. There is an army of cameras outside, but I am too tired to notice. We make our way up to the third floor, past the many campaign staff who are watching the final results trickling in, through to the office towards the back of the building that we have made our own. There is no mood of celebration. We sip our cups of strong builder's tea apprehensively while we wait for George to return from Cheshire.

It is still too early to call, but it looks as though we have fallen short of the golden number needed to form a government on our own. There are 650 seats in Parliament, so strictly speaking, we need 326. But historically Sinn Féin have never turned up to Westminster, as they refuse to say the oath to the Queen, so you can achieve a working majority with 323. At 6 a.m. we are some way off that and heading for the first hung parliament for thirty-six years. No party commands a majority in the House of Commons, so no party will be able to get their legislation through (in other words, govern) without an alliance of some sort with another party.

We consider our options. There is the possibility of a 'confidence and supply' agreement with the Lib Dems, which guarantees their support for key votes (such as the Finance Bill) without actually forming a government with them. But we all fear the instability that comes with a minority government. The country is in crisis and fixing it will be a nightmare with no majority. We would have to chase every vote, including within our own party. This feels too precarious when we can see the difficult things which need doing. This points towards striking a more formal agreement with the Lib Dems . . .

In the early hours of Friday morning, with results still to come in, David does not want to make any decisions. He wants to return to the hotel, await the final numbers, and then regroup after he has had some sleep. So, we head back to the bleak Westminster Bridge Plaza and agree to meet again in just over an hour. I set my alarm so that I will have time for a shower. I feel surprisingly rejuvenated after it, despite my lack of sleep.

The morning bulletins declare a hung parliament. The country is already in economic turmoil and now we seem to be in political stalemate. The markets open and react badly to the lack of firm leadership. The news then turns to Greece, where people are rioting on the streets as the Eurozone crisis continues. The world feels very fragile. My phone is filling up with a barrage of texts – some from friends and family being supportive, others from anxious MPs and journalists wanting to know what is going on.

The end result has us on 36 per cent, with 306 seats in Parliament. Labour are on 258 and the Lib Dems on 57. In just one Parliament, as Leader of the Opposition, David has pulled the party out of its rut. For about a decade, the Tories consistently polled at around 33 per cent; last night, we won 97 new seats, the biggest Conservative gain since 1931 and the end of thirteen years of Labour rule. It is certainly a defeat for Gordon Brown. However, it seems it was simply too big a stretch to reach an all-out victory in one go. We are 20 seats short of a majority, with too few to form a government on our own.

Now we are stuck in a no-man's land at the Plaza. I wander down the corridor to David's suite. I don't feel despondent though. Looking out over the river Thames, my coffee in hand, it seems like the game is not yet over.

'I've thought about it overnight,' says David, as we reassemble for breakfast in his suite. 'I want to form a coalition.'

8

A COALITION IS BORN

These are needy times. Which is why David wants to make a big, bold offer to the Liberal Democrats. A coalition is definitely the more radical of the options on the table, and it will be the least popular with the party, who dislike and mistrust the Lib Dems. We also have no idea if they would even contemplate it. There has not been a formal coalition in British politics since the Second World War, but a minority government will lack the strength to take the tough decisions we need for the country. With the Lib Dems, we will have force in numbers.

For now, Gordon Brown remains fully ensconced as Prime Minister, which constitutionally he is obliged to be – that is, until an alternative government can be formed. The convention is that it falls to the party with the largest number of seats to try to form a government first. But if the Lib Dems were to refuse to play ball with us, it's over to Labour to try. So, there is a very real possibility that Labour could stay in Downing Street propped up by the Lib Dems and others, and that we will have won the most seats but failed to win power.

In the haze of the morning after an undecided result and one hour's sleep, Labour stealing away our victory (of sorts) doesn't yet feel like a very real threat. We drink our coffee and nibble croissants. We are the clear winners, we say – we just need to work things out. However, this possibility of it going against us will grow in the coming days.

The first thing we need to do is get David to speak to Nick Clegg, who is at home, licking his wounds. His seemingly triumphant campaign of change has failed to deliver at the ballot box. In fact, the Lib Dems have lost five seats. Nick is definitely interested by David's offer, but he has to get a lot of people onside – as do we. They agree to speak again later in the day.

Outside our hotel the world is waiting. We need to show we are gripping events and that the momentum is with us. So, we plan a public statement for early afternoon and get to work. There is a lot to do in a very short amount of time. Liz starts looking for a venue. Steve starts drafting a speech. Ed and I sit down with David and make a list of whom we need to talk to: senior members of the Shadow Cabinet, party grandees, and Graham Brady, the current head of the 1922 Committee.

We hit the phones. Some calls go better than others. The weight of opinion amongst the Shadow Cabinet is with David, with only Chris Grayling and Theresa Villiers coming down against. There is a mixed reaction elsewhere in the party, especially from the more traditional wing; they're wary of an alliance with the Lib Dems, who are so disliked on the ground. Also, the Coalition risks drawing the political balance towards the centre. We need to carry the party – and it's going to be tough.

William Hague, who is part political historian, understands why we would want a coalition – but why would they? A cursory glance at history shows minor parties destroyed by participating in coalition governments. Fortunately, the Lib Dems seem less spooked by the past than perhaps they should be. Or maybe they just want power more than we realise.

I walk down the corridor to the small office we have created in the hotel. Steve, wearing shorts, a T-shirt, and no shoes, is writing away. He is in a state of agitated excitement. This is the political breakthrough he has dreamed of. It speaks of a new politics, of capturing the mood of this moment. He is full of optimism for the future. Words pour out of him onto the page.

The final speech is still warm from the printer when it is passed to David to underline in the short car journey to St Stephen's Club in Westminster. It is around 2.30 in the afternoon. Liz is fending off the crowds to get David into the building; they close in behind him, making it virtually impossible for us to follow.

'I want to make a big, open, and comprehensive offer to the Liberal Democrats. I want us to work together in tackling our country's big and urgent problems – the debt crisis, our deep social problems, and our broken political system.' David's words are carefully chosen: the word 'coalition' is not yet used, though it is hinted at. The thought lingers across Westminster and the country. When the speech is over, we head back to CCHQ and start putting together a negotiating team for the coalition talks. The Lib Dems put forward Chris Huhne, Danny Alexander, Andrew Stunell, and David Laws. For our side are George, Oliver Letwin, William Hague, and Ed Llewellyn. As well as working for Paddy Ashdown in Bosnia, Ed had spent time working alongside Nick Clegg at the European Commission, and this seems to be paying off. Ed is a man the Lib Dems know and can trust. It is agreed that both sides will keep their leaders out of the talks, so things can be thrashed out without jeopardising what might be an important future relationship.

We have both played safe with our teams. Which is possibly why the Coalition agreement is put together quickly and efficiently – but also why it causes some consternation in later years. Neither team represents the wide-ranging views that lurk in the wings of our respective parties.

Team Cameron has their orders. Our manifesto is our negotiating mandate. We know our red lines. The economy is most crucial. After all, we are trying to form a coalition so that we have the strength to do the difficult things the country needs. There would be no point in coming together if we negotiated away Plan A. So, five days of tough negotiations begin.

As our team head off to do battle, David and I leave CCHQ. It is late Friday afternoon and neither of us has been near our children for days. And although everything is up in the air, it feels so good to be home, if not quite settled back into family life. I walk round Battersea Park with my children, feeling slightly detached from the election machine for a short while.

WE RECONVENE ON SUNDAY evening to take stock. It is odd to be back in our old offices. I am extremely fond of the place, but I wonder if it is my fate never to leave the bright green rooms looking out across the Thames at the London Eye. We sit around the long, green felt-covered table eating pizza and 'chewing the cud', as David puts it, late into the night. We can almost feel the brooding presence of Gordon Brown, who remains ensconced down the road in No. 10.

By Monday morning, the momentum feels like it is shifting away from us as the Lib Dems pursue parallel coalition discussions with Labour. Later that afternoon, Brown announces he will stand down as party leader by September – presumably to eliminate any hurdle that his leadership might pose to a future deal with the Lib Dems. A Lib-Lab pact would still fall short of a majority, but there is talk of forming a rainbow coalition supported by other left leaning parties like the Scottish National Party and Plaid Cymru.

We watch events unfold on the twenty-four-hour news channels while we wait for updates from our negotiating team. If we are going to shift things back in our favour we need to move quickly – and address some of the unresolved issues that are slowing us down. The Lib Dems have long campaigned to reform our voting system, seeing the first-past-the-post system, which gives preference to the two main parties, as undemocratic. A referendum on the Alternative Vote (AV) system, a variant of proportional representation where voters rank their candidates in order of preference, is one of their big asks, but it is also something that offends our party to the core. While we have been dragging our feet, Labour are showing signs of giving them what they want.

We are being outmanoeuvred.

That evening we call the parliamentary party together under the auspices of the 1922 Committee. The committee meets each week,

traditionally in Committee Room 14, which is part of the problem.
The room – dark-panelled and church-like with its pews – speaks
to old-fashioned values rather than to progress and change. And
it is impossible to hear a word anyone says from the back, which
is where Ed and I always stand, amongst those who generally like
David the least. Sometimes these meetings can go very badly wrong,
with MPs speaking out, one after another, against a government
minister, or even a prime minister. Losing the room can mark the
end of a political career. But handle it right and the 1922 can row
in behind you.

It is difficult to know how this meeting will go. The MPs are
naturally anti-coalition, anti-Lib Dems and anti-AV, and we are
asking them to put up with all three. I stand with Ed, trying to
gauge the mood.

David comes in to great banging on desks and 'hear hear's; MPs
don't clap. David addresses his MPs (or 'colleagues', as they prefer
to call each other). Almost a hundred of them are brand new to
Parliament and very excited to find themselves at the centre of
history. David appeals to their sense of duty to their country. He
asks why they should turn their back on running the country when
it so desperately needs strong leadership. We have sat on the
opposition benches for over a decade. Why retreat to them again
and allow Labour to steal victory from under our noses? Labour
are offering AV without even a referendum, so we must offer an
AV referendum, at the very least, if we have any hope of forming
a government, he says. David expresses it as a simple choice: do
we concede and take the reins of government, or slink back to the
opposition benches and sit on our hands while the country falls
apart? David leaves the room with the full support of his colleagues.
Only later is there a question mark over how far Labour had really
gone on AV, and whether David had, in fact, bounced his party
into the decision, giving away something that it was not necessary
to give. But for now, we have what we need. We are able to return
to negotiations with the Lib Dems on firmer ground.

Though the tide has changed again, with Labour moving away

from a deal and us towards one, I make my way into Westminster prepared for another day in limbo land. I have arranged to take my daughter and her friend to a Rihanna concert at the O2. When I booked the tickets months ago, it seemed like a reasonable bet to arrange a special outing for after the election. Now that it is imminent, I feel uncomfortable. But she is 11 and this is a very big deal.

Jeremy Heywood makes contact. He asks to meet up to discuss our initial thoughts on what a Cameron No. 10 would look like. Jeremy has the role of principal private secretary to the Prime Minister at the more senior level of permanent secretary, in recognition of his years of experience and ability. If we ever manage to get through the door, we will be working hand in glove with him.

We need to find somewhere discreet to meet and suggest our old favourite – the Westminster Plaza. 'Surely it is a good sign that they are reaching out to us?' I say to Ed. He is not convinced. Jeremy is a professional to a tee. It is his job to prepare for any eventuality, and at this point in time, that's exactly what we are: one of the possible eventualities.

Over coffee with Jeremy we share details of our current team and our daily operation – both of which we hope to bring with us to No. 10. We feel that gathering our key people – David, George, Oliver, the senior team, and the Chief Whip – together twice a day, first at 8.30 a.m. and then at 4 p.m., has given us the structure to deal quickly and efficiently with a range of issues during our years in opposition. Jeremy is delighted with the format. We get the impression that Brown's No. 10 are not overly fond of meetings. Brown is more of a 'sit in his office and call for people' kind of guy – leaving the meetings to Jeremy. We hope to create a more ordered and functional No. 10.

'What is "Cx"?' I ask, pointing to the list Ed is writing for Jeremy of who comes to our meetings. 'That is code for the Chancellor', explains Ed, reminding me that he has served in government and I don't know the lingo. 'Why don't you just say George?' I say. 'Things just work a little differently in government,' he replies. I can see I will have a lot to learn. But at this point No. 10 still seems a long way away.

By lunchtime we are nearing a deal with the Lib Dems. There is finally a package on constitutional reform to please them: Reform of the House of Lords. A referendum on AV. Boundary reform. And an agreement to a fixed-term parliament, which will effectively bind us into the Coalition for a full five years.

Most importantly of all, we have a firm commitment on Plan A – our deficit reduction programme. It is Plan A that forms the central impetus of the Coalition government. It is the glue that binds us, giving us common sense of purpose.

We call the Shadow Cabinet to David's office in Norman Shaw to talk them through the deal. The idea that Labour might still steal the election away from us has strengthened David's hand around the table; there is a growing resolve for the Coalition in the room.

In the early afternoon, Samantha calls me from the Camerons' home in west London. 'What do you think?' she says. 'Should I get ready?' 'David thinks you'll be fine for today,' I reply. We haven't yet finalised the deal and Brown is supposed to stay put until an alternative government is in place.

But as afternoon draws into evening, things start to feel different. We are hearing things – from the most reliable grapevine in political London, the detectives. Brown's protection team have told David's that things are moving swiftly at No. 10 and to be prepared. At first we are dismissive. We are still some way off forming a viable government, and it would be unconstitutional for Brown to step down pre-emptively. It is also getting very late in the day for these sorts of fireworks. I think the concert will be fine, I tell my daughter, but I put my husband on standby just in case.

Then it all happens. Gordon Brown announces he is finally stepping down as prime minister with immediate effect. We are in shock. David rings Samantha to tell her to put on her dress and get over here as fast as she can.

It is evening when Gordon and Sarah appear outside No. 10

with their boys to say their goodbye before making their way to the palace to take leave of the Queen. We can hear the helicopters circling overhead. David's speech is tweaked, printed, and then changed one last time. A smart tie is tracked down. And although this is what we have been waiting for, for days, it still feels surprising. My daughter heads off to see Rihanna without me.

We gather round the television and watch David and Samantha make their way to the palace, driving slowly up the Mall live on TV. It feels incredibly emotional, a culmination of years of hard work for us all. But it is most especially a moment of deep personal pride in David, who at 43 is set to become the youngest prime minister for nearly 200 years.

A woman called Kristina Murrin who is in charge of our 'transition' to No. 10 has arranged for us to enter Downing Street through the back door. Ed, Steve, Andy, and I follow her, slightly bewildered, up Whitehall and in through the door of No. 70. People greet us but I have no idea who they are or where we are. None of us are familiar with No. 10 – except Ed, who spent time there as a young man in the last days of Thatcher. We ask whether we can stand outside in the street to see David arrive.

We are ushered out of the door of No. 11. It is after 8.30 p.m. and dark now, but the street is lit up by a small battalion of cameras. Helicopters are circling overhead once again. I feel as if I am on a film set, only this is real life, in real time. David steps out of the car, walks up to the podium positioned in front of the famous door, and addresses the nation as prime minister for the first time. Samantha is standing just behind him, now very pregnant with Florence.

'Our country has a hung parliament . . . and we have some deep and pressing problems – a huge deficit, deep social problems, a political system in need of reform. For those reasons I aim to form a proper and full coalition between the Conservatives and the Liberal Democrats. I believe that is the right way to provide this country with the strong, the stable, the good and decent government that I think we need so badly.'

As David finishes, he turns to enter No. 10 with Samantha. The door closes behind them, and the gathered staff 'clap in' the Prime Minister as the couple make their way down the yellow corridor to the Cabinet room at the end. We follow a few minutes later, looking mostly at our feet. In the Cabinet room, Jeremy Heywood and Gus O'Donnell, the Cabinet Secretary and the most senior civil servant in the country, are waiting to greet us.

Then we are ushered into the den. This is the office from which Blair operated as Prime Minister.

'Well, here we all are,' says Oliver Dowden, our senior policy fixer and attack dog. Ed, George, Andy Coulson, 'Olive' Dowden, Rupert Harrison, Steve Hilton, and William Hague. This is the core Cameron–Osborne team from day one – small and close. Andy will be the first to leave us, eighteen months later. Then Steve. The rest will stay the course of the Coalition.

We relax into the comfortable chairs, looking round at each other in amused wonder. A growing realisation dawns: we have achieved what we set out to do. We are starting to see that, in one sense, we have finally come to the end of a long journey. And yet, in another, we have only just arrived at our beginning.

PART 2

No. 10

9

WELCOME TO THE BUNKER

I am up early and make my way to the office – which is now No. 10 Downing Street. It all feels a little odd, though hugely exciting. I am holding a cup of coffee as I walk up the street past a bank of photographers, who start clicking merrily away. I remember I have failed to pass the Isabel Spearman make-up test and now there will be evidence to prove it. Will the photographers be here every morning, I wonder? The answer is, yes, they will be. Sometimes they take pictures of you, sometimes they don't. The papers are always careful to have an up-to-date image just in case you land yourselves in the news – generally because you have done something wrong.

I feel a bit overwhelmed, honestly. The new place, the new people. It feels a lot more like the first day of a new job than merely an extension of an old one than I had anticipated. But then again, I am not sure what I was expecting, or whether I had ever really, in my heart of hearts, envisioned working here at all, despite working towards this moment for the past five years. And over the coming months, I would discover that although my government job looked the same as my opposition one on paper, that little extra dimension of helping to run the country makes it a whole new ball game.

I hammer on the big black door and the policeman opens it to let me in. There is no side entrance for staff. I make my way down the corridor. I have no idea where I am supposed to be sitting.

A tip from George: just find yourself a desk as close to David as you can. Then everything will be fine. Proximity is power.

I walk into the room next to the den, which we have decided to make our private office. There is an empty desk just outside the door to David's office. Someone has got to sit here, so it might as well be me. I sit down and turn on the computer and am amazed to find a few emails addressed to me at my new email address, which is so long and complicated I cannot believe I will ever remember it. A few hours later George finds me there. 'Well, you can't get closer than that,' he says, approvingly. And it is here that I sit for just over six years.

Opposite is Ed Llewellyn. We have already spent five years sitting across from one another. By the time we leave No. 10 it will be eleven. Along with Jeremy Heywood, who also inhabits our office, we are the CEOs of No. 10. Working hand in glove, we divide up the tasks, taking on the difficult ones together. This is why Ed likes to say that we box and cox.

At the far side of the room is the duty clerk and diary secretary, the person in charge of all that the prime minister does. It's a high-security job, 'red phone' at the ready. Behind their desk, in the corner, is a dumb waiter that is used to bring official papers up and down from the garden rooms. With them comes a smell of dead mouse. There is also a desk designated for the use of the other private secretaries, who take it in turn to sit with us in the hot spot. There are two chairs by the door for people to sit in if they are waiting to see the prime minister, which we mean to get rid of (but never quite do) on the grounds that you never know who might turn up. Outside, the military band practises 'Land of Hope and Glory' in the parade ground. Coming into Trooping the Colour, they will be at it all day and all night. 'In the flat you have to choose between fresh air and noise', says a tired David.

'Is this the moment when you get told about the alien in the basement?' I ask, perched forward on my chair and speaking to David, who is working at his desk, door slightly ajar. (This is how we discuss a great number of things over the coming six years.)

'No,' says David, 'at least, not yet. I think this is the man with the nuclear codes.'

Tom Fletcher, the Prime Minister's foreign affairs advisor, keeps putting through calls from foreign leaders ringing to congratulate David. They started the night before: 'Prime Minister – President Obama on the line.' It feels completely surreal.

Green and red files start piling up on Ed's desk – put there courtesy of the duty clerk. 'Why have you got all those files and I don't?' I ask Ed. 'Because I've requested them,' he answers. And I realise there is no one telling you what to do here, not even Ed.

The green files are for box notes – in other words, notes written to the Prime Minister for his evening box. The red files contain more sensitive documents.

It takes me two more weeks before I realise I haven't even scratched the surface. 'Why do you all seem to know what David thinks about everything?' I ask Ed. 'I just read the reply,' he responds. They circulate to a select few; I add my name to the list. The puzzle fits together piece by piece. But no one offers to show me how, especially the people who know already.

I go in search of my scattered colleagues. We have all been working together in an open-plan office and now I have no idea where everyone is. I find Ameet Gill, David's speechwriter, ensconced with the official speech team, and Andy settling in to the press office two doors down in No. 12. Nos. 10, 11, and 12 Downing Street look like separate houses from the outside, but inside they are all connected.

'Where are you going to sit?' I ask Steve when I bump into him. 'It's going to be great!' he says. 'Polly and I are sharing an office.' Polly Mackenzie is Nick Clegg's policy advisor. This raises eyebrows. The idea is for the Cameron and Clegg teams to work closely together – but not fuse. The shared office does not last.

To our new colleagues in the Civil Service we want to look like we are dignified professionals taking our first day at No. 10 completely in our stride. In reality, we are like school children who want to huddle together in a corner and laugh at our good fortune.

I learn fast that it is easy never to leave 'the bunker'. When you work at Downing Street, everyone wants to come to you. My daily walk out the back and across Horse Guards to get my lunch becomes my one defiant bid for freedom.

ON DAY ONE, OUR first task is to launch the Coalition agreement – our official programme for government. We are planning a joint Cameron–Clegg press conference, and talk through the format and one or two likely questions with Nick and his team – Jonny Oates, soon to be Nick's chief of staff, and Lena Pietsche, his head of comms. We meet upstairs in what they call the Terracotta room. We eye each other up across this grand state room. Only a week ago we were adversaries and now we are colleagues (of sorts). Everyone is excited and upbeat.

Outside, the weather has changed for the better, so the press conference is moved to the rose garden. The two men, standing side by side, speak of optimism, of rising above party politics in the national interest. It is an historic moment that seems to capture the country's mood, though it grates with some in the party, who feel that David is moving too far from his roots. Many are about to feel even more aggrieved when they realise they have to share government posts with the Lib Dems.

Government posts are to be allocated roughly in proportion to votes won, so around three Conservatives to every Lib Dem. But David is more generous in Cabinet. Nick is to become Deputy Prime Minister and get four more Cabinet positions, so five in all. This annoys the Tories, not least because there are fewer jobs to hand out. Many members of the Conservative Shadow Cabinet fail to make the government. Most of those who make it are demoted. Sue Gray, a warm and down-to-earth woman with the scary *1984*-style title of head of propriety and ethics, sets up in the small study by the Cabinet room to sketch out where we have got to with the make-up of the government. Names keep dropping down or off the chart. Those who fall off altogether join a core of MPs who feel disappointed and disenfranchised by the Coalition right from day one.

Now, though, it's full steam ahead with appointing the government. David starts with William and George. William as Foreign Secretary and First Secretary of State – David's effective deputy – and George as Chancellor of the Exchequer at just 38 years old. Both head off to their departments to address their own staff, which are considerably larger than ours.

David sits at the centre of the Cabinet table next to either Ed or me as MPs are brought in one by one and sat opposite. It is all very formal – even with those we know the best. 'I am asking you to join my government as . . .' David says, before outlining his priorities for the job. Fresh from opposition, the formality feels a little strange. Later, once we are ensconced in No. 10, it becomes more the norm. The government machine separates and formalises relationships. Ministers work through their officials rather than picking up the phone to a colleague, which can be damaging over time.

There are a few surprises, such as Iain Duncan Smith's appointment as Welfare Secretary and Theresa May's as Home Secretary. It is the last thing Theresa is expecting – and she is stunned and a little giddy as she leaves the Cabinet room. Nick sees his own people first and then hands them over to be formally appointed by David. Vince Cable is to represent the Lib Dems on the economy at the Department for Business, Innovation and Skills (BIS). Chris Huhne goes to Energy. Danny Alexander is to be Secretary of State for Scotland. David Laws is to be number two at the Treasury, taking up the Chief Secretary role.

Before the day is over, David wants the National Security Council to meet. This is a new invention, borrowed from the Americans. He wants to show that he is on top of the security side of the brief, and that he expects a one-government approach. Cabinet will have to wait for the following morning.

The new Cabinet members arrive keen and early the next day. Cameras are invited in for a few minutes at the start of this first meeting. David sits in the large chair bang in the middle of the coffin-shaped table. On his right is the Cabinet Secretary, Gus

O'Donnell; on his left, David's deputy, William Hague. Across the table is Nick Clegg and right next to him, George. David wants to be able to catch George's eye when he needs to. Over the course of the Coalition, David will usually pick George to speak on an issue straight after Nick, so George can add his weight to any decision. After a decade of warfare between Blair and Brown at Nos. 10 and 11, this signals a period of alignment. And although there are differences of approach and sometimes of views between David and George, they operate as co-heads of one team throughout. The message to the Cabinet is clear: there will be no playing one off against the other.

I sit next to Ed and Jeremy Heywood in the row of chairs just behind David. Here we can survey the scene and pass him notes if we need to. 'Remember to flag X!' 'Don't say Y!!' Or 'We've just heard, such-and-such has happened . . .' At this first Cabinet, the contrasts – of politics and character – are still yet to emerge. Even Vince Cable looks faintly pleased to have finally gained office after a lifetime dedicated to commentary. And Michael Gove has not yet started to eat his breakfast during the meetings, which becomes a regular occurrence. Looking across at Oliver Letwin, Michael, and George, I smile to myself. What a long journey we have made from the Camerons' kitchen to the Cabinet room.

Over the weekend, there is a kerfuffle about the courtesy country houses. Following tradition, William, as Foreign Secretary, has been given the grand, Grade I-listed Chevening, which is suitable for entertaining foreign dignitaries. But the question is who gets Dorneywood – Nick or George? It has in the past been home to both deputy prime ministers and chancellors. George has his eye on the house, not least because it is only half an hour from Chequers, the prime minister's country retreat, and thus a good way of keeping in touch with David over the weekends. But Nick wants a house too, and as Deputy Prime Minister he is, in theory, senior. William hums – normally a sign that he has a view about something that he may or may not choose to reveal. George decides to take matters into his own hands and heads to Dorneywood first thing on

Saturday morning to claim the place as his own. In the end, it is decided that Nick and William are to share Chevening.

A FEW WEEKS LATER, I go down to Chequers for the first time. It is half-term and Samantha has taken the children off on holiday. David is hunkered down in his new house. The plan is for us to give a series of thank-yous for people who helped us with the election.

It is an early summer evening when I pull up outside the Elizabethan manor. Everything is in full bloom, including the variety of trees, in their different stages of life, which have been planted by visiting prime ministers and presidents over the years. The house is more romantic than I had expected, with its panelled rooms, open fires, and large old masters. The housekeeper greets me. 'The Prime Minister is in the den,' she says with Mrs Danvers formality, then points me in the direction of the small study off the main hall. She stares at my jeans and seems relieved when I change for dinner. 'Lovely dress,' she coos.

DAVID WILL WORK IN the den off and on throughout the weekends – near enough to his family so they don't notice how often he pops out to take a call or read a newly sent memo. Chequers works because it allows a prime minister to work and relax in an atmosphere of privacy.

David already looks very much at home here. But he is clear with his family right from the start: this is not our home; home is in Dean. The Camerons start to run the house in an informal, family style. I suspect that shepherd's pie for Saturday lunch is not what the cook has in mind. Unused fireplaces are opened and swept; fires are lit. David sets up a sound system in the great hall. Over time, the place begins to feel less like a government guest house and more like a family home.

George is on the phone when he arrives. 'I've got a problem,' he whispers, continuing his conversation. David and I have a walk round the lavender-infested terrace waiting for him to finish. When he finally does, it is bad news. Just two weeks into the government, David Laws is going to have to resign over his expenses. This is quick, by anyone's standards. And it is a blow to George, who was working well with Laws on his first budget, which is just weeks away.

We sit down for dinner at a small round table by the window in the large state dining room. It is almost cosy. A fleet of uniformed staff on secondment from the armed forces serve us a complicated plate of very English food. It's all roast beef and homegrown vegetables, purees and jus. Afterwards, we wander round the upstairs gallery looking at the extraordinary things in the house – Elizabeth I's ring, Cromwell's swords. We can't quite take it in.

The following week we are due to meet Nick Clegg for our now weekly PM–DPM bilateral. With the budget just weeks away, David suggests that George join us. Nick wants to bring Danny Alexander, who has replaced David Laws on his side. The four of them sit down to discuss the budget. The 'Quad' – the driving force of the Coalition government – is formed.

Then, it is late June. George delivers his first budget, and austerity is born.

10

HOW No. 10 WORKS

No. 10 never sleeps, or takes a holiday. Along with the colony of mice who enjoy the freedom of its corridors at night, are people working shifts – monitoring emails, answering phones, guaranteeing the security of the current prime minister – ready for every eventuality. These people are part of what makes the place so unique.

Chris Martin, who will become David's principal private secretary after Jeremy Heywood leaves to become Cabinet Secretary, likes to call it 'the House' (he calls the machine of government 'the System'). This seems a strange way of dehumanising the efforts of many people, but it fits with the sense of duty and public service of the people who work here. The House and the System are there to serve its master (or mistress). Full stop. They served the master before and will serve the master (or mistress) after. This is a highly professional service devoid of emotional attachments – collectively, that is. Individuals, of course, have their own feelings.

Instructions seem to be issued to a slightly abstract entity. 'I'll get the House ready,' Chris might say, or 'I'll give the System a kick' – meaning what exactly? Or more to the point – who? When something goes wrong it is always 'the System failed' rather than so-and-so has messed up. In this other world of politics, when something goes wrong, somebody 'gets a bollocking'.

Also, in 'the House' lives the famous No. 10 switchboard, or 'Switch'. This refers to the diligent (mostly) women who operate the house switchboard 24/7, 365 days a year, Christmas included.

They work shifts and have beds upstairs, operating in an almost wartime atmosphere of duty and camaraderie.

'No. 10 Switch here,' they say, in their now virtually extinct 1950s' BBC English. They can get hold of anyone, anywhere on the planet, keeping a whole range of numbers for any one individual (mothers, aunts, friends), but they will never, *never* give out a number. I have tracked down the most random people across time zones through Switch. They also plagued my life for six years. Constant calls at all times of days and night, so many walks round the park where I have held my phone to my ear, half talking to my children, half listening to some foreign leader discussing world peace with David.

Switch offer a bewildering set of options for communicating. There are conference calls, one-to-ones, calls which I am invited to speak on and calls which I am simply supposed to listen in to. In the beginning, I am not sure which is which. David on the call to a head of state: 'patched in', or in other words, listening only. David on the call with his team: free to speak. More complicated is a call from David to, say, Nick Clegg. Here, I have a great deal to say – their conversation is going seriously off kilter – but find I am unable to speak. I complain to David how frustrating it is not to be able to interrupt his weekend conversation with Nick. 'I cannot tell you how relieved I am you can't!' he says.

Ed accepts the 'mute' button when it comes to calls with foreign leaders but finds it frustrating nonetheless. He starts giving David advice through a series of notes (when David is in the office) or emails (when he isn't). 'You're talking too much,' Ed often writes. On a call with Angela Merkel, the note comes through: 'Be more charming!' David replies, 'Just piss off.'

There is even a strict etiquette to how the calls are set up. Switch start with the most junior. Last on the line is the most senior. You cannot ignore your place in the pecking order; Switch will gladly remind you. Doing a large(ish) conference call this way means people hanging on the line for quite a while as everyone is tracked down. Then finally, 'Prime Minister on the line,' Switch announce chirpily, and everyone stops gossiping, or whispers to their children to leave them alone.

The custodians form another important component. They are a bizarre combination of custodian, butler, and historian in one. They uphold the traditions of 'the House' and are also responsible for a diverse set of duties, which they fulfil with help from the 'front of house' team: marshalling events, bringing teas and coffees to meetings, hosting tours round the building, even organising the Prime Minister's takeaways. The custodians have seen a few prime ministers come and go. So be offhand with them at your peril: they will definitely outstay your time in 'the House', and they have the collective memory of a tribe of elephants.

I get to know Michael and Anne the best. Michael has seen it all. He always brings me water (and offers me harder alternatives) in the event of a crisis. Serving tea and coffee for meetings is cancelled early on in my time at No. 10 due to austerity. (This is Jeremy Heywood's idea of setting a good example.) There isn't a biscuit in the place. Except if you know how to ask FoH the right way. Then biscuits might make a miraculous appearance.

Standing guard outside the Cabinet room with a determined expression, Anne sometimes looks more like she is preparing to wrestle visitors to the ground rather than welcome them nicely to a reception. Her favourite day of the year is the annual No. 10 children's Christmas party. She usually dresses up as an elf – hat daggling down her back, but with the same determined look on her face. I am not sure what the children make of it all, but perhaps they are too excited by the live reindeer from central casting to give it much thought.

The festive season begins with the lighting of the large Christmas tree outside the front door by the Prime Minister, normally followed by some carol singing. No. 10 staff gather outside, wearing coats and scarves to see the lights switched on, often bringing their own children along for the occasion.

Switch and the custodians are not the only group who work shifts 24/7. Downstairs are the famous 'garden rooms girls'. This is the name given to a now mixed gender but once female-only group of prime ministerial support staff whose office in No. 10 looks out on the rose garden. They fulfil a huge range of functions: overseeing the paperwork and organising diaries, calls, and events.

Next door, the duty clerks fulfil a more complicated function. They keep the show on the road – dealing with official material, fielding calls from heads of state, picking up the red phone when it goes off, and alerting us to matters of urgency. There is always a duty clerk and a garden room girl on duty. Always.

Then there are the police. There are those who look after the building (armed police) and those who look after a prime minister (the detectives). These are two distinct groups of people, who have been trained very differently. Both are dedicated, good people, there to look after their 'principal', or 'the boss', as the detectives are fond of calling David. But be clear: these people are *not* there to look after you.

Detectives allocated to protect a person is known as a 'security detail'. And running a 'detail' is a complicated business. For the person being protected and their nearest and dearest bang goes your privacy as your team are with you day and night.

Security could also be maddeningly inflexible for those of us trying to get on with our day jobs. We already have the bank of photographers to contend with, but another, less predictable local obstacle is being caught up with random 'lock downs' which may make perfect sense from a security perspective, but it does not help at all when you are running to make the morning meeting.

ONE MORNING I FIND myself in lock down with minutes to go before a crucial meeting and the agenda still to write. I realise the police still think David is planning to take Florence to school, only he isn't anymore, because an issue has blown up overnight and he has called us in early to discuss it. I say to the policeman, 'If you are in lock down because you think the PM is about to leave, he isn't – there's been a change of plan.' Policeman does not respond; it is not his job to question. I ring the custodians. 'Can you pop into the police ops room and tell them tell him the PM is not going out anymore?' Not our responsibility, they respond.

I ring the duty clerk and ask the same question. By now, most of the meeting is being held up at the back gate while David is sitting by himself in his office wondering where we all are. I finally ring David direct. I offer to pass him to the policeman. 'How do I know that is him?' says the policeman.

For those arriving early, at least they have Marg and Alison to greet them. This sunny duo is the heart of No. 10, running the small canteen downstairs with a cheerful familiarity lacking else-where and handing out bacon butties to most of the staff each morning. A sausage sandwich for Oliver. Porridge for Olive. An espresso for George. Most would agree the food is not the biggest attraction of the No. 10 canteen but rather the people who run it. When I first arrived, I was asked what I might like to see on the menu. I mentioned the word 'yoghurt' – only to find a large yoghurt pot on the front page of *The Sunday Telegraph* a few days later: 'Cameroons bring healthy to No. 10'. So, I decided against any more adjustments. I was more than happy to buy just a cup of tea (given the ongoing tea ban upstairs) and have a chat.

NOW ENSCONCED AT NO. 10, David is surrounded by a mass of new officials, all of whom call him Prime Minister or PM (we mostly still call him Dave, at least in private) and eager to make their mark. They impress him with language about security and codes, which we are yet to be versed in. At first this drives a wedge between us, but over time it wears off. As we get to know each other – 'politicals' and officials – we become one team.

George too is soon in his element at the Treasury, with so many bright, slightly nerdy people who appreciate his intellect and humour. Before long, he is running the ship as if he had been born its rightful captain. But then, No. 10 and the Treasury notoriously attract the brightest and most professional of the Civil Service. Others are certainly having a bumpier ride – Michael Gove taking on what he sees as the vested interests of the Department for

Education, for one. These different experiences invariably colour individual attitudes towards the Civil Service. On the one hand, some view it as a scandalously closed shop in need of radical overall, while others see it as a finely tuned machine that serves the government of the day with the highest quality of brains, altruism, and integrity. The truth probably lies somewhere between the two. No organisation is so perfect that it does not need a watchful eye looking over it, especially an organization of this size that is essentially self-regulating and paid for by the public purse.

In No. 10, we must work hand-in-glove with our Civil Service officials in management of the government. We of course set the direction of travel; they are there to help us get to our chosen destination. Though aligned and respectful of each other, we are very different animals. Politicals vs. Officialdom. We the politicals prefer to contact each other via text, while the officials use BlackBerries or phone through Switch. Politicals never take minutes (dangerous), while officials are always supposed to. We speak out at meetings, they wait to be asked their views. They take annual leave and expect to be left alone, we take holidays (not often) and expect to be bothered a lot. They are assessed properly by their line managers, while we know all is well if we have not been fired. When something goes wrong they blame 'the System' and we blame ourselves. They will not gossip with us (only with each other). We discuss things with David. They ask for the Prime Minister's 'intent'.

Of course, there is sometimes a definite cultural clash, especially of humour. David brings with him to No. 10 his boyish sense of humour, which many of the officials struggle with. A particularly hapless delegation from the foreign affairs team interrupt a difficult speechwriting session.

'I'm busy with the speech,' David says, less than pleased.

'Sorry, PM. It's just the Chinese are really pushing us to know . . .'

'Know what?' he replies, short and not in the mood.

'Well . . . whether it's to be Golden Era or Golden Age for the state visit.'

'I don't care . . . anything golden will do . . . as long as it's not a golden shower!'

The delegation shuffle to the door. 'Thank you, Prime Minister.'

Although strong relationships develop, a respectful distance remains. In the end, our lot was thrown in with David and theirs with 'the System'. In difficult times, the risks fall on *our* shoulders. The political team arrive together; we fight political battles, elections, and referendums together. And ultimately, we will leave together while the others remain to serve another boss.

ALTHOUGH THE MAIN CEREMONIAL function of state remains safely with the royal family, No. 10 has its duties to do in hosting prime ministers and heads of state. 'The House' always rises to a big occasion – and there are plenty of them. David greets visiting heads of state with a handshake at the door – this is the picture they want for their front pages back home. And then it is over to Carol Kempton, who is in charge of events at No. 10. Bedecked in black, Carol heads up what looks remarkably like a Victorian funeral procession. Slowly and purposefully, the dignitaries follow her along No. 10's corridor, up the stairs to the state rooms where meetings take place. Us meagre staffers are supposed to keep out of sight and sound. Forget the meeting you are late for. You will just have to wait. No one dares cross Carol with her VIPs.

The Queen comes to Downing Street twice during my time there – once with Prince Philip to have lunch with David and Samantha, and once to attend Cabinet. The lunch is a private affair. No. 10's tradition of clapping in and out their prime ministers is only extended to a very select few during my time there – namely, the US and the UK heads of state. The applause for the Queen is respectful – and it is hard to curtsy and clap at the same time. Upstairs, a group of us are lined up to be presented before they go into lunch. I am standing next to Steve, who has decided to play by the rules for once and wear a suit and even a pair of shoes. He has stopped short of a tie.

A year later the Queen is back. This time to attend Cabinet as part of the celebrations for her Diamond Jubilee. It is the first time the monarch has attended Cabinet since the eighteenth century.

ALTHOUGH THE MANAGEMENT OF 'the House' itself is really controlled by the officials – not by the political staff – the officials know I am their best bet if they need a decision out of David. Which is why I become embroiled in all matters furnishing. 'Why not ask Ed?' I suggest, feeling it is a bit sexist. The problem is, Ed just doesn't care. Samantha is of course responsible for the flat upstairs, which she soon turns into a haven of good taste and tranquillity. Downstairs lands in my lap.

Jeremy Heywood suggests that I choose some pictures for David's den and the private office next door. By the time I get round to booking an appointment with Penny Johnson, head of the Government Art Collection, George – who is something of an art connoisseur – has already taken the best pictures for his various offices. I choose some photographs of West Country beaches that I think David will like, as well as a print of Oxford, to remind him of his university days and constituency. John Piper's *Sheffield Suburb*, which Brown hung above the fireplace, we decide to keep; even though it is a little gloomy, it is still a beautiful picture. I search for an image of Churchill but am told none are left – until I find a charming one in George's dining room. And above the sofa in his study is a beautiful Nevinson – an image from the First World War, perched within the clouds – which I long to hijack for our end of the corridor.

Even though the den looks so shabby with its stained sofa, torn armchairs, and drooping curtains, David is reluctant to spend a penny on it while we push ahead with austerity. We agree to let things be. So, we are slightly put out when George redecorates his rooms with Osborne & Little – courtesy of his parents, not the taxpayer. We feel like the poor relations; David grumbles as he passes the newly laid carpet. When George's lovely new wallpaper seems repelled by the old walls we are not overly sympathetic.

But there are some things which cannot be left forever – whether

David likes it or not. This is an official house; it cannot simply be allowed to fall into disrepair. So, every year, Helen, whose job it is to oversee the building, makes a small change where it is needed most. When it is the turn for the main carpet, which runs along the historic corridor and up the main staircase, Helen suggests we simply renew the existing carpet. But in a back room, up on the third floor, I find an older, subtler version of the design, which turns out to be the original from Thatcher's day. When it is laid, I feel a ridiculous sense of achievement. I have a feeling this will be my most permanent legacy to No. 10.

There are no pets in No. 10 when we arrive, only the memory of a bygone age of Humphrey, the Blairs' cat. Andy Coulson sets about trying to put this right early on. He wants a dog – a bulldog, even. This is perhaps an attempt to capture the nation's imagination, but it is obviously out of the question. No bulldog. No dog. In fact, David and Samantha have no desire to have a pet, full stop. But Andy persists. And when a mouse runs out from under David's desk we agree: it is time for a mouser. This will strictly be a house – not a Cameron – cat. The cat's food is paid for by an annual quiz night, which becomes the most popular staff event of the year.

Liz Sugg goes off to Battersea Dogs & Cats Home and comes back with Larry. The cat people think he has the right personality for No. 10. They are right, he does, roaming the corridors like the alpha predator he is supposed to be, sitting wherever he likes, including on David's chairs, and covering his suit with a layer of cat hair. Only the Chief Whip, Sir George Young, dares remove him from the sofa when he finds him in his favourite spot at the 4 p.m. meeting. He is very nearly never asked back.

Does Larry ever catch a mouse? I think not. Possibly because he is so spoilt. Fed by a doting staff. Sent presents from all over the world – toys, blankets, even bow ties. Larry has a girlfriend who lives in the keeper's cottage in St James's Park. It is an abusive relationship; he eats her food. But he is still welcome. Larry even has a blog. There is no doubt about it: Larry is a celebrity. They erect a blue plaque for him at Battersea.

But Larry's glory days are to be short-lived. Somewhere across London, an elderly lady dies and her family bring her cat to the vet. They don't want to take on a pet, so the vet suggests they track down the former owners, who turn out to be a family called Osborne. Freya has been gone quite a while, having run off with the neighbourhood alley cats a few years back. Her brother, Oscar, went missing in action around the same time. In Downing Street, George presents his delighted children with their long-lost cat (or at least one of them). But the reception to Freya is a lot cooler elsewhere. Carol – who is nominally in charge of Larry – is against. Larry won't like it, she says, shaking her head. And soon there is a growing clamour of Larry supporters who make it clear: George's cat is not welcome. This does not deter George.

Freya arrives – a comfortable, overweight female, used to a sedentary life at the side of her elderly owner. The real Freya is yet to emerge. In a few months, she morphs from house cat to full-blown minx. With her trim little figure and adventurous streak, she begins to throw her weight around, soon becoming a well-known sight not just around Nos. 10 and 11 but all over Whitehall. She regularly attends meetings in the Foreign Office, where William's team think she has been bugged, either by the Russians or possibly by George. But her reputation is truly defined by her relationship with Larry, whom she loves to torture. She displaces him from his favourite sunbathing spots and fights with him openly in front of the cameras, undermining his 'cred' in 'the House'. With Freya around, Larry becomes a bit of a recluse, sleeping for hours on end in the lesser-known corners of No. 10. His supporters are not happy. The cat soap opera is brought to an abrupt end when Freya is hurt by a car and taken home by Carol for her own safety.

Some less charitable people in the building think Carol has catnapped George's tabby. But I suspect George (being more of a dog person) and Carol have conspired to find Freya a new home. No one is happier than Larry . . . until Lola, the Osborne dog, arrives.

11

THE HOUSE, A HOME

No. 10 is the heart of the UK government, but it is also a home. And it was my goddaughter Florence Cameron's first home. This is what makes No. 10 so unlike any other place of work. It requires the utmost dedication and professionalism from its staff. But juxtaposed with the weighty daily duties of helping to run the country is the softness of family life buzzing around you.

In August, David and a heavily pregnant Samantha head off for their annual family holiday in Cornwall, their first since arriving at No. 10. Although Samantha's due date is some way off, her babies have a habit of coming early. Florence is no exception. Off they rush to the Royal Cornwall in Truro and Florence Rose Endellion – Endellion after the Cornish village – makes her entrance to the world.

The No. 10 press and ops teams rush down for the requisite photo call. But by this time Samantha has learned to push back on the enthusiastic comms team. She is not being frog-marched outside for a photo call straight after a Caesarean, as was done after Elwen's birth. *Click* – a nice picture of David holding Florence is released to the press. The family photo op will wait for their return to No. 10, where baby Florence is ensconced upstairs in the flat in a cardboard box with her name on it. She was Queen of No. 10 for the time she inhabited it and possibly loves it more than any of us. When the moment comes to leave in 2016, she tries to attach herself to the railings. We are supposed to make a dignified exit, Samantha explains. 'But I don't want to go,' says Florence.

Florence's popularity grew with her mobility. Her first fans are the custodians, policemen, and gardeners, who admire her daily trips to St James's Park, where she is pushed in her pram by Gita, her devoted nanny. It seemed hardly any time before she is propelling herself with speed and dexterity around the carpeted corridors of No. 10 on a pink scooter, with matching helmet, visiting her favourite members of staff (noticeably those who had sweets).

It's clear to us that Samantha's great gift to David is in not being a 'political' wife but in creating a 'safe haven' for him away from the spotlight. He is naturally a balanced person with a positive outlook, whose happiness is rooted in his commitment to his family. All this gives him great strength to navigate the ups and downs of life as well as politics – and makes him unusually suited to the job of prime minister.

David got his 'glass half-full' philosophy from his father, who was a much stronger influence on him than many people think. Ian Cameron was a man who was handicapped by being born with no heels, yet marched determinedly through life without them.

But then, barely a couple of weeks after Florence's birth, David loses his father, leaving him heartbroken. We console ourselves by being thankful that he was alive to see David walk into No. 10.

As Samantha points out some years later, for those of us in the core team, half our adult lives were spent in the all-consuming Project Cameron. So, it is hardly surprising that we shared so much – not just our political journey, but in life, including some we lost along the way.

Like Ivan.

AROUND 7.30 A.M. ON Wednesday, 25 February 2009, my mobile rang. This was towards the latter part of our years in opposition, and I was busy preparing the children for school before heading off to the office. I wedged the phone under my chin. It was Ed. 'I've got awful news,' he said, 'so prepare yourself.'

'What's happened now?' I replied, not too concerned. Most days in politics tend to start with a drama.

'No really,' he said. 'This is different.'

And he was right. I certainly did not expect to hear the terrible news that David and Samantha's son Ivan, aged six, had died in the night after a severe fit. They had rushed him to St Mary's in Paddington, but the doctors could not save him. Of course, all David and Samantha's friends knew that Ivan, who was born with the rare Ohtahara syndrome, was fragile. But somehow nothing prepared any of us for the reality that he might not live forever – least of all his devoted parents.

Since his birth in 2002, David and Samantha had spent days and nights with him in hospital, trying to control his seizures and make his life more bearable. Their terrible anxiety was that he might be in pain but they would not know. How could he tell them – not being able to speak or really move? More painkillers, while allaying their concerns in this respect, lost him his beautiful smile, and his parents a great deal of joy. For while Ivan could not sit up, and I never saw him eat other than through a tube in his stomach, he was a beautiful child with a serene presence, always watching his parents from his chair, or from the special mound they had made for him in the garden. A large picture of Ivan smiling hangs on the wall of Samantha and David's kitchen, and a smaller version of the same picture always sits on David's desk.

On the many occasions David has spoken with grateful respect for the men and women who work tirelessly in our health services, he often singles out the doctor who worked so patiently to bring Ivan's smile back. A little tweak here and there to the dosage, the doctor said, might just bring the light back into Ivan's face and cause him no additional pain.

Still, there were the all too frequent nights when a seizure, above and over the usual, would terrify them into A&E. While most of the 2001 parliamentary intake was busy networking, David spent much of his time at St Mary's with Ivan.

David would readily admit this was the first time that fate had delivered him any sort of blow. His had been an idyllic upbringing – a loving family, a brilliant education, always popular amongst his peers. By the time I first came across David at Oxford he was already marked out as someone to know. Samantha, who was younger and definitely 'cooler', brought a lighter touch to the more serious and conservative (with a small 'c') David. And then Ivan came, and rather than break them, he brought them closer together, as they supported each other through the emotional and practical difficulties that having a disabled child inevitably brings. Samantha and David were immensely proud of Ivan and they never stopped worrying about his welfare.

Much has been made of whether Ivan changed David, and how he affected David's perspective as a man and later as a politician. There is something in this, of course; we are all shaped by what happens to us. Ivan certainly brought to David a sense of humility and patience, and a consideration for the weak. The pride David and Samantha showed in Ivan, I think, also helped other parents of disabled children hold their heads high and be proud of theirs.

On that Wednesday morning in February, I could barely take in the heartbreaking news of Ivan's sudden death. My phone started to ring. Another call from Ed. He had been speaking to Andy and it was their decided view that someone had to go round to the Camerons'. The story was about to break any minute and they would need the support. I headed over to Notting Hill with a heavy heart, calling George on the way to break the sad news to him. I didn't want him to hear it first on the radio.

Nancy and Elwen were alone with their babysitter when I arrived. They were young and clearly confused about what was going on. Soon after, David and Samantha returned. Shattered, they collapsed into chairs in the sitting room. After tears, hugs, and a lot of tea, we drafted some words for the press and I set off back to the office. I found George, Michael Gove, and William Hague working on a statement in David's office. They were visibly upset but trying to be professional. Gordon Brown cancelled PMQs; he would pay tribute to Ivan instead, reflecting of course on his own terrible ordeal after the death of his baby daughter, Jennifer Jane, years before. It fell to William, as David's deputy, to respond. No one was more skilled for such a sad task than the great orator and scribe who is William. Gordon began movingly: 'The death of a child is an unbearable sorrow that no parents should ever have to endure.' Michael and George, seated on either side of William, looked close to tears.

The funeral of a friend's child is not an event that I would wish on anyone, and sadly I have had to sit through two. There is someone inside us who never recovers from this inexplicable sadness – the loss of life, of hope, of so much grief for our friends. And this family tragedy was complicated by it being so much in the public eye.

We were asked not to wear black to Ivan's funeral, which was held at the beautiful country church in Chadlington, near their home in Dean, which they will always keep, because Ivan is buried nearby. Samantha wore her 'best dress' – polka-dot blue. The small congregation was made up of family, close friends, and Ivan's carers and doctors.

Most of us arrived in sad little groups, to support one another. Steve Hilton was next to me in the pew. Ivan was his godson and he had been asked to read the lesson. He seemed a bit confused at first, looking round at the church, and then he saw it: Ivan's small coffin at the front. 'Oh my God,' he blubbed, the tears pouring down his face. I didn't know how he was going to get through his reading. It still makes me sad, thinking back on Steve that day, remembering all that he and David meant to each other.

When Ivan died, there were people who said it was probably for the best. That is not how the Camerons felt about it. I cringed when I heard people say this to them, for I knew how painful they found it. He was their first child and they were devastated.

A week later, David was back at work. Opposition is a one-man show. It was too soon. How do you keep going when you are weighed down with grief? Yet he did. Years later, David told me he wished he had taken longer after Ivan's death, that the sadness had come in waves. I wish I had sent him home for another month. But then perhaps no time would have been enough.

When David prepares to move the family out of No. 10 and back to North Kensington, many years later, it is there, intact – Ivan's mound, like a lighthouse, guiding them safely home.

MY CHILDREN ARE 11 and 8 when I start working at No. 10. They come to visit for the first time one Friday after school. Michael, my favourite Front of House, devises a special 'ghost tour', lining up some of the others to jump out at them from under sheets. It's all very exciting, seeing the famous house and my new offices. Also a bit strange, because No. 10 is that odd hybrid – an official residence, a family house, and mummy's office. Just as it consumes me, it begins to pull them in too.

In the beginning, it is a big adjustment for us all – especially the formality of the place. In opposition, we have operated as a band of 'sort of' equals. We have lived in the same city and come to work by public transport (or by bicycle). We were free to move around as we pleased. But this changes overnight when David becomes Prime Minister. And with it, some of the intimacy of those years is lost.

David is now master of two new households. He has a police escort, an armoured car, and a patrol of bikes. Some prime ministers have liked the bikes, but David thinks they irritate, and should only be used in cases of emergency. The bikes are duly sent home and he sits in Boris's traffic jams like everyone else.

Guarded by a protection team, there is little spontaneity in David's life, save for the occasional run at short notice, or maybe a visit to the House of Commons, which is a protected area. At first he finds this difficult, and then he learns to bend to it. In the end, this is the reason prime ministers spend so much time in their official houses. At No. 10 or Chequers the detectives leave you alone – giving you a sense of freedom within the confines of the secure compound. Outside means the 'protection' are always in tow.

The fact that his family is in residence, rather than him having to travel home to west London to see them, grounds David and helps to keep him sane. David has a ferocious work ethic, but part of what keeps him balanced, and able to make good decisions, is his ability to switch off. He will go for a run or spend time with the children. At Chequers, he often plays tennis – with a friend, if one is around (they are supposed to lose graciously), or if not, with his ball machine, nicknamed (by the press, originally) 'the Clegger'. There is the possibility of a swim in the indoor pool – a gift from President Nixon. I don't love swimming, I say on one occasion when Nancy is trying persuade me into the water. 'Mum got over that stage a while ago,' she says critically. I say I don't have my swimsuit and she points to a rather tired-looking one-piece hanging in the changing rooms. 'You can use that one   it was left here.'

Late at night, David might watch TV – whisky in hand – before turning in. This earns him some criticism: David, the 'chillaxing' Prime Minister. In fact, David, like his tennis machine, is a tireless worker. And he expects everyone else to be as committed as him.

The Camerons follow the example set by the Blairs, who lived here with four children, and move into the flat above No. 11, not the one above No. 10, which is traditionally for the prime minister. The No. 11 flat is much larger – a house within a house, with lovely views.

Here Samantha erects a fence round the family while, with the help of the highly able Isabel Spearman, also fulfilling her range of duties as wife to the Prime Minister. Isabel has great personal style – we are all terrified to be caught looking untidy by 'Belles'. Samantha carefully carves out a life for herself and her family that hits the right balance – supporting David when he needs her, but focusing primarily on her children and her interests.

Right from the start, Samantha sets down her rules. This is not going to turn into a 24/7, Clinton-style, pizza-eating 'meeting-a-thon'. The minute David walks through the door of the flat, it is family time or red boxes. Unless we absolutely have to, we mostly don't intrude. We already operate on eleven- or twelve-hour days.

Out of hours we do as much as we can on our official No. 10 BlackBerries from home. Of course, I am on email and take calls late into the evening, but I am at home. If there is an emergency we all come back in. This is important. There is a time at night when I know I can return to be with my own children.

The wife of the British prime minister is in an interesting position. Her role is very much in the public eye, but it is a far cry from the role of FLOTUS – the First Lady of the United States – who, as official consort to the US head of state, is required to be more high-profile and perform a set of ceremonial duties. In the UK, we have a royal family who does that job excellently for us.

Samantha decides very early on to keep quite a low profile, which seems to both fit with what is expected from her and works for her and her family. Other prime ministers' spouses have attempted more prominent roles – and they have not always been well received. There is a balance. As a rule of thumb, being supportive and seen to care – advisable. Being seen to meddle or in any way take advantage of your position – not advisable.

Samantha has her own ambitions of course, but they are not in politics. Halfway through her time in No. 10, she starts preparing for her lifetime dream, to launch her own clothes label. She busily tries out her new designs in the upstairs flat. 'You can be my standard size-8 model', she says cheerily, pinning me into her latest dress.

The difference between what is expected of Samantha and how things are done on the other side of the Atlantic, draws my attention when I join her for tea with Michelle Obama and a close advisor. It is a private chat – just the four of us. The stunningly attractive and powerful Michelle Obama is adept at steering the conversation; much of it is about how to manage the role of a leader's wife while bringing up a family, about how to set boundaries. This supporting role could become all-consuming. You need to be careful to protect what is your own.

I was always proud of Samantha for standing by David but not forgetting to be herself.

* * *

ALTHOUGH I SOMETIMES ENVY David's ability to 'pop upstairs' to see his children, I value the freedom of being able to get in my dilapidated VW Golf and drive myself home, away from the Westminster bubble, even more. I like knowing this is my home, whatever happens. I am a diplomat's daughter, and so I grew up in fancy houses that weren't my own.

My journey to work has another benefit. At 7.30 a.m. every day, Rupert Harrison, George's right-hand man, and I meet at our favourite coffee place and I drive us both into work. We have been travelling in together for nearly four years now, dropping my son off at school on the way. The *Today* programme is on in the background as we cover whatever school or work issues arise. For example, my son's choice of poem for school poetry recital competition.

This is in 2014, the anniversary of the start of the First World War. It's got to be 'Dulce et Decorum Est', says Rupert. And the (ultimately) prize-winning poem is duly rehearsed for weeks from the back of the car. We joke to David and George that their bilaterals are nothing as compared to the issues we resolve in this half-hour every day. There is a lot of truth to this.

I miss our journeys to work in my final year, once Rupert has departed for a new career in finance. But I gain the bonus of having my daughter for company – when she can propel herself out of bed in time – after she moves to a new school in Westminster. On the rare occasion the 8.30 meeting is cancelled, we sit with our coffees at a café we have discovered in St James's Park, looking at the child-sized pink pelicans perched on a rock in the lake, discussing the challenges of the day ahead. Sometimes she comes to No. 10 after school, setting out her homework on an empty desk, so that we can drive home together when I am finished.

My daughter also helps me with the less important but nevertheless anxiety-inducing question about what to wear every day. Quite apart from being photographed on the way in, there is the sense of every day being special when you work at No. 10. Here is where the men have the advantage. Deciding which suit, shirt, and tie to put on each morning is easy compared with the complications of a woman's wardrobe. It's a long day. You've got to wear something that will work from morning to night. I opt for dresses, as they can be dressed down with cardigans and are still fine for the evening without. Nothing risqué, but nothing too corporate either. Nothing too tight or too tiring. Mum wears party dresses to work, is my daughter's take on my 'style', if it deserves such a word.

She makes signs for my hangers, Monday to Friday. We pick the dresses out on Sunday night – her advising me from the bed – so that, first thing each weekday morning, I don't have to think.

NO. 10 IS MORE than just an office for those who work there. Taking up so much of your life, it comes to signify a way of life. Over time, No. 10 becomes like family, with all the good and all the complications that go with that. Venture outside and you are a sitting duck for criticism. It's one of the hazards of the job, and people weren't afraid to constantly give it. Some vicious. Some personal. 'No, David does not use hair dye,' you say yet again. We live in a democracy, so it's fair enough for people to say what they think – but it can be trying and at times unpleasant. Which is why those who work at No. 10 often revert to a smaller and smaller group of trusted friends during their time there. It is a protective mechanism. But it is also creates a bubble – which can be a bad thing.

We are all quite wrapped up together. Even to the point where our children seem to follow the same nit cycles. This can sometimes take its toll on others, and other relationships. Relationships collapse. Some under the stress of never being put first. Some from the preoccupation of running the country, and the uncertainties this brings. Three marriages break down after the 2010 election (including my own). David worries he has taken 'our prime', but actually I think he has made it – whatever or whenever 'your prime' really is.

12

MEN AND MEETINGS

From the moment my radio alarm clicks on, discharging *Today* directly into my ear, I am thinking about the agenda for the 8.30, our first meeting of the day. We simply don't have the time to schedule separate meetings for every issue that crosses our desks, especially if they need to be dealt with swiftly, often by roughly the same group of people. So, we bookend the day: a news-driven meeting at 8.30 a.m., and then, at 4 p.m., one focusing on larger issues and strategic problems. This is the basic infrastructure by which we try to keep the show on the road.

We have always worked like this, from our very first days in opposition. Sitting down together first thing – considering what needs to be done today. Of course, once you are in government, nothing is quite that simple. Very quickly, everyone figures out that these two meetings are when the key people meet and the important decisions are made. As their fame extends across Whitehall, so too does the number of people who wish to attend them. I am very aware I am losing the battle to manage the 8.30, which is growing like a pregnant elephant. However, I have put my foot down firmly about the 4 p.m. This is for our core team – no outsiders. We simply can't get anything done otherwise. If you are going to have a proper argument about important issues, which is our modus operandi, you need to trust the people in the room. You need to trust that the discussion will not leak into the newspapers.

Before I can leave the house, I have two children to get out of bed, breakfasted, and off to school. I check my emails and browse the papers online with one hand, a cup of tea or hairdryer in the other. It takes one second to reach for the designated dress on its designated hanger.

The timing is on a knife-edge. This morning the traffic is piling up and I am running late. It's my responsibility to put together the agenda, and it must be ready and printed by 8.30. I have done this so many times now that I can compile it in my head. I get an email from George and a text from David and mentally add these items to my list. Time is ticking. Sometimes I get Rupert to call the duty clerk while I dictate the agenda. The first item is always the media summary. Today I add: Eurozone crisis, troubled families, vote.

I arrive at my desk and swap my flats for my heels, trying not to feel too stressed and dishevelled. The increasing noise from the hall means they are all arriving – George, William Hague, Chief Whip Patrick McLoughlin, as well as David's parliamentary private secretary, Jeremy Heywood. And there's Andy Coulson and the press team, as well as the foreign team. I open the agenda and look over the page before I nervously press print. I am dyslexic, but there must be absolutely no spelling mistakes.

Bang on 8.30 we go into the den and the meeting begins. David is extremely punctual. Ed and I are responsible for what we discuss because we write the agenda. So, while David chairs the meeting, we 'host' it – explaining why an item has been brought to everyone's attention. I sit in the same place every day, in a strategic position on the far end of the sofa across from David's and George's armchairs so that I can catch their eye and scowl at them if I have to. When he is able to, William Hague will attend the meeting and displace George from his usual armchair. George, always respectful of his former boss, draws up another chair.

This morning I'm hot and bothered from my dash into the office. Sometimes I wear my coat to the meeting, which David thinks is a passive-aggressive act. Actually, it's just survival instinct. David is a hot-bodied person, whose body temperature seems to increase with stress. Sometimes he puts the air-conditioning on in winter. I feel the cold, and I am pretty sure everyone else is freezing too but would not dare to add a layer and risk annoying the Prime Minister. I have no such compunction – though I do stop short at a beanie.

To my left are Ed and Jeremy Heywood. Together we form half an inner circle. Rupert stands behind George, madly working away on his BlackBerry – unless David sees him and he gets hollered at. (David has an intense dislike of people playing with their BlackBerries during meetings.) The entire press team seem to be here, even though I have told them a hundred times not to come. There are members of the foreign affairs team too, as there never seems to be a day without a foreign or security issue.

One of the main reasons I battle so hard to avoid this meeting getting any larger is simply that there are not enough places to sit. And even if there were, in practice the issues are discussed and resolved by only a handful of people. Those of us who sit in the chairs tend to do the talking, whilst the outer ring seems to just look at us as we talk. This creates an awkward sort of voyeurism. An audience brings a circus mentality to the whole thing.

After a bumper meeting we agree a cull of attendees is needed. I go through the list, crossing out names. The cries of dismay are heard across Whitehall, but for a few weeks the meeting returns to a level of efficiency. Then, bit by bit, the numbers creep up again. David is often partially to blame. His weakest moments always come in a reshuffle. Someone is offered a new job, which David wants to present as a sideways move when we all know it is in fact a demotion. David takes a friendly line – you'll be part of the inner team. And suddenly they're on the list for the 8.30 meeting.

Given that I am quite small and speak with a terrible lisp, I find the meetings quite daunting at times. The simple task of entering the fray and expressing my point in a half-coherent fashion has taken time for me to master. And while newcomers at the meeting are clearly thrown by my struggle with the English language, David is so used to it he doesn't bat an eyelid. However, over time I have gained in confidence and relaxed, and even started to enjoy them. I have a brilliant vantage point from which to view and understand the psychology of what is basically a group of mostly alpha men, whose primary objective is to show off to each other.

Watching closely, I see that the men use language to enhance their credibility. George is taken more seriously than me, obviously because he is Chancellor. But he is also a master of 'power language'. For example, he doesn't have an 'idea'; he never 'suggests'; he doesn't ask 'how about we say' this or that. George 'creates narratives' and then 'deploys' them – to which everyone nods approvingly, and William hums.

George is also very good at bringing everyone back to focus on the 'big picture' when we have got lost in the weeds. He raises our sights, making us think about what is really going on. This may be the right thing to do – but I've observed it is also an extremely useful tactic if you ever find yourself having to deal with the 'extremely learned man' in a meeting. (There are just as many learned women, but they tend not to display the same characteristics.)

The 'extremely learned man' is someone who was busy learning every statistic in the history of statistics while the rest of us were going to parties or playing sport. This enables them to (seemingly) back up their points (which may or may not be right) with the confidence of gods – and a contempt for opposition that makes the rest of us feel too intimidated to protest. I've learnt that the only way to deal with these people – other than go back to school – is to get back to the 'big picture' or in other words, what the discussion is really about. And to remember that there is a difference between being learned and having good judgement. You can have both of course. But you can also have the former and lack judgement in spades.

In contrast to George, Gavin Williamson, who becomes David's parliamentary private secretary in 2013, has never knowingly deployed a narrative. But he understands his worth, which is measured on his ability to read the party, something he does with great skill. He navigates the lion's den with dexterous charm and agility while also being an extraordinary font of knowledge – some of which is entirely scurrilous. Gavin's network of spies fan out across Westminster, lurking on stairwells, and feed him information that he leverages as his own personal power. He is a strategist and a first-class political game player.

Craig Oliver, when he replaces Andy Coulson as head of comms, sits next to me on the sofa and takes the lead on giving advice on the media. He is clear that he takes a dim view of anyone who attempts to second-guess it, so they mostly don't dare.

Ed rushes off to call another foreign leader, while Olive Dowden defies the classic alpha male norm, mostly sitting quietly in the firm knowledge that the worst jobs are bound to come hurtling to him anyway – but if he opens his mouth, he will no doubt be given another. 'Yes, Prime Minister,' he says and sighs. 'Another turd to polish,' he whispers to me, as he heads off with his task for the day.

Once you have a feel for what is going on, the environment seems less daunting and the meetings easier to deal with. You can always just ignore these men at their power plays (the most tempting option), or else you can learn to take them on using some of their techniques. 'Let's get back to the big picture,' I suggest. Or, if all else fails, and you really have to get something done, you can always set up your own meetings without them.

I want my daughter to learn to stand her ground. This really matters. There's no denying that it is tough – women often feel intimidated by male-dominated environments, not just in politics but in many walks of life. There is a latent sense that a man's view carries greater weight. Women can be put off from speaking their minds, and often don't go for jobs which pay you for what you 'think', opting instead for being paid for 'doing things' – when they could easily do either. In politics, this often translates to falling into ops, leaving men to do policy. It also, I suspect, puts off some women from going into frontline politics. That men thrive in these environments is a factor in keeping women from this sort of work as well. Mostly it is not intentional – but sometimes it is.

Luckily, David surrounds himself with strong women – including his wife. And we have one another – Gabby, Isabel, Liz, speech-writers Clare Foges and Jessica Cunniffe, diary secretary Lara Moreno-Pérez, Kate Marley, Georgina Graham, and also Simone Finn, Kate Shouesmith, Laura Wylde and Kate Rock, to name a few – for support, when the going gets tough.

THOUGH THE 8.30 MEETING throws up various logistical issues, as well as providing a showcase for a few alphas, if I were to give a prize to the meeting with the worst culture, it would be the one in which we prepare for PMQs. Even when I am being most generous, I'd say this meeting pretty much mirrors the event to which it owes its existence in the first place.

Prime Minister's questions takes place every Wednesday at 12 p.m. when Parliament is sitting. The Prime Minister is asked questions from MPs, including up to six coming from the Leader of the Opposition. It is supposed to last for exactly half an hour but the Speaker, John Bercow, seems to have invented his own time, which extends the session depending on how long the two leaders have spent in one-to-one combat. The exact timing is a mystery to all but him.

It is part bare-knuckle fight between the PM and the Leader of the Opposition, part town hall meeting, as the MPs who have won the ballot get to ask questions. You need to be across your brief: the MPs can ask on any topic they chose, without warning. The challenge for the opposition is to find a set of questions that expose the PM's weakness, usually around the political issue of the week.

The weekly process to prepare for this showdown kicks off with a small meeting in No. 10 on Monday afternoon to go through the week's likely topics. From this, a bulky file is constructed for David to comb through on the evening before PMQs. It includes notes on nearly every topic under the sun. The diary secretary knows never to put a late engagement in on Tuesday night.

On Wednesday morning, a larger group gathers straight after the 8.30 meeting. In attendance are officials with their files of facts as well as MPs and politicals armed with clever one-liners (or so they hope).

At its best, this weekly ritual helps to keep the executive on its toes. Under the intense examination of the PMQs process, policies are altered or abandoned altogether as the starkness of their failure is set out in the defensive lines to take that are presented to a prime minister in his or her briefing pack. It is no coincidence that floundering ministers may find themselves 'let go' on a Tuesday night as a prime minister rehearses the defensive footwork needed to justify them remaining in post to a Commons baying for blood. It is a game – but there is a point to it.

The Wednesday morning prep for PMQs quickly descends into a war of words – a political rap competition. Michael Gove is rapper in chief. He perches on his seat, Pret coffee in hand, producing ingenious but mostly unusable couplets. In intense game-player mode, George arranges the moves in his head. Neither of these men are new to this. George has been helping prime ministers prepare for PMQs since he was in his twenties, working for John Major.

The job of the parliamentary private secretary – a role fulfilled by Desmond Swayne, then Sam Gyimah, and lastly Gavin Williamson – is to find out what the MPs on our side are planning to ask and 'persuade' them of something better. The MPs will be conflicted. For many it is a rare chance to get the limelight, so they will be tempted to ask something a bit edgy. But it also gives them an opportunity to win brownie points with the Prime Minister by asking something helpful. This is where Gavin sets to work – moulding a question that works for us and, if he is clever, has a constituency angle. 'You know it makes sense,' Gavin says with a broad, slightly menacing smile. Later he gathers his group of supportive MPs – his 'Q team' as he calls them – ahead of PMQs to practise their chant or hand gesture of the week, to be deployed from the backbenches.

This raucous parliamentary chorus is a reminder of another purpose of PMQs: to cheer up the troops who are sitting on the benches behind a prime minister. In this, PMQs is a curious tribal ritual. A victorious David will keep the MPs happy for a while, or certainly happier than if he comes off the loser. There is no doubt that a leader who fails to deliver at these weekly exchanges will begin to fade in the estimation of their colleagues over time.

I am supposedly in charge of keeping PMQs prep focused and appropriate. In this duty, I invariably fail. Ed sensibly sits out these meetings. His take is, 'The louder the laughter from behind that door, the worst the results.' He's generally right. The meetings can take on a momentum of their own – everyone forgetting they are there to serve a purpose rather than to engage in a furious game of one-upmanship.

This meeting breaks up at ten, giving David an hour on his own to work through his answers. He likes to do this at his office in the Commons with his team on standby if he needs any facts found. At 11.15, the group gathers for another round of question prep – 'net practice' as we call it. Olive Dowden, acting as Leader of the Opposition, bowls a set of six questions, and we all pile in.

David was often criticised for being a bully at PMQs – the worst type of male, public school one. In April 2011, his Michael Winner-style 'Calm down, dear' – meant as an amusing put-down to Angela Eagle – earned him the reputation of being patronising to women, something he never quite shrugs off.

I try to impress on him the need to be less bombastic. 'Don't bother,' he says. 'It's a bear pit, so you have to be a bear. If you want different behaviour, put me in a different habitat.' He has a point.

Of course, the whole event is predicated on who David faces in PMQs. At first, when David was Leader of the Opposition, this was Tony Blair. David often came off as young and promising against a tainted and tired Blair. But Blair was still good – light on his feet, agile, witty. David landed the occasional punch, but Blair was hard to beat. Then came Brown – that 'clunking fist'.

Here it mattered less if David landed a punch, because Brown did not seem to notice. He just kept going, like a digger over a field, repeating set lines that bore little resemblance to the questions.

After Brown resigned following the 2010 general election, we watched, captivated, as the two Miliband brothers battled it out for leadership of the Labour Party. David was the better known of the two, and we considered him by far the strongest – and potentially a much more problematic adversary. As Ed's campaign took off in 2010, David and George's smiles broadened. George welcomed the news of Ed's triumph in front of the television on bended and grateful knees.

Of course, Ed Miliband has his strengths too, as well as his moments. Here is where PMQs can provide a platform for the opposition as an issue hots up. Most memorable are Miliband's proposed cap on energy prices and his campaign in 2014 against News International and David's 'wilful negligence' in hiring Andy Coulson. Though Miliband at times did cut through, he often failed to land the killer blow, leaving David mostly the victor of these encounters.

Then Corbyn arrives in 2015. We are too amazed even to get down on our knees. Corbyn tries to move away from the adversarial, so-called 'childish' encounters of PMQs, choosing to ask questions he has received from members of the public. Although it is clearly a worthwhile endeavour to remove the bear from the pit (or at least the teeth from the bear), the problem remains: we are still in the coliseum, surrounded by the braying crowd. Soon, as he fails to make an impact and interest in his 'new' style of PMQs wears thin, Corbyn returns to more standard practice. A set of random questions is unlikely to bear fruit in the way that a six-question interrogation can.

Before and after Ed Miliband, David faces Harriet Harman as acting Labour leader. I have to admit I am biased in favour of her. I admire her. So does Steve Hilton. She is genuine and has real poise, speaking from the heart about issues that clearly matter greatly to her. In 2010 David asks how he should deal with her in

PMQs. 'I love Harriet,' says Steve, unhelpfully. 'Respectfully,' I say, annoyingly. Then she is back in 2015. David asks again. 'More respectfully,' I say, more annoyingly.

With his Michael Winner moment behind him, David does indeed tread carefully against Harriet. Not just because she is a woman. Because she is good.

'DOESN'T DAVID KNOW IT'S Valentine's Day this Wednesday?' asks Nick forlornly, when he realises that David has planned a Quad dinner for 14 February as Samantha has taken the children skiing.

The Quad first convened to resolve budget issues, but it has been going from strength to strength as the Coalition has progressed. It has proved so successful a device for making decisions that we use it to navigate all the central issues of the government. The dynamic of four have very different characters, which is part of what makes it work. As ever, David is the leader and strong decision taker, while George is the creative intellect who always wants to push the boundaries. Danny Alexander is bumptious like his partner in crime at the Treasury, George, and enthusiastically tries to make things work . And then there is Nick – cautious, sensitive, prevaricating. As they grow into their roles within the group, they play up to them; George, for instance, starts to bring more radical proposals to the table, so that he can land the one in the middle. But generally the Quad succeeds in creating the 'checks and balances' system at the heart of government, with each side refusing the other's more outlandish plans. This small group basically like and trust each other.

Now, however, we have a problem. A conflict. I go to David and explain that we have to move the Quad dinner date; otherwise the Clegg household is going to go into meltdown. 'We're talking about the stability of the Coalition here,' I add, when he looks at me askance.

So, the dinner is moved. This in turn creates another problem. David has a free night. He finds himself at a loose end, and when this happens, it somehow always ends up being my problem. Think of a plan to entertain me, asks David. So, we start arranging a singles night for Valentine's Day. No couples allowed (unless one half happens to be away). They should be together, the Prime Minister, aka head of the 'marriage police', points out.

I am deluged with texts when word of this new dinner hits the grapevine. 'No, you aren't allowed to ditch your other half to come,' I say, fending them off.

We end up with a rather eccentric group of waifs and strays up in the No. 11 flat. I cook dinner, doing battle with the Camerons' fancy kitchen appliances while David hovers over me, issuing instructions. Luckily we are awash with alcohol, courtesy of Jonathan Marland, the Trade Envoy, so most people don't notice the food.

In addition to the Quad, David meets with Nick every week. David likes Nick a lot, but he cannot resist putting the boot in from time to time. On the whole, Nick brings sensible, sensitive, and mostly quite conservative (with a small 'c') judgement to our deliberations. When he veers a bit too far to the right, he has his more political chief of staff, Jonny Oates, to remind him he is a Lib Dem. Experience has already taught us that leaving Nick to mull something over the weekend is a bad idea. Jonny will stiffen his spine and then the Liberal grandees will pile in with calls. By Monday Nick will have changed his mind.

Nick is a mild, charming, measured man who always has a faint air of being downtrodden by the more powerful people in his life. These include his wife (who he clearly worships and is terrified of in equal measure), David, George, and Theresa May. Obsessed by *Game of Thrones*, we come to think of him as a Jaime Lannister figure.

Nick struggles in particular with what he perceives to be an impossibly Tiggerish George and an unmovable Mrs May. George bounces one step ahead of him – creating a Powerhouse in the North, where Nick is supposed to reign supreme, and getting more attention and wider audiences for his speeches. George even goes to Sheffield! And then there are George's fatal words to him on tuition fees which went something along the lines of, you're an idiot to change your mind – but it's great you are. What an unmitigated disaster that decision turns out to be. In politics, you are only really judged on a few things. *Boom* – that's it – the public have made up their mind, crystallised their view of you forever. Nick had made an election promise not to put up tuition fees, and seemingly the minute he gets into power, he changes his mind. All of his fresh-faced 'new politics' posture is undermined in a moment. It is a game changer from which he never recovers.

Theresa May presents still more of a challenge for Nick at the Home Office. The Lib Dems sit on the more libertarian side of the argument about liberty versus security. This is hardly surprising. These are difficult judgements to make, often falling between safeguarding your country and its citizens, and protecting individual rights. David and Theresa lean towards the security side, Nick towards the individual. In the battles between Mrs May and Mr Clegg, Mrs May does not move – not one inch. Nor does she ever smile at Nick. He comes to our weekly meetings begging for mercy, for some recognition that both sides have a point. So, it falls to us to find a way through.

We too have trouble navigating Mrs May. Her inflexibility is at times a force for good, but at other times much less so. For example, in the discussion around homegrown terrorism, we try to get to grips with the very difficult issues around national cohesion. David has been one of the first to challenge the existence of separate, 'parallel' communities, placing a greater emphasis on the importance of forging a stronger national identity. Theresa takes the view that we must target resources at the violent extremists only. David thinks we must ask more difficult questions about how terrorists have emerged from our own backyard to begin with. It is a battle we fight throughout our years in government.

Although she tends towards the workmanlike in her approach to her job, I cannot but admire Theresa in a way. She is our most senior and formidable woman. Her frosty and immovable style – backed by a fearsome duo of advisors, Nick Timothy and Fiona

Cunningham, who are difficult to work with but deserve credit for their loyalty – works during her years as Home Secretary (though is less well-suited to the role of premier).

A large part of the day of any prime minister is spent in meetings – large or small, private or public, official or political. Meetings to plot your agenda; meetings to drive it forward. Every day hundreds of decisions, some very significant and others less so, are made in this fashion. I am in most of these meetings, and help steer the conversation towards some of the outcomes. David chairs Cabinet, he does not just convene it. He listens and he leads. Meetings are made up of people, and inevitably, in politics, personalities matter.

13

CIRCLE OF TRUST

What defines a term of government? Often a far-reaching policy decision, or its consequences. A war. A referendum. But often there is much more to it than that. Look back on any government and what do you remember? A period of good, relatively stable governance, run by a group of people basically trying to do the right thing? Or a period of instability, intrigue, chaos, and leaks? Were there bold decisions taken or a vacuum of creativity? Much of the atmosphere of a government – which in its turn dictates what the government accomplishes – comes down to leadership, and to the team that the leader chooses.

David was a brilliant if demanding boss – intellectually rigorous, pragmatic, decisive, and extremely funny. He was fond of humour, not to undermine the seriousness of what we were doing, but as a means of lightening our load: humour to humanise. What was not tolerated was sloppiness and laziness in his staff. Everyone was expected to be 'on it', 24/7. He didn't suffer fools gladly.

Ed and I try to run 'the House' in this spirit. Our team is expected to give all to their work and to always be professional. It is not a rude or bullying sort of place. We do not replicate the Alastair Campbell screaming at the press years, nor do we seek publicity for ourselves, or encourage others to seek it. We are aware that MPs find the power of the unelected staff around the Prime Minister to be grating; to read about it in the paper endlessly seems to us a needless distraction from our real work. As far as we can, we also discourage internal politics. Everyone knows why they are here and what they are here to do.

For us, No. 10 at its best is an efficient machine of governance, with the various parts working together smoothly. It feels focused but not too introspective. It is free of internal politics. It is driven by that solidarity which comes from a common sense of purpose, of helping the Prime Minister to do the right thing in running the country. This is unique and hard to replicate outside Downing Street.

Much was made of the Cameron 'inner circle' – the so-called 'Notting Hill set' – being an elitist group of friends. There were some strong friendships, but also some serious fallings out. Although there was a high density of Oxford graduates amongst us, we came together through politics – mostly from working at the Conservative Research Department – rather than from meeting at school or university. And we came from very different beginnings: Steve Hilton, the son of Hungarian immigrants; Michael Gove, the son of a fishmonger; Ed Llewellyn, the son of a naval officer; Andy Coulson, the Essex boy who became a journalist straight out of school; George, whose parents set up a wallpaper company; and me, the half-American daughter of a diplomat. David – himself the son of a stockbroker and a magistrate – hired each of us because we brought something to the table. Ed was not made David's chief of staff because he knew David at school, but because he had already clocked up years of experience working for Chris Patten and Paddy Ashdown.

The criticism stuck though, and in some ways it was a good thing, making us all the more determined to reach out. Craig Oliver, Olive Dowden, Ameet Gill, Liz Sugg, and Gabby Bertin were completely unknown to David when he hired them to the team. Soon they were counted amongst his closest advisors.

It's important people do not feel disengaged. This means they need to be able to have a relationship of sorts with David, and not just through Ed and me. We do try to include people in meetings, not shut them out. David likes to hear new ideas and have his view challenged.

The layout of No. 10 doesn't help, however. Consider an open-plan office at one extreme and No. 10 with its higgledy-piggledy corridors and random rooms at the other. This is a building that lends itself to closed doors and inner circles – which themselves give rise to a feeling that anyone who doesn't sit close to the prime minister has to guess what's actually going on. This can at times create an unhealthy sense of being left out. And although it is impossible to get away from a tight inner circle at the centre who trust each other and make the key decisions, we know that if you want the best out of the people who work for you – your speechwriters, your policy thinkers – they need to spend time with the boss.

The No. 10 machine has been honed over many years with the purpose of allowing the person in charge to inhabit the role of prime minister. But if left unchecked these mechanisms can isolate them, driving a wedge through relationships – professional and personal – and creating a bunker mentality.

My job, the job of gatekeeper, is therefore a more skilled and nuanced one than people might imagine. You need to protect your boss from the endless calls on his (limited) time, but protect him too much and he loses touch with reality. Stops seeing his friends. Can't remember the names of his colleagues. Has not heard a fresh view for months. You have done him no favours. The gatekeeper must know when to open the gate.

Ed and I often have a long list of difficult things to discuss with David day after day. Some are issues that others feel more comfortable with us raising rather than them. This too is an important part of our job. We perch on the chairs in the den, and David asks, 'What have you got for me now?' – looking at us suspiciously as we tried to cancel yet another family holiday.

So, David needs to be as accessible as possible to the people who need to see him. And of course, we need him chairing essential meetings for the management of the government and performing at PMQs. We also want him out and about – and sometimes out of the country altogether. We mastermind where he goes and what he says, through ruthless management of his diary and the infamous Grid, which plots our announcements

We made it a rule that David did nothing without me, Ed, and the principal private secretary agreeing to it. The Prime Minister's time is both precious and finite. Bids for his time have to come to a diary meeting for assessment and approval. Full stop. And this is how the weekly diary meeting becomes one of the most notorious meetings in No. 10 . . .

Over time, the diary meeting becomes a female-only meeting. We do not have time for the sort of alpha male posturing that often takes place in other meetings, and our male colleagues quickly learn that the jury of no-nonsense women do not appreciate random, poorly thought-through bids on the Prime Minister's time.

David walks in while I am chairing the meeting from his favourite armchair. 'This must be the scariest gathering in Whitehall,' he says, looking round at the group of formidable women. 'Don't mind me,' he adds, trying to get out of the room as quickly as possible.

Once he's left, we continue, working through the diary bids. Requests for meetings, interviews, visits, speeches. No, no, no, possibly . . . down the page we go. We have learnt it's better to be polite but firm to avoid future disappointment. Foreign bids? I ask. And now the room fills with the entire foreign team, who have come collectively to make a case for a prime ministerial visit to Kazakhstan. 'Last time I checked the good people of Kazakhstan could not vote in the UK,' I say, aware that local elections are looming.

All this sounds draconian – and it is. But it serves a purpose. There are lots of calls on David's time and it is our job to make sure his time is managed properly. If he is to do all he must and also have time to think – and spend some time with his family too – it means not accepting everything which comes his way, however nice it sounds. Worst of all is to accept and then later have to let people down.

My admiration for the diary secretaries at No. 10 knows no

bounds. Once we approve (or decline) the countless asks on David's time, theirs is the thankless task of painstaking scheduling and managing the diary. More often than not, it has to be unravelled at last minute for yet another emergency. The diary secretary is hounded with email requests, and faces angry, disappointed people whose meetings are rescheduled again and again. They are caught in the middle of feuds – across Whitehall, within No. 10 – and, most difficult of all, the clash of the personal with the duty of government.

The sight of Samantha's chief of staff, Isabel, making her way down the corridor is enough to make the private office shake. There's a clash: Flo's nativity vs. the Summit. It is hard to remain calm, and yet the women who do these jobs – Kate Marley, Lara Moreno-Pérez, and Georgina Graham – are the most professional and unflappable people I have ever known.

EFFICIENT GOVERNANCE IS THE very least of what people rightly expect from their government. Which means, in practice, that you are responsible for what happens across a vast array of departments, from the well-being of our citizens, to the pothole on the street, to the trains running on time; from the education of every child to the defence of the realm. What goes wrong is ultimately your fault.

While you keep track and take care of the 'old', you also have think about the 'new', if you want to do new things. Change things. Enact your manifesto. The best governments drive their agenda forward with creative political ideas that speak to their values and which are fresh and new. Without this, the government will soon seem stale and stagnant.

So a successful government must be able to multi-task: you need to keep up the momentum of your own agenda while also fire-fighting, 24/7. In reality, this means that our tiny team at No. 10 needs to exert control over the vast bureaucracy of government, often using guerrilla warfare tactics, backed up by the power of the prime minister.

To keep the train on the track – and preferably travelling forwards – we organise our week around a set of objectives. Achieving a good, strong 'intervention' at the start is one. This means an announcement of some sort by the Prime Minister with a visit, speech, and round of media interviews. You can see the headlines. Cameron announces Troubled-Families programme. Cameron launches new wave of free schools. Cameron launches dementia challenge.

For ideas on policy announcements, we try to harness the creative brains of the policy unit on the third floor of No. 10, with mixed results – not because they are not very clever, committed people, but because of the conflicting nature of their jobs. The policy unit is there to do a range of things. Shadowing the departments is a key role. The health advisor, for example, will oversee the Department of Health and keep watch over all health-related issues. We also want our policy unit to be blue-sky thinkers – looking for big, new innovative ideas – as well as coming up with a series of more day-to-day announcements to keep the Grid ticking along. Rarely does one person, however brilliant, thrive at both these functions – and understandably so. In reality, feeding the beast that is the 24/7 news cycle is not something many of them are either attuned or even sympathetic to.

So, it is often a small group of us at No. 10, along with George and his team, who come up with the ideas for the announcements in the first place. We are just nearer the coalface; we have a better feel for what might fly. George is especially gifted at this, driving a creative, dynamic policy machine from No. 11 supported by talented thinkers like Rupert, Neil O'Brien, and Eleanor Wolfson. Sitting above all of Whitehall, holding the purse strings, George has a bird's eye view of policy and the ability, as Chancellor, to glide in everywhere, sometimes to the chagrin of the resident Cabinet minister. Again, the headlines. Osborne announces Northern Powerhouse. Osborne announces high speed rail and new road schemes. Osborne is filmed standing by the potential bypass while his transport minister is nowhere to be seen.

Beyond our Grid, which is built around the Prime Minister, is another Grid, which extends to the wider government machine and which it attempts to coordinate. Whitehall's natural inclination is to churn out announcements in a completely random way any day of the week – the good, bad, and ugly egged on by politicians who long for the limelight, oblivious of the potential outcomes. So, it is the job of our Grid master, Ameet Gill – who has been promoted from speechwriter – and Andy Coulson (and after Andy, Craig Oliver) to stop them, or at least try to bring some sort of rhyme or reason to the plans. This earns No. 10 the reputation of being bossy and interfering – and always will.

Of course, there are lots and lots of times when people do what they want without telling us, often going straight to the Sunday papers too. Then all hell breaks out. What is Ed Vaizey's library announcement doing in the middle of crime week?

WHILST WE ALL GRADUALLY adapt to working in the confines of government, we create some dynamic and strong working relationships. But it also pushes some of us apart.

Steve Hilton finds the transition to No. 10 unsettling. He increasingly chooses to circumvent our meetings, saving his energy for more worthwhile things – such as his one-to-ones with David. In opposition years, he would often visit David in Dean, where they would talk informally over the issues we are grappling with, and discuss an overall strategy. Then, Monday morning, back at the office, the rest of the team would arrive to find the entire strategy had changed.

In government, this method doesn't work. The Prime Minister cannot make decisions and then be persuaded out of them by Steve in private. Even if David wanted to change his mind (and occasionally he does), when decisions are made, minutes are taken, and hordes of civil servants begin implementing them. Steve can only put the clock back so many times. And it is this which largely undermines Steve and erodes his spirit in No. 10. He despises 'the System' – and never finds a way to work successfully inside it.

Early on, Steve starts to operate a sort of parallel government, taking meetings across Whitehall with those who at first think of him as David's representative on earth. He is deep in a 'bromance', for example, with Rohan Silva, George's entrepreneurial and talented young aide whom we all like and admire. At first, we don't really notice Steve's pursuits, as we are so busy with our own work. But when he appears to go completely freelance, avoiding our meetings in favour of his own, or commissioning random work streams, we try to draw him back. This results in a volcanic erup- tion. Then Steve comes to us with a solution: to give him a formal role as head of the Policy Unit on the third floor. David pushes back; he wants Steve as a special advisor to the Prime Minister, not driving the Policy Unit – and not quite sure where to. It's another nail in the coffin of their relationship. We try to find ways to bring Steve closer. Come to the meetings, we suggest. Share our office. We set up a hot desk for Steve in the private office, which he never uses.

Steve's disillusionment grows, haunting the building like an unhappy, shoeless ghost, and spills out into the newspapers. Underlining this is a growing sense of alienation from the one person he came into politics for: David.

In the beginning, Steve saw it very much as a joint project: David and Steve. When they became friends in the CRD in the late Eighties and early Nineties, David was attracted by Steve's compelling intelligence and radical, reforming zeal. Their friendship gave David a political confidence. He could be more than just a boy with a privileged upbringing. Steve encouraged him to think out of the box, and together they came up with ways to move the party forwards after its introspective years. For David, Steve repre- sented Dumbo's lucky feather: with it, he can fly. But David finds, as Dumbo does, that he can fly without the feather – and he always could.

David still admires Steve's blue-sky thinking and creativity – and loves him as a friend – but he wants him to find a way to operate that does not put him at odds with everyone and everything. Yes,

Steve has brilliant ideas, but not all of them are either workable
or advisable. Moreover, David no longer has time for the 'Are you
with me or against me?' game.

The rift grows and saddens me. I wish we could find a way
through it, because I value and care about Steve. But we don't.
And when Steve goes back to California in 2012 to join his wife,
who is working for Google in Palo Alto, I think we all underes-
timate his sense of betrayal, which comes back to haunt us too.

14

ON OUR WATCH

One of the foremost jobs of any government is to protect the people it serves. So, it is unsurprising that the security side of the brief accounts for about half of the Prime Minister's time. Not just the country-to-country diplomacy, but also the homeland security issues, intelligence assessments, military planning, and, from time to time, the very hardest decision of all – risking a life, sometimes to save another.

As leader of a country you are responsible for what happens on your watch. Even if you wish to take the ostrich approach to your foreign and security brief, it may not take an ostrich approach to you. Things happen which prompt a response. Require moral courage. Action or inaction. The legacy of this is likely to stay with you for ever, not necessarily because you made the wrong decision, but because any decision is likely to have a cost.

My father's generation of diplomats were Cold War warriors. They knew their enemy and fought their fight. We inherit a more complicated, fragmented world, where allegiances are constantly shifting.

And a lot happens on our watch. Libya, Somalia, Syria. Crimea, the disappearance of the Malaysian airliner, Ebola – to name just a few. The most consistent threat comes from Islamic State with their aggressive expansionism abroad and threat to our security at home. We watch horrified as they execute our people in orange jumpsuits and groom young British girls in their front rooms.

All governments are shaped and tainted by what comes before, and in turn, they shape what is to come. The shadow of Iraq hangs heavily over the 2010 Parliament, just as it does the Obama White House. We must operate within the confines of a post-Iraq political environment, where there is little support for foreign intervention of any sort.

DAVID FINDS HIMSELF DRAWN to the national security brief, and he is good at it. He has the intellect to navigate tricky situations and is not afraid to be tough, however uncomfortable. He is far from a Foreign Office dream – partly because he wants to do too much of the work himself, and also because he likes to challenge 'the System' – thinking out of the box even if in the end he returns to it.

By introducing the American-style National Security Council to Britain for the first time, we hope to signal a new, holistic approach, shifting away from the battling fiefdoms of the past: Foreign Office battling Ministry of Defence battling MI5 battling MI6. We want an era of more joined-up decision-making. The power of the NSC model is in effectively knocking heads together – and meaning it. Which means having an effective team behind it, so that the decisions are ruthlessly implemented across Whitehall. And for this to really work, it also needs the sustained interest and time of the Prime Minister as 'head knocker in chief'. David is supported in this by Ed Llewellyn, his foreign affairs supremo.

The goal of NSC is to be agile enough to cover a range of topics, from counterterrorism and military strategy to energy security and aid, whilst including a wide range of people. Not just senior Cabinet members – the Chancellor, Defence Secretary, Foreign Secretary, Home Secretary, and Secretary of State for International Development – but also the Chief of the Defence Staff and the heads of the intelligence agencies, with other ministers attending when necessary. Their first challenge: a full Strategic Defence and Security Review (SDSR) spanning all NSC ministries. Our first

National Security Advisor is Peter Ricketts, a very decent and highly thought-of diplomat.

But David doesn't want NSC to turn into a 'talkathon', so he steers it away from endlessly discussing strategy. He fears such discussions will be too broad-brush and easily ignored. Instead he favours specific problem solving. He asks for slides that set out the choices: what should we do next, and with what resources? The more specific, the better. Detailed action points are noted and followed up.

NSC remains a large and formal meeting, sitting in the Cabinet room. But in operational (Libya) or crisis management (counter-terrorism) mode, or in dealing with homeland security (Olympics or fuel crisis), it comes together in another format: COBR(A). This stands for Cabinet Office Briefing Room A, but the room is renamed, so it's just COBR. It is ideally suited to getting key people at ministerial and official level together quickly and efficiently at all times of day and night. Once it is recognised as the critical crisis management mechanism, the phrase 'The Prime Minister will chair COBR today' carries great weight with both media and public.

We spend a lot of time there. After a while, though, the glamour of COBR begins to wane. COBR is really just a secure, high-tech basement briefing room that is set up to 'beam in' teams from all over the country or the world, depending on the nature of the problem. For homeland security or a natural disaster – which might range from a terrorist incidence to a major flood – you have the police 'gold command' as well as the army, intelligence services perhaps, and an array of relevant ministers run by the civil contingencies team. For overseas issues, you may lose the police but add embassies, who are connected by video link. These are run by the National Security Secretariat.

COBR is in almost daily use for running the Libya campaign (February–September 2011). Then, when there is an earthquake followed by a tsunami near a nuclear energy plant in Japan, we are faced with a row of men with a beards. 'These must be the scientists,' I say to Ed – this is not a hipster beard sort of place.

Despite the array of bigwigs of one kind of another in attendance, if badly chaired the COBR meeting can still come to nothing, disintegrating into a talkathon with nothing ever pinned down and the buck being passed round and round the table at breakneck speed. Not under David's watch. He is king of chairing COBR, and he dedicates a great deal of his time to it. The point of COBR is to bring coordination to what is often an uncoordinated set of resources, and the prize, as always, is found in the detail.

Often the 'real' meetings take place in the Prime Minister's den, especially if they involve the intelligence chiefs. The den is more leakproof than COBR. David likes to draw on an inner security circle – essentially the Quad plus William Hague, as well as senior officials such as the National Security Advisor, 'C' (head of MI6), and CDS (Chief of the Defence Staff). The functional way in which this runs is yet another example of how the Coalition was cemented by a group of people who basically trusted and worked well together.

Some situations require impossibly difficult decisions – like whether or not to mount a plan to rescue someone who has been kidnapped. It has been UK policy for decades: the British government does not pay ransoms. For good reason, as it encourages more kidnaps. But David is also clear that we will do everything we can to rescue our people, so be warned. Deciding to mount a rescue attempt involves weighing up risks that only the most experienced of our military personnel can give us guidance on. Wait another day or two and the person might be taken up country, their chance of survival diminishing by the hour. Go in, and they might be freed, but there is the risk that the rescue will go wrong. These decisions can revolve around details like the brightness of the night sky. Even with all the best advice and most experienced people around us, they are harrowing decisions to take that will stay with all of us forever.

These meetings require high-level security clearance to attend, a process which involves hours of invasive interviews and quite a lot of general sniffing around. I sit for mine early on in my time at No. 10. It lasts three hours, with a man asking me a range of intimate questions and writing away in his small notebook. Phone calls are made to colleagues and friends. Few topics are untouched. My finances. My alcohol consumption. My previous boyfriends. My sexual preference. My marriage. My views of the Iraq War. My years at Oxford – how well had I known David? They know that we are a close-knit group, and I have an idea they are trying to assess a possible conflict of loyalty between boss and country. 'I can conceive of no such conflict,' I say.

Ministers don't have to go through this interview as it is seen to be corrupting of the democratic process. They sign the Ministerial Code instead.

Our constant dread is a terrorist attack on British soil. We plan for every eventuality, aware that the intelligence community are daily risking their lives to prevent and circumvent it. When a British Army soldier, Lee Rigby, is attacked and killed near his barracks in May 2013, we are devastated. The murder is a terrible reminder of the deadly effectiveness of random acts of terrorism – and played out live on social media. We are regularly drilled on our own security. 'Just don't do the same thing every day,' we're told. Which is difficult if you are a creature of habit, like me.

David is helped in this by a new type of appointment to No. 10 – the military assistant. From the start, David was convinced there should be a military person in No. 10, and so a representative is seconded to the foreign team. But David doesn't want an MOD 'desk man'. He wants someone who knows how it feels to take brave men and women into battle, to feel responsible for their lives. I feel deeply honoured to have worked with these people during my time at No. 10: Colonels Jim, Gwyn, and Nick. We are lucky to have people like them dedicating their lives to protecting our country.

In addition to a military assistant, David also brings in a legal one. There is much that lawyers are asked to adjudicate on in government, but none more so than in decisions around national security. In this, the Attorney General wields not just a veto, but has a say on whether or not to use force – and if so, how much. 'Are we going "kinetic"?' the Americans say. Having a lawyer of our own in 'the House' helps us navigate the issues and give us a bit of support.

IT IS MARCH 2011. Gaddafi is bearing down on his own people in Benghazi. David is working with President Nicolas Sarkozy to put an international coalition together to protect the Libyan people and impose a no-fly zone. Obama is reluctant. There is a muttering from some angry backbenchers keen that we stay out of it, thinking perhaps of Iraq. But David is thinking of Rwanda and of the Balkans, desperate to prevent another Srebrenica. He feels these deaths in Libya are too avoidable. Just because you can't stop every atrocity doesn't mean you don't move to stop one when it falls on your watch. The intensity of the moment bears down on us. This is a decision that will play out in terms of people's lives. David presses ahead with intervention, aware that he is taking a personal political risk in doing what he believes to be right.

It is late evening at No. 10. We have Arab League support and a UN resolution but need the Americans on board too if we are going to mount an intervention. David has a call scheduled with Obama. We hotfoot it down to the video teleconferencing room in the basement so that we can hear. There are only a handful of very high security phones in the building. One is on David's desk; the other is by the duty clerk's. There is no way of listening to the call if you don't make it to the VTC room. And they won't open the door once it's shut.

Obama's voice booms through the vaulted, secure room. He is still reluctant to get involved but feels the mounting pressure. So, he'll lend his support at the beginning – with American 'shock and awe' – but doesn't want to get embroiled with a longer-term commitment. No. 10 suddenly is swarming with military types and foreign policy advisors. The trolleys of food on their way to George's dining room remind me I haven't eaten. I wonder if they'll notice a bread roll go amiss.

By the time I return the next morning, it feels like there has been a military coup. Everyone is in uniform. 'We're in a campaign,' says David's defence attaché in a clipped tone – top to toe in khaki. The diary has been cleared for 'campaign' meetings – military not political. The rest of the political team are left twiddling their thumbs as Libya dwarfs everything.

Later, there is much controversy surrounding our intervention in Libya, given how things turned out. Would things be better today had we not intervened at all? Who can ever really know for certain? I believe there is a strong case in saying we should have done more, not less, in the aftermath. We may have inadvertently allowed room for the extremists to gain ground. What we do know is that the near-inevitable massacre in Benghazi was prevented.

WHEN OBAMA IS RE-ELECTED in November 2012, we feel a sense of relief and growing confidence across the ocean. Released from the pressures of re-election he is liberated. And we wonder how this will play out in his foreign policy.

David and Obama have been mulling over the ongoing commitment of both countries' troops in Afghanistan for some time. We have been there for a decade. British lives are still being lost and it is now unclear what success might look like going forward. There is growing support around a transition to an Afghan lead, and the gradual withdrawal of our troops, first mooted by both leaders in July 2010. Obama goes first – and announces US withdrawal in his State of the Union address in February 2013. David follows, announcing a future drawdown of troops from the front line during a Christmas visit to the troops later that year. When we finally do begin to pull back, the number of deaths begins to decline, and with them the steady stream of heartbreaking letters David has to write to the families whose sons, daughters, sisters, or brothers have sacrificed their lives serving our country. The memory of writing them will never leave him.

Then there is Syria. The behaviour of the Assad regime becomes increasingly hard to bear. Over the course of months and years, what began as a series of protests as part of the Arab Spring evolves into a full-blown, violent civil war. There is a lot of talk but little action, save for the lifting of the EU arms embargo on Syrian rebels. Then Obama warns that the use of chemical weapons would constitute a 'red line' for America.

In August 2013, the red line is crossed with a chemical attack in eastern Ghouta. The sarin nerve gas kills more than 1,000 people, many of whom are children. The images are horrifying. David is on holiday in Cornwall. I am in Ireland with my children. The world takes a deep breath.

The Americans go deep into their cave to work out what to do. Obama is not a natural interventionist, but he has drawn the battle lines and now, faced with such a sickening act, he has to make a decision. When the Americans finally emerge, it is to announce their intention to strike Syria. David is clear in his mind that to join the Americans is the right thing to do. But we are a long way off achieving this.

There is a debate about whether we need to recall Parliament. Strictly speaking, their permission is not a requirement for engaging troops or firepower. But politically, in a post-Iraq world, it is highly risky to bypass them. William is particularly cautious. Then, when Obama decides to delay the bombing because of pressure from the UN, there is no excuse of time pressure.

Parliament is duly recalled. I speak to Ed Llewellyn from Ireland. He is in 'controlled manic' mode but seems confident of getting the cross-party support we will need to win a vote in Parliament. He says Nick Clegg is onside, and Ed Miliband is being supportive. 'Are you sure?' I ask nervously. I can tell I am annoying Ed, quite understandably. He is in COBR and I am in the bogs of Ireland. I make arrangements to fly home in time to help with recall. The following days are spent building a coalition of support. There is the legality to certify. And we need a UN resolution, if at all possible. And there is still the House of Commons to get onside.

I land from Ireland and drive into Downing Street. Things are already blowing off course. A UN resolution is now off the agenda, as the Russians have indicated they will veto. I put my bag down by my desk and open the door into David's office. William is there with George, Ed, Chris Martin, David's principal private secretary and our Chief Whip, Sir George Young. They all look crestfallen. 'Miliband's just pulled out,' says David. I am not in the slightest bit surprised.

Now the Lib Dems are wobbling all over the place and the Chief Whip is not at all sure about the levels of support on our own side. William is doing the numbers in his head; he takes after the Lyndon Johnson view that the first rule of politics is that you have to be able to count. The Chief, who is charmingly old school, admits we might be in a spot of trouble (none of us are sure whether he can count or not). He draws up a list of MPs for David to see. We decide to up sticks to David's office in the Commons to see as many as we can before the vote. (In fact, there are due to be two votes – one on the motion and one authorising action.)

The long afternoon draws into evening, and our conversations are not going well. The intelligence from those we haven't seen is even worse. Many MPs are not picking up their phones. I sit with David while his PPS and Ed Llewellyn scour the building for Tory MPs. David and I know we are going to lose. We can feel it all around us. We are not converting anyone. Some are strongly against intervention, questioning the upside and morality of Britain meddling in another country's affairs. Some are downright rude. Crispin Blunt tells David that he deserves to be humiliated. At 10.30 p.m. the vote is announced. We lose the motion and concede defeat. Thirty of our own vote against and a further thirty-one abstain.

We have made a political miscalculation. Just because we had Nick Clegg onside didn't guarantee him delivering his party, especially with no UN backing. And Miliband, who is not exactly keen to support us in a crisis anyway, presides over a party collectively traumatised by Iraq. There is a sense of all the party leaders being brought into line by their backbenchers in one form or another. It will take the next Parliament to shift the shadow of Iraq, even just a little.

William looks uncomfortable sitting in his chair and I have a feeling he is considering his (figurative) position. Always with an eye on history, William, I know, will think a lost vote in the Commons should lead to a resignation. He quietly leaves the room and I tell George to go and find him. They are close, and a conversation between them is sure to help.

David is preparing a clip for the news. When I finally leave the Commons, it is midnight. It is my first day back after the summer break. To lose a vote of such magnitude normally spells trouble for any government, but somehow I think, on a political level, we'll be fine. This Parliament feels strangely detached from the executive – more congress than parliament – choosing to keep it in check rather than offering unconditional support. Perhaps this is because we are in coalition with the Lib Dems and there is less of a sense of ownership from the various wings of our party. The vote is a kick in the teeth but not worse than that. I am more worried about Britain's standing in the world.

In the end, there is no American intervention either. Obama's red lines are crossed with no response. We have to live with the fact that chemical weapons have been used against hundreds of innocents, and the world has stood by in silence.

Just over two years later, in December 2015, the new Parliament votes with a majority of seventy-four for Britain to join a coalition of countries in airstrikes against the Islamic State in Syria. It is not quite the same thing as our previous call to arms, but it feels like some ghosts have been laid to rest.

15

THE PITFALLS OF FOREIGN TRAVEL

Prime ministers have to travel, whether they like it or not. And they often do – like it – quite a lot. At home, they are subjected to the daily grind of political life. *Primus inter pares* in Parliament, they face the usual trials by tabloid. Abroad, they fly high, representing Britain against a backdrop of red carpets and guards of honour.

There is the foreign travel a prime minister has to do, like attending the summits: EU Council, G8 (Group of Eight – later G7), G20 (Group of Twenty), NATO, Commonwealth. And then there is the travel he chooses to do, because he wants to focus on bilateral relationships, such as with India and America, or countries in the Middle East and Africa, or, nearer to home, in Europe.

I spend a lot of my time fending off the foreign team at No. 10, who would have had David on a plane every week if they had their way. The irony of the diplomat's daughter pushing back on foreign travel is not lost on the team. But it is important to get the right balance between domestic and foreign affairs. However enticing, there are no votes to be gained by travelling abroad, and a few to lose if a trip goes wrong.

With the British lobby in tow, you are subject to a daily grilling, and more often than not, it has nothing whatsoever to do with the trip. The worst is when something blows up at home, leading to an inevitable attack from the press pack, who howl insults at a globe-trotting prime minister 'absent while Blighty burns'. I still remember how David, as Leader of the Opposition, was accused of being absent whilst Blighty was sinking in floods.

Ed Llewellyn is reluctant to let David leave the country without him, so I let him go on the bulk of the trips. One of us needs to stay in the country. And anyway, it keeps me at home. However as tempting as the foreign trips are, they are pretty disruptive for my children.

Our first foreign trip, just weeks after assuming office, is a big set-piece summit. We're going to the G8 in Muskoka, Canada. On the whole, we are excited, not nervous. What greater privilege could there be to represent Great Britain abroad?

The G8 started life in 1975, when France issued an invitation to five other highly industrialised countries – Germany, Britain, Italy, Japan and the US – to a summit to discuss global issues. A year later, they met again with Canada. Then Russia joined in 1997, making it the Group of Eight. At its best, the G8 follows its original design – of a fireside chat about the critical issues of the day between the most powerful people in the world. At its worst, the leaders meet and just read out pre-prepared scripts, leaving the real discussions to their 'sherpas' (the senior officials whose job it is to negotiate the meetings). The real, big issue of the day is often left off the formal agenda to avoid a punch up between premiers, which could have lasting repercussions.

Arriving at the royal suite at Heathrow on the way to our first summit, I find I have no seat number. Instead my name has been put next to David's at the front of the privately chartered Virgin plane. He has two seats in fact, one for working and the other one for ignoring us all and having a nap. There is a huge entourage – accompanying ministers and officials, the protection team, duty clerks and garden room girls, and the red phone. It is the job of the duty clerks to recreate a mini version of No. 10 wherever the prime minister is, ready for all eventualities, even the outbreak of World War Three (literally). So, travelling light is not an option. Not does it seem to be an option for my own suitcase, ever expanding. What is the dress code for a summit?

There is no time for a shower and a change when we land; the red carpet and guard of honour are waiting to welcome us. We quickly learn to keep the window shutters down for landing so the cameras can't film everyone as we're getting ready.

David is the new kid on the block amongst a group of mostly experienced world leaders. First challenge, the requisite 'family' photo. Andy's worries that David might look nervous and side-lined prove to be unwarranted: he sets off to join the other leaders as if he has turned up for his school house photo. Watching the G8 leaders gathering is like viewing a very particular type of nature documentary. Power matters. So too, it seems, does size. Everyone wants to be near Obama but not look like they are trying too hard. Sarkozy is bobbing up and down. I can see other leaders struggling to make sure they are seen on camera, in fear of being eaten alive by their own public opinion, which will be wondering where their leader has gone to on taxpayers' expense. Only Angela Merkel seems serene, cool as a cucumber in her trouser suit.

David unknowingly causes a bit of a stir. On the first morning, he had decided to go for a swim in the lake. (David has a habit of swimming in lakes, rivers, or even the sea, whatever the season.) It was colder than he'd anticipated and also not so private (there were armed divers everywhere). News has now got round of his antics, and this has clearly upset some of the older leaders. They see the young David as a bit of an upstart – making them look tired by being all fresh and vigorous. Prime Minister Stephen Harper, our host, is far too professional to show any irritation, and quickly changes the subject to his own his fitness routine. It is Berlusconi who is visibly put out. Who is this young Turk showing off in his swimming trunks? This is what I call a man in swimming trunks, he says, producing a series of pictures of himself by the sea in Italy. By the looks of them, they are quite a few years old. I can't help but wonder what Chancellor Merkel did to deserve having to see Berlusconi in his Speedos.

As our first G8 meeting draws to an end, the plan is to join the G20, who are now gathering in Toronto. There was going to be an exodus by helicopter from the camp, only the weather has changed abruptly and no one has a helicopter capable of flying out – that is, except for POTUS on Marine One. As the Americans get ready to go, leaving the rest of us grounded, our team suddenly realise we have quite a serious problem. David has a bilateral scheduled with Obama that afternoon. Unless the weather changes again, he is going to miss it, and the chances of a reschedule are next to zero. As the brand-new Prime Minister, missing your bilateral with the President of the United States at your first summit looks and smells like failure, even if it is a tornado's fault. Our press pack is certainly not going to write it up sympathetically.

Liz hops into operation 'save the day'. First action, search for the American ops people. The phone rings. It's Gabby, from Toronto. 'I am dying here,' she moans.

'What's wrong?' I ask.

'I'm all alone trying to entertain the entire press pack with no stories, no David . . .' she trails off with a heavy sigh.

'Just keep them busy,' I say cheerfully. 'You're doing a great job!' I add, for encouragement.

'Please tell me you are nearly here,' she replies. I explain that there's a slight hitch. There is silence on the other end.

I am standing with Andy and Tom Fletcher, the foreign affairs advisor we have inherited from Gordon Brown's days. Tom is from the 'serious operator' school of diplomacy. Obama's notorious Chief of Staff, Rahm Emanuel, saunters over and we try to look in control.

'OK, guys . . . This is how it is,' he says, with one of those slightly 'bad guy' types of American accent. 'There's room on Marine One for Prime Minister Cameron plus one.' He eyeballs each of us. 'And when I turn my back you can start arguing amongst yourselves about who gets to be that one.' He saunters off, sniggering.

I look at Andy and Tom and realise I don't have a cat's chance in hell of making Marine One. There is a strong case for Tom (who is supposed to be briefing the Prime Minister ahead of the meeting) and for Andy (who is supposed to be briefing the press after the meeting). Even I admit my purpose is more obtuse. They flip a coin and Andy wins. David and Andy leave on Marine One (and oh god, do we never hear the end of it) and the rest of us are left, stranded with no 'principal', which at a summit, we soon discover, is tantamount to being cast into oblivion. All the other delegations head off in their cars, flags waving.

George and Rupert Harrison call from Toronto, excited to be at their first G20. 'Where are you? Where's Dave?' 'Well, he is on Marine One and I'm stuck in a car park waiting for my ride,' I say. General amusement from both. First rule of travelling with the Prime Minister: never fall off the convoy.

HOURS LATER I MEET up again with the team in Toronto. Andy is in a state of high excitement – he has arranged for us to watch the Germany–England World Cup match with Merkel and her team later that evening. 'Why would we want to do that?' I ask, bemused. Andy looks at me like I am the stupidest person in the world. Andy, who is a bit of an authority on football, has convinced himself that England is set to win and that he has secured a once-in-a-lifetime opportunity to watch Germany being beaten by England whilst sitting next to the German Chancellor. I know nothing about football, although I am aware of what usually happens when two teams are up against each other. So I say, 'But Germany always wins Andy, so it's going to be a shocker.'

We gather in a special room for the match. David sits next to Merkel. George takes a seat next to his opposite number, the distinguished Wolfgang Schäuble, who is confined to a wheelchair because of a failed assassination attempt. The game starts badly, with Germany scoring two goals. There are a lot of 'Ahhs' and polite utterances of 'Shame, David' from Merkel. Andy looks like he might explode. Then, oh joy, Frank Lampard gets a goal! We stifle our yelps. This is the beginning of the great British fightback! Only the referee has not seen the goal and declares it void. An un-goal. At this point a decidedly frosty atmosphere descends in the room. We lose 4–1. It is fortunate we don't have a scheduled bilateral with the Germans, as this would have been awkward.

Whereas the G8 meeting is a cosier affair, strictly leaders only, the G20 is a slightly more obese relation, with many more people attending. This makes it a little less constructive and far harder to navigate. It often becomes all about the meetings taking place on the sidelines.

I am lent a 'gold pass' for ten minutes to see what the inside of a G20 looks like. The first thing I notice is that there are a lot more than twenty people in the vast room. There seem to be endless representatives from the European Union, for a start. The leaders all sit behind their national flag, with their finance ministers and chief advisors behind them. George points out that most of the finance ministers are actually not sitting behind their prime minister, but roaming round the room, probably 'plotting' to replace them.

The financial crisis is eating through incumbent leaders – 'like Angry Birds', as David puts it – and he quickly goes from being the new boy to a seasoned world statesman. The effect of the economic crisis is that a divide emerges between more left-leaning governments trying to boost their economies out of recession, and those on the right favouring austerity. No one really knows for sure which strategy will work – but they know they must have one, and stick to it. Later, as they see our economy coming round the corner into growth, there is an extra respect for and interest in the British-style Plan A. Little gives a premier more power on the international stage than a growing economy – save maybe a strong defence budget and popularity in the polls.

David often surprises his international colleagues by speaking his mind, unscripted – a legacy of the British parliamentary tradition. And he likes to press for tangible action points from the summits. Otherwise, why bother? He also likes to use the G8 and G20 gatherings to knock heads together, especially when he comes upon an entrenched problem. David's view is, Yes, it's complicated, but that doesn't mean you shouldn't try – and you're probably going to be criticised either way. He calls summits on Somali pirates and

corruption, long-standing problems that he believes are not insur-
mountable – with a bit more political will.

IT WAS A VERY different story in opposition, when there were a
tiny number of us organizing high-profile foreign visits from
scratch. In opposition, you're always vulnerable to the pitfalls of
cancellations from the most prestigious people you are trying to
see, with the press declaring you a 'nonentity'. Or they're accusing
you of undermining Britain abroad if you offer any hint of criticism
of the existing government.

Shortly after David became party leader, we kicked off our time
in opposition with a trip to India, where David opened a new
British-owned JCB factory. The ops team spent weeks negotiating
the details. 'There is a small problem concerning elephants,' Liz
said one day. She was adamant. It would not look serious to have
David pictured with elephants. No elephants.

We arrived in India to find . . . three large elephants. The pictures
were certainly jolly: David, George, and Anthony Bamford, chair
of his family-owned company JCB, with garlands round their necks,
red dots on their foreheads, and elephants' trunks sweetly nestled
around their smiling faces. 'It's not quite what we had in mind,'
admitted George Eustice, David's then press secretary, looking at
the papers the next day.

We toured one of Mumbai's many ghettos with a local charity
– we didn't want to come to India and ignore the poverty. Then,
realising we were running late for David's *Today* programme interview back at home, we started to head to the hotel. George Eustice
jumped in the car with David and I joined a minibus behind with
the journalists including a friend of mine who was working for the
Financial Times at the time, Jo Johnson.

The convoy set off at breakneck speed, our minibus at the back
straining to keep up. The journey was all acceleration followed by
screeching brakes. Then the rain came down in buckets. I was
terrified – and it wasn't just me. We urged the driver to slow down,
explaining very firmly that we were not in a hurry; we knew where

we were going, so there was no need to drive this fast, in this rain. Someone is going to get hurt, we warned.

Then it happened. A great thud sound and blood on the side window. There was an eerie silence in the minibus. The driver stopped and got out. Someone had been hit. I feared the worst and literally couldn't breathe. An angry crowd gathered and began remonstrating with our driver. A bystander opened the bus door and tried to pull out one of the journalists with us. We pushed the door shut, nervous at what might happen. Then the crowd surrounded the bus and started to rock it. At this point I was pretty sure we were in serious trouble. I rang David. 'Dave – I think I'm about to be killed.' 'I can't talk now, I'm about to do the *Today* programme,' he said. 'I'll ring back afterwards.'

And then, magically, our driver, looking a bit worse for wear, reappeared, started the bus, and drove us to the nearest police station to give statements. By the time we arrived, the story had already been filed by the Press Association guy sitting in the back: 'Cameron in Indian car crash rushing for VIP lunch.'

I was a wreck, sure that the victim could not have survived. Yet she did – thank god. And our embassy got her to one of the top hospitals in Mumbai.

THE NEXT TIME WE are in India, David is Prime Minister and it's a whole new ball game. The plane is heaving with half the Cabinet, half a dozen vice chancellors, scores of businessmen, and officials; the hacks are at the back. When we arrive, there is no traffic. None. The streets have all been cleared to make way for the convoy, leaving unimaginable chaos beyond the marked route. David is immediately whisked off to a private dinner. Jo Johnson – now an MP – persuades me to come to a party an Indian friend is giving for George.

'All Delhi' is at the party and I am having a whale of a time – until I realise I have drunk far too much. Though the food is finally arriving (at midnight), it is time for me to leave.

The next morning, the Indian sun pours into my room. My

head is pounding as I try to read my emails, check the newspapers, and get showered and dressed in time for breakfast in David's suite. I let Andy lead off our meeting with the press summary whilst I try to eat something (surely food will help?). Liz comes in. 'We leave in ten for the formal welcome,' she says. 'Kate, do you mind joining the delegation? We are bit short on numbers.' I don't know what this means, but I suspect it will not be 'hangover friendly'. I am right.

I stand in the heat and dust with David, George, William Hague, and the High Commissioner as the Indian military perform an elegant guard of honour welcome in front of the extraordinary Lutyens-designed parliamentary building. David and Prime Minister Manmohan Singh inspect the troops, and then the intro-ductions take place, Singh to his team and David to ours. I am at the very end of our line-up. It is 35° and I think I am going to pass out.

The rest of the day goes according to plan – and it is a very busy one. There are speeches, openings, visits, and wreath-layings. As usual the formal end of the trip is marked by a joint press conference or 'presser', as the No. 10 press office call it. Our team gather in a quiet room to go through David's statement and some 'net practice'.

Foreign affairs advisor Tom Fletcher comes forward with a list of people David needs to thank. Minister Sheila Dikshit is top. Andy asks if it is really necessary to single her out. No disrespect meant, Andy says, but we have the whole British lobby on the front row of this presser and her name is, 'excuse my English, *Dikshit*.' Tom glares at Andy. The Indians will be very offended if she is not thanked properly by the Prime Minister. David under-lines his statement: *thank Minister*.

We each take our seats in the front row. Prime Minister Singh begins with warm words about the relationship between our two countries and the usefulness of the meetings. David follows with his words of thanks – and without a bat of an eyelid, Minister Dikshit is duly thanked. The British lobby snigger in their chairs.

Afterwards, Chris Patten, Chancellor of Oxford, comes up to me, shaken. 'Have you heard the terrible news?' he says, clearly upset. I haven't. 'Dinner is dry!' Still privately nursing my hangover, I am quite content with this.

The flight back after dinner is certainly not dry. Although I sleep almost the entire journey home, many of my colleagues join the party at the back of the plane. There is not a drop of alcohol left on board when we land. At least Gabby Bertin stops David having the traditional huddle with the press at the back of the plane. A high-altitude, high-alcohol gathering of press, together with a not altogether sober PM, high-spirited after a successful trip and dreaming of statesman-like flags and fireplaces plastered all over the papers, usually ends badly.

FOR SHORTER TRIPS, SAY, to European capitals, we use the Queen's flight, a military plane, if it isn't otherwise engaged. On these flights – as so often with life around the Prime Minister and No. 10 – it is all about where you sit. Everyone wants to be near a prime minister. Sit down too quickly and you'll have to move along to the window seat – out of range. Board too late and you might be bounced into the second part of the plane. Then you might as well go home.

If it is just the No. 10 team, I am allocated the throne opposite David's so we can discuss our strategy for each meeting. I sit on my feet, dwarfed by the enormous chair. Our favourite parts of the brief are the 'ice breakers' drafted by the Foreign Office – two-liners suggesting ways for David to start a conversation with a particular foreign leader. 'Congratulate X on his/her recent election/re-election' (probably a Western ally). 'Congratulate Y on his/ her launch of the "new way"/"next path", a ten-year programme for government' (subtext: probably having done away with elections altogether, this leader may be a little less keen on democracy). And sometimes things are more personal: 'Congratulate Z on his recent marriage' with '(this is his fifth wife)' written underneath, with no irony whatsoever.

16

A SPECIAL RELATIONSHIP

The relationship between a British prime minister and his or her American counterpart is always going to be a focus of attention. Arguably, it is not the most important relationship. You could, for instance, make a good case for why the German chancellor might matter more. The British prime minister certainly sees the German chancellor more regularly, and Germany affects our immediate neighbourhood to a greater degree. There are the various Commonwealth leaders with whom David is on friendly terms – the centre-right Aussie, New Zealand, Canadian prime ministers to name a few. And then Nordic prime ministers like Fredrik Reinfeldt of Sweden, who shares our more pragmatic view of Europe. But undervaluing the Americans is like pretending you don't have an uncle with clout who lives in the huge house at the end of the street, drives around in a Hummer, and has half the neighbourhood on his payroll. Whether you like it or not, they are hard to ignore, and they are family.

An opposition leader's contact with the US incumbent is generally fleeting, and rightly so. Presidents are naturally mindful of not offending a prime minister, so will not allow a formal meeting with the prime minister's opponent in the Oval Office. Instead, standard practice is to offer the leader a meeting with the National Security Advisor, with a 'brush by' from the president. This is the lingo for POTUS supposedly just dropping into someone else's meeting (but it is in fact scheduled).

This is amongst the most precarious of all diplomatic manoeuvres. For a start, the meeting itself is far from guaranteed, and even if the president does turn up, you have no idea how long he is going to stay. The first question the press pack will ask is: 'How long was the meeting?' The answer is all-important. If it is 'one minute', then you look pretty stupid.

In late 2007, when meeting President George W Bush, David's tactic was to bowl a highly strategic, last-minute question at the President – about his exercise regime. Fortunately, Bush's very lengthy response pushed the brief meeting well into the so-called 'golden' time zone, deemed by the press team to be 'long enough'.

Even if you manage to pull off a brush by, and push the conversation to last long enough to gain the approval of the press, then there is the negotiation about whether or not you get a picture. Without a picture, no one will remember you have even been there anyway.

Ultimately, David's most important transatlantic relationship is not to be with the forty-third President of the United States but with the forty-fourth, Barack Obama.

People will have differing views of Obama's presidency, but most would agree that he deserves huge credit for the extraordinary way in which he emerged from the American political system in the first place – a system so geared to incumbency – with little more than hope and astonishing personal charisma to help him. I am half-American, so for me, when I contemplate Obama's election in 2008, I think of the America of my late grandmother – born in 1901 – and of *To Kill a Mockingbird*, and the battle it represents. And there, he has won me over for life.

In summer 2008, Democratic presidential candidate Barack Obama is a wow. He lopes onto the world stage and inspires huge crowds with his beautiful prose. He passes through London on his European tour and we are desperate to meet him. Ed goes into operation 'deliver Obama'. Meanwhile, the Brown government is busy trying to pack Obama's agenda, so that he won't have time to see us. But after a near miss, he arrives at our offices in Norman

Shaw. Tall and in control, he moves purposefully and precisely – and not before his team is ready for him. He understands that it's all about getting the picture right. David is still a novice in this respect and strides ahead, even when told not to.

Alone in David's office he wants to mull over all the issues. This sets the tone for their future encounters. Hours of discussion. We quickly learn that Obama is a cautious, thoughtful thinker. He deliberates, takes his time. Andy Coulson organises the official photos, but his mind is on the real prize – a picture of himself with Obama. At the end of the formal Cameron–Obama handshake, Andy cheekily springs the question: 'Group photo?' Obama is too polite to say no, and we all jump in – *Click* – before he has time to change his mind. This picture still makes me laugh. It looks like an office snapshot from our early years, with David, William, George, and Andy at the front, but there, lurking at the back, is Barack Obama, almost as though he's a new member of Team Cameron.

The second time they meet, Obama is President of the United States and David and Samantha have just lost Ivan. The financial crisis is beginning to cast its shadow, and Prime Minister Brown is in his element, touring capitals trying to build a consensus around his plans to rescue the world.

Obama is in town for the G20. His staff agree to a meeting with David at the US Ambassador's residence in Regent's Park, while Samantha is to have tea with Michelle.

Just as I am leaving work, we hear that there is to be an exchange of presents, including for the children. All hell breaks out. The shops are already shut and the meeting is the very next morning. We have literally no time to buy a present, even if we had any ideas about what to buy. Then Samantha has the idea of a bracelet for Michelle, and we agree on a book for the children – a trilogy by Susan Cooper that Samantha and I both loved when we were young. I volunteer to pick it up first thing on my way in to work. We have exactly half an hour from opening time to gather the presents before we get into the convoy to the residence. I am waiting outside the bookshop impatiently and when the doors open I rush in and head straight to the children's section. My phone rings – it's George. I explain I can't talk because I am on mission critical to buy the Obama children a book. 'What book?' he asks. I reply, '*The Dark is Rising*.'

There is a silence. 'The what?' He does not sound happy.

'*The Dark Is Rising*,' I say again. 'It is a wonderful Arthurian trilogy . . . Samantha and I really loved these books as children.'

'It doesn't matter how much you and Sam loved the books or what they are about,' he says. 'What matters is, it's called—' he says each word, slowly, '*The Dark . . . Is . . . Rising*. Think of the *Daily Mail*! You can't give them that.'

I see that, however inconvenient, he has a point. I now have fifteen minutes to choose something else.

The Obamas are kind and gentle with David and Samantha when they meet, reaching out to them as fellow parents. David begins to build up a rapport with Obama. Iraq and Afghanistan feature in their discussions, as does the economic crisis. There is a glimmer of a future awkwardness around our differing economic strategies. Obama's more 'Keynesian' approach (throw money at the problem) contrasts with our own emerging strategy. We haven't fully spelt out Plan A, only made clear that we don't intend to spend our way out of a recession; the cuts narrative is yet to come. These viewpoints are dictated by very different circumstances, however. Our deficit is much larger, and the Americans are strengthened in having the dollar as reserve currency.

IT FEELS STRANGE TO be back in the British Embassy in Washington, DC, a place I know from my childhood. The vast palatial residence sits alongside other mansions, each of totally different design, that mark the suburban streets of the American capital. I was at a party here with my twin sister in December 1988 when the tragic news of the Lockerbie bombing broke. We had crossed the Atlantic the day before to join our parents for Christmas.

Today, we are all trying to take things in our stride, or at

Celebrating Hugo's birthday and the final hustings of the leadership election, 2005. With (left to right) Hugo Swire, James Cecil, Liz Sugg, Sophie Pym and David.

Early 2010, Davos. With David and George Osborne.

In campaign mode, on the way to Birmingham, April 2010.

Putting the final touches to a statement, and discussing the possibilities of forming a coalition, May 2010.

Early meetings in Downing Street with the newly-elected Prime Minister.

Daily meeting in the Prime Minister's 'Den'. With (right to left) George Osborne, Ed Llewellyn, David, Jeremy Heywood, Simon Case, Ameet Gill and Stephen Gilbert.

Meeting President Obama at the White House, March 2012.

Preparing for the worst and hoping for the best on Election day, 2015. With (left to right) Craig Oliver, Claire Foges, Liz Sugg, Ed Llewellyn and David.

Landing in Prague, with Press Secretary Gabby Bertin, January 2016.

David's last day in office as we say goodbye to the staff, July 2016.

least look like we are. This is slightly challenging under cannon fire. I stand behind David and Samantha on the White House lawn as the Marine Band plays our national anthems followed by a nineteen-gun salute. We move inside to meet the President formally, then sit down for talks before a joint press conference in the garden. My deputy chief of staff is an American citizen, David admits to an amused Obama. (I am a dual citizen.) There are White House-branded packets of M&Ms everywhere. Gabby Bertin is munching her way through her second. 'Most people don't actually eat the M&Ms,' an attendant says to her. 'They are supposed to be mementos.'

That evening they throw a big party for us at the White House. Everyone is dressed up to the nines. We are positioned for the receiving line, but then I look behind me to see my colleagues have disappeared to talk to George Clooney. I am whisked away to the Obamas' private apartment upstairs, and out on to the balcony for drinks. There are just a few of us here, sharing stories and jokes. Looking over the lawn onto the memorial park below, I think of my late grandmother and smile.

The next morning, George and Rupert Harrison catch the early flight home to work on the budget speech and the rest of us head off to New York City. Ed and I have a drink downtown before meeting the others for dinner. We are thrilled with what feels like a successful visit. Ed, always the pragmatist, says, 'It'll probably all go pear-shaped after this.'

Sure enough, arriving at the restaurant we spot Craig Oliver ahead of us, phone firmly planted to his ear. 'There's been a leak,' he whispers. 'They want to know if we're going to get rid of 50p tax rate.' It is a long flight home and we have a budget to land when we get there.

THE LAST TIME I meet President Obama in person is when he visits London before the EU referendum, six months before the end of his time in office. He is over to have lunch with the Queen and see the Cambridges, but we get a brief look in. We gather in the Cabinet room with the US team to discuss the joint presser, including potential questions around the referendum and any future US–UK trade deal. Obama tries out his line: Britain will be 'back of the queue'.

For the six turbulent years that this prime minister and this president overlapped in office, they came together to make important decisions – on Libya, on drawing down troops in Afghanistan, and on air strikes against the Islamic State in Syria. I look at David and Obama and think how they both now have grey hairs and seem to bear the weight of their years in office. I suppose we all do, to an extent.

As he stands next to David telling the British press how much he hopes Britain will stay in the EU (with an inevitably mixed reaction), I think how Obama, in the end, has tried to be the very best friend to David, and to Britain, that he can.

17

JUDGEMENT

'Events, dear boy, events,' is the rather old-fashioned phrase to sum it up. Or, as Olive Dowden would put it, 'Shit happens.' It all amounts to the same thing. Sometimes things just happen to people, and sometimes it's their own stupid fault. Politicians are not immune to the pitfalls and complications of life – they are human after all. Some are decent, others less so. Some make mistakes. And sometimes their hearts just don't beat in a way that fits easily with the tempo of public life. The cacophony that follows can be entirely unpredictable.

The rule of thumb is that you know you are in trouble in politics if the story is still going strong after two weekends of headlines. When this is the case, no matter what the individual scenario, two further rules usually seem to apply.

Firstly, the head of comms will always demand the victim's head, whether or not they are guilty. They are only interested in saving a prime minister's reputation; everyone else is expendable. This sits at odds with the rest of us who want to be fair and not unduly swayed by the court of public opinion.

Secondly, whatever anyone thinks, the person hasn't a cat's chance in hell of surviving if the issue comes down to judgement or, more to the point, a lack of it. Judgement is everything in politics. The more senior you are, the more it matters. In the end, the job of a politician is to make decisions on our behalf. We give them that power through the ballot box. But if they show no judgement in exercising their power, we are unlikely to ask them to do it again. And there is the simple fact that no matter how high-profile they are, just like everyone else, politicians are people who can get depressed, get into fights, and change their minds about all sorts of things, from their political beliefs to their sexuality. Only they are in the public spotlight – so chances are, it will become a story.

Our first 'scandal' was the ten-day assault on David about whether he did or didn't take drugs as a young man. We emerged from this storm resting on the simple statement that everyone deserves a private life and a past. It held because most people thought that David was a sensible guy and it was a reasonable position to take. People don't want their politicians to be preparing for public life from the age of 10. And they also don't want them to have to be insincere about it.

Fast forward a few years to 2008. We are having supper at David's house in North Kensington. George is late and arrives looking out of sorts. It turns out with good reason. His childhood friend has written a letter to *The Times* accusing him of lacking judgement in allegedly trying to raise money for the Conservative Party from a Russian billionaire whilst staying with him over the summer – a story that only has legs because George had invited his friend Andrew Feldman to join, as he was holidaying nearby. Andrew happened to be party treasurer at the time. Had Andrew not gone, it would have been: 'Shock, horror: George has a drink on a large boat owned by a dodgy Russian.' The story runs and runs because it features so many good ingredients: billionaires, famous people, vengeful friends, money. And, of course, politics.

Corfu and drugs were mere scraps compared to the first real scandal we have to deal with: MPs' expenses. This matters more because it threatens the entire political establishment and would leave an enduring legacy, both in how society view politicians and how Conservative MPs view their leader. Neither, of course, in a good way.

At the heart of the expenses scandal is the national condemnation of a system that had long since passed the 'smell good' test, with the sheer scale and extent of the payouts unfathomable to most. It centres around a system of allowances to support MPs in their parliamentary duties. This system had been allowed to grow as MPs' salaries stood static. Some had bought into a culture where the money was 'rightfully theirs' rather than keeping to a sense of decorum around what is appropriate to take from the taxpayer. In the individual stories themselves, there is a huge range of culpability, from fraud at one extreme to nothing very much to see at the other.

In early 2009, the *Telegraph* buy a leaked file, which has apparently been 'doing the rounds', recording MPs' expenses over the years. They publish the stories day after day, to an outraged country. MPs lie awake at night waiting for the email informing them they are next. There is a feeling that no one is safe, no one could be innocent. The stories glare from the pages of the newspapers, brought to life by some of the more absurd expenses claims – for cleaning moats, or building duck houses.

There is a sense that all MPs are being judged by the worst cases – and there are plenty of those. What respect the public had for their local MP diminishes by the minute and the political class unravels in disgrace.

We have a very big problem on our hands. In fact, we have two – and they conflict. On the one hand, the public are very angry and are being fed a daily diet of stories, which threaten to bring down the entire political establishment a year before a general election. It seems we are looking at the possible collapse of the mainstream parties – especially the Tories, who are hit the worst. There is the risk of 'anti-sleaze candidates' running against incumbent MPs up and down the country. On the other hand, we have a lot of very furious MPs and their families to deal with, many of whom think they are being hard done by.

We have no choice but to act – and to act quickly, to stop the whole thing unwinding further. David is a strong believer in apologising when something has gone wrong. Sorry – because the public deserve an apology. Sorry – so we can establish a clean break with the past, and hopefully move on and start trying to put things right. In practice, this means setting up a system for dealing with existing grievances, the 'clean-up'. Which needs to be tough but also fair. Next we need to put a process in place to make sure whatever went wrong won't happen again.

So, we start reviewing the expenses of our own MPs, one by one. It is a hard slog, and ultimately we are judging the MPs against homemade standards of what seems 'reasonable' and what passes the 'smells good' test. Our team deliberate day after day – advising MPs to apologise when necessary and, in the most difficult cases, pay money back to the taxpayer. It is judgement day all round. Even David pays back money for having his wisteria cut.

All this comes at a cost. Because now we have a very unhappy group of MPs on our hands, furious at being dragged through the mud. And they are angry about what they consider the root of the problem – their pay. Most of all, they are angry with David for not standing up for them. Many of the MPs can't see that we are trying to save the party. Or help them save their seats. Some don't seem to even care that David is trying to do the right thing by the public. They feel David should ignore the fuss and stand by them, come what may. Many of them look at David – who they view as well-off compared to them – and resent him for it.

All in all, a generation of politicians is caught up in what is a very ugly episode that leaves public regard for and trust in politicians at an all-time low – not to mention the lasting legacy of a parliamentary party who feel betrayed by their boss.

The sour aftertaste never really goes away.

AN MP FRIEND OF mine is taking his young daughter's class round the House of Commons. He asks if anyone can tell him what 'MP' stands for. There is an embarrassed silence. Well, I know who can, he says, smiling indulgently at his daughter. 'It stands for "Miserable Person",' she replies.

When things go wrong for MPs, especially ministers, too often they don't have a lot of people to turn to. The nearest thing there is to an HR department are the whips, but they aren't altogether a sympathetic lot. Their job is to police the party, and above all they are colleagues who love to gossip and probably want your job. So, it often falls to us at No. 10 to deal with very sensitive personal issues. We end up being the psychiatrists, firefighters, walking hankies, and executioners. It is us who have to talk them into a manageable place, and find a way through if a solution is required. Sometimes at relative speed.

The problem is that if you are told something potentially inflammable, from the moment you are in receipt of the information, the clock is ticking. Doing nothing is not an option, because when the scandal breaks – which it inevitably will – the first questions people are going to ask are, How long have you known and what have you done about it?

When a married MP with a family declares he is gay the press have a field day. Watching an MP's personal life unravel in the public eye, people often wonder, why did such-and-such go into public life in the first place? Because they didn't know what issue might unravel – or perhaps they did, but hoped for the best. But do we want our politicians to all conform to a bland stereotype, or do we want them to more truthfully mirror the experiences of the rest of us? I fear we want both. We dislike the machine politician, but sometimes find the truths of their real lives less than palatable.

Coming into government, all this intensifies. As MPs become ministers, they take on the responsibilities of their departmental duties, some extremely sensitive, and this often brings them more in the public eye. It's no longer just the leader's office and the party whips they need to answer to.

All ministers sign the Ministerial Code, where they promise to uphold the dignity and propriety of the office they hold. If they are accused of impropriety, it is generally up to the Cabinet Secretary – guided by Sue Gray, as head of propriety and ethics – to adjudicate whether or not they have broken the code. Sue is a rare breed in officialdom, in that she has a high level of emotional intelligence in a place that does not really value it. She often has to make difficult calls. Some find her too representative of 'the System' for their taste, but her role means she *is* the system. That's the point.

Liam Fox was the first Conservative Cabinet Minister during our time in government whose career hit the wall due to an error of 'judgement'. He resigned in October 2011 after a story concerning his travelling on official business with his friend, and unofficial advisor, Adam Werritty. The perception of a conflict of interest was deemed a clear breach of the Ministerial Code. Andy and Ed were dispatched to Admiralty House to talk to Liam, but by the time they arrived he had already decided he had to go.

Mark Harper's failure to spot that his cleaner had a forged working permit was unlucky for him. No one thought he was really at fault – but he was Immigration Minister, in charge of toughening rules around employers checking the status of their employees. His credibility was shot to pieces. Again, it goes back to judgement. The Commons would have had him for breakfast the minute he rose to his feet. Mark knew the game was up and resigned. And because he did it quickly, and everyone was sympathetic, we were able to bring him back into government within months.

We were relieved that the most gripping saga of the early years was not our problem but Nick's. The Chris Huhne affair began as a story about a broken marriage and ended as a sad tale of two parents 'doing time' – a disastrous finish to a political career. It all started with a question of who had accepted the penalty points for speeding – Chris or his wife. Nick was in despair. Our press team offered their sympathies to their Lib Dems colleagues. We knew what they were thinking: *This is the sort of thing that happens with Tories, not our nicely behaved Lib Dems.* But we had plenty of our own problems brewing.

And when things go wrong, they don't just go wrong for the politicians. I sense something is really wrong by the look on Ed's face when I walk into the office one day in spring 2014. 'Is something up?' I ask, slightly defensively, because if there is one thing

I dislike above all else, it is if Ed has been working on something important and not shared it with me. Sue Gray appears with a 'We've got a problem' look about her, compounding my suspicions. 'I'll tell you after the 8.30,' Ed says. I try hard not to scowl.

When we meet afterwards I quickly sense this involves something well out of the ordinary. Ed, Sue, and I sit in the private office along with one of our senior officials. They all look tired and tense. Their faces say: who's going to fill Kate in on what happened last night?

Patrick Rock has been around Conservative politics for years. He was special advisor to Michael Howard at the Home Office, and contested a few seats in his time. Halfway through the Parliament we had decided it was time the No. 10 Policy Unit was redirected away from serving the Coalition to focusing on the (Conservative) Prime Minister. We suggest to Nick Clegg that he form his own policy unit. We need some more political animals upstairs. 'The Rock', as he is known, is duly hired.

His old-school style does not sit easily with our professional, modern No. 10, and we have had some issues with him over the past year. But recently he's seemed more agitated than usual. He has been spending time on work close to my heart – trying to make the internet safer for children, and in particular, bringing the search companies to bear some responsibility for the ease with which bad things are so easily accessed through their search engines. We have pressed them to clean up their act, but they are of the mindset that the search engine is a neutral common good – like the air we breathe – and the responsibility for any ills should be borne at the point of use.

When Patrick goes missing from work those closest to him worry that he may be seriously depressed. Then we hear troubling news of an arrest.

'So where exactly is Patrick now?' I ask.

He is in a police cell awaiting bail. We all look at each other in despair.

Months later, Patrick is charged. When the trial is finally heard, he is convicted of downloading indecent pictures of young girls and gets a two-year conditional discharge. The very man who was helping us devise a safer internet for children. The whole thing is awful, shocking, and sad on so many levels.

Lawmakers cannot be lawbreakers. If you discover that someone has done something wrong, then you are duty-bound to act on it. That doesn't mean it's easy, and that you don't feel the tensions and conflicts. Nor does it lessen the personal impact. If anything, it exacerbates it.

18

PHONE-HACKING

A few years into opposition we were on the hunt for a senior figure to join our team as head of communications. We had an excellent press secretary in George Eustice, but there was an overall feeling that we were undergunned in our media operation. We didn't have strong support from the *Telegraph* or the *Mail*, and the Murdoch press was still not won over. There was a view that we needed a heavy hitter. Such people aren't very easy to find. Traditionally, they come from the media, often from a newspaper – Alastair Campbell, for instance.

At the beginning of 2007, Andy Coulson had resigned as editor of the *News of the World*. The paper's former royal editor, Clive Goodman, and private investigator, Glenn Mulcaire, had been convicted of hacking phone messages. Andy denied having known anything about it all, but he took the hit because it had happened on his watch. He was respected and well-loved by his staff. His name emerged as a possibility.

George liked him a lot. So did Steve. And soon Andy was brought in to meet the rest of us. He seemed to have a great deal to offer, but there was still that black mark by his name. So, soundings were taken. Yes, there were warnings, but not of a specific nature; most of the feedback was positive. The noise around phone-hacking at the paper was certainly ugly, but the view was that the problem had been endemic on Fleet Street. The police had done their job, two people had been found guilty:

case closed (so it seemed). And Andy had had the dignity to resign.

David believes in giving people second chances, but he wanted to be clear in his own mind that Andy had had nothing to do with the phone-hacking itself, which we view in a very dim light, not least for the profound hurt it causes. He asks for assurances from Andy when they meet. Later, both men are adamant about what was said – David that Andy gave him full assurances, and Andy that he did not lie to David. I was not there, so I cannot say.

To start with, we view one another with some trepidation: Andy from Mars, the Cameron inner team from Venus. But soon we fall for each other. We value and seek Andy's advice. Above all, we find him to be one of the most professional people we have worked with, a brilliant manager and a rare advisor, in that he gives as much to his relations with his team as he gives the boss. He is also very good company – and quickly David enjoys having him around.

Andy also brings with him his network of media friends, including his relationships with the Murdochs and their editors, who form a sort of extended Murdoch family. Rebekah Wade, then still editor of *The Sun*, is the most formidable of these, with her flamboyant red hair and compelling nature. After she starts a relationship with and then marries an old friend of David's in Oxfordshire, Charlie Brooks, she becomes a neighbour and friend of the Camerons.

It is hardly new for a politician to strike up a friendship with a journalist. The days when 'hacks' critiqued the political class from a separate world is long gone. And Rebekah had form. She was close to Blair; she went to Sarah Brown's Chequers pyjama party. But when the spotlight shines on their friendship, it feels uncomfortable, not least because of the some of the texts that emerge. LOL (by which he meant 'lots of love') is etched in people's minds.

When Andy accepts the job with us, he makes it clear that he will try to help us win the next general election but not come with us to Downing Street if we win. Judging by where we are in summer 2007, this is not looking too likely anyway. But then things pick up.

In January 2009, I sit next to Andy on the plane heading to Davos. Our conversation turns to a general election. 'Think, if we win, you'll be head of communications at Downing Street,' I say, forgetting that Andy is not supposed to be coming with us. He reminds me, and I cannot think why he would have made such a commitment. And it seems that Andy may be changing his mind. Whatever was worrying him then has either gone away or is worrying him less. He asks me whether I thought David would like him to join him in No. 10. I cannot see a good reason why he wouldn't.

This proves to be a fatal move. Had Andy kept to his original plan – to help us win and then to leave in a blaze of glory – the whole phone-hacking saga might never have been brought to the boil in the way it was.

For although there were questions around what happened at the paper at the time, the motivation behind the story was largely political – driven by Tom Watson from the backbenches of the Labour Party. Their goal was to attack David through Andy, and have a go at the Murdoch empire.

But the past came knocking on his door even while we were still in opposition.

One afternoon, in summer 2009, a link from *The Guardian* pops up on my screen. I need to talk to Andy about a couple of things – so I make my way along the corridor to his office. Just as I am about to leave, I remember – oh, there's something about you on *The Guardian* online. Andy looks a bit agitated and searches for it straightaway. Later Steve claims to have warned Ed about a specific allegation from a friend at *The Guardian*, around the hiring of a private detective at the *News of the World*. Ed has absolutely no recollection of this conversation – and he is a very meticulous person. Of course, it is not impossible that Steve mentioned it in passing, for example, while Ed was on the phone and wasn't listening. Either way, this conflict between Ed and Steve adds to the tensions in our team.

Later that summer, Andy is summoned to give evidence to the Culture, Media and Sport Committee on their investigation into phone-hacking. They conclude that it is 'inconceivable' that more people had not known about it.

With months to go before the election, Andy takes up pole position in the team. A combination of Steve's year in California and the financial crisis has strengthened his hand. George wants to put the economy at the centre of our campaign – and so does Andy. He views Steve's Big Society agenda with raised eyebrows. Hard-working families have other things on their minds right now, like their jobs. They grate against one another – the blue-sky thinker and the political realist.

On 11 May 2010, Andy comes with us into No. 10 as director of communications. He is in his element. He settles into Gordon Brown's old office in No. 12, with its views over Horse Guards, presiding over the press office and gets to work building up David's stature as Prime Minister. He soon earns the respect of those across the Coalition as well as those in officialdom who do not already know him well.

But this period of relative calm is interrupted in early autumn when the *New York Times* publishes a piece on its website claiming Andy had known about phone-hacking all along. We have grown used to this story rumbling away in the background, but now it grows into a storm. Things get still more tangled when Vince Cable declares war on the Murdochs by threatening to block a proposed takeover bid of BSkyB by News Corp. Cable is supposed to be impartial in his quasi-judicial role, so David has no choice but to take the responsibility away from him and give it to the Culture Secretary, Jeremy Hunt, instead. There is a view that we are too wrapped up with the Murdochs. Trying to protect them.

By January 2011, things have reached fever pitch. There is an unpleasant moment when we all realise that we cannot go on as we are. Andy is the story – and the story is not going away. Our operation is in paralysis. David is under attack. We have a lot of other things we need to do. It is Andy, not us, who calls it a day.

As he says, 'When the spokesman needs a spokesman, it's time to move on.'

We travelled the uncertain road to Downing Street with Andy. He is part of the small, tightly knit team that propelled David to power. We rely on his advice and good judgement. Most painfully of all, he is our friend. And now he leaves under a huge cloud. Andy wants no goodbye parties – or goodbyes, full stop. There are a lot of tears on the day he leaves, mostly from the political side of the building. The officials look at us like we are slightly unhinged.

Now we need to find a replacement. We are wary of looking to the newspapers again. It is Nick Robinson's idea that we meet the editor of the *BBC News at Ten* – a guy called Craig Oliver who he rates highly. It is difficult for Craig in the beginning. We are a close team and we have just lost someone we like a lot and trust. Craig is accepted as a professional colleague, but everyone is a little wary of a more emotional connection. Craig senses he has a lot to prove.

Andy has left the building but he hasn't gone away. Allegations of who knew what about phone-hacking at the *News of the World* continue, but the political story is now centred on David's judgement in hiring him in the first place, whether he was too loyal in keeping him on while the background noise grew louder and louder. Ed Miliband goes in for the kill, taking aim at the Murdoch press at the same time. This and his attack on energy prices are the most successful political campaigns of his leadership.

Rupert Murdoch flies in to clean up the mess. The entire paper is shut down overnight. The only person left standing is Rebekah Brooks. And Andy looks precariously isolated – although he does have loyal friends, who stand by him the whole way through. I am not alone in being one of these. I take a dim view of people who drop friends when they fall on bad times.

Months go by, and then on 8 July I wake to hear on the radio that Andy Coulson has been taken into custody in the early hours. My children are in a state, thinking of his young boys who they have played with. 'Will Andy go to jail?' I am upset. I make my way into work. Craig reads out the morning media summary. 'Andy Coulson was arrested this morning.' People look down at their feet. I catch David's eye. He too is upset. He is also worried.

Miliband is in full war cry and we need to work out what to do. There is enormous pressure for David to apologise but he is careful to avoid this. After all, Andy is an innocent man, awaiting trial. For the Commons statement, we pick his words carefully. 'If it turns out that I have been lied to, that would be the moment for a profound apology.'

To put out a big fire you need to set in place a process to ensure – and most importantly, show why – the past won't be repeated. The classic device is some sort of review or inquiry. But this is a more difficult decision to take than you would think, because whilst you might solve today's problem you are creating another one further down the line. Put the report date in your diary – because that's when the issue will be back in the public domain once again. And worse, if it is an independent inquiry, you will have absolutely no idea how it will turn out.

For these reasons, we at first push back against a full independent judge-led inquiry. In the end, however, with the firestorm still raging and no support coming from our Coalition partners, we give in and announce Leveson. Days later, Rebekah Brooks resigns and the Murdochs are subjected to a grilling by the Culture, Media and Sport Committee – made more memorable by Wendi Deng's extraordinary leap to save her husband from an incoming flying pie of shaving foam, launched by a protester.

The specific allegations around phone-hacking, in so far as they relate to Andy and others, is now a matter of criminal investigation. So, the inquiry, chaired by Lord Justice Leveson, will focus on press regulation, ethics, and the relationships between media and the political class. Although there is a sense that the relationships are often uncomfortably close, what might they do? Ban all relationships between journalists and politicians? That's a few marriages over, for a start. Press regulation is a can of worms. On the one hand, there is the hallowed principle of the freedom of the press.

On the other, the criticism that the current system of self-regulation is fairly toothless.

The storm quells but never quite subsides. The press now sees everything through the prism of Leveson – which they view as an all-out attack against their freedom, unleashing a torrent of terrible headlines day after day. Miliband is on a roll, and turns his attention to whether Jeremy Hunt has broken the Ministerial Code over his handling of the BSkyB takeover. And we haven't even started the official inquiry.

The inquiry opens in the summer of 2012 and is played live on television. It feels unsettling to watch David and George grilled under oath by Brian Leveson for hours on end. It is certainly compelling footage.

We wait anxiously for the report, knowing that Leveson's verdict might mark the end of this circus. A harsh judgment is sure to undermine David's authority and credibility. The report arrives at Downing Street with an ominous thud – a small mountain of paperwork. A few of us are allowed to read it ahead of its release, each copy named and numbered. We sit silently thumbing through the text looking for killer lines. We will regather in an hour.

'I can't see anything too difficult,' David says. 'What have others found?' We all agree. There is no accusation of any wrongdoing or impropriety. The relief in the room is palpable.

Leveson's main condemnation is reserved for the newspapers, and the inadequate way in which they are regulated. In the end – up against a divided press – one self-regulated body is merely replaced with another.

WAY FURTHER DOWN THE road, in summer 2014, the phone-hacking trial finally begins. Seven years after we hired Andy.

Until this moment we feel we have never wavered in our support of Andy, despite the huge pressures to do so. Everyone knows and believes that a man is innocent until proved guilty; we will stand firmly behind that tradition. If it turns out we were wrong, David will make a full apology.

We are sitting with a group of officials when the news comes through – Andy has been found guilty of conspiracy to hack phones. There is a silence. David continues with his meeting, professional to a tee. As soon as I can, I send everyone away. I have texted George to come. We shut the door behind us and sit in silence. We feel incredibly sad. It is horrible to think a close colleague, a friend, is actually going to jail. We think of Eloise and their three boys. We know the time has now come for us to shift our ground and say sorry. Any minute now Craig will be knocking on the door. But we just want a moment in privacy, to reflect.

Craig arrives; he wants David to make a statement immediately. But there is an issue around whether this is appropriate given the jury is not yet out on the other charges against Andy. We take soundings, including from the Attorney General. The overwhelming view is that the judgment has been passed on phone-hacking, and the world and his dog are out there commenting on it. Had the judge wanted to keep things closed, he would have waited and given all the convictions together. By not saying anything, it looks like we are dragging our feet, yet again.

David goes out to make a full and frank apology. 'I am extremely sorry that I employed him. It was the wrong decision.' An hour later, the judge hammers David for his intervention, and worst of all, suspends the rest of the trial. We are completely mortified.

In the end, Leveson reports. Rebekah is found innocent. The press remains self-regulated. A Sunday paper is closed. Lots of people lose their jobs. Rebekah resigns. The Murdoch empire remains. Rebekah is rehired. A new Sunday paper is born.

And what has actually changed? One man is sent to jail while another's reputation takes a good kicking for hiring him in the first place, and then for standing by him. And, allegedly, for showing a lack of judgement, that cardinal political sin.

No matter how much we valued and liked Andy – which we all did – it had been a risk for him to join the team, especially when we went into Downing Street. A risk that hadn't paid off. Especially for him.

19

THE DOLDRUMS

Halfway through the electoral cycle we hit choppy waters. George's 2012 Budget unravels almost as soon as it is delivered. The main problem is the juxtaposition of a cut in the top rate of tax from 50p to 45p, with tax increases, including on hot takeaway food such as pasties, making the whole Budget look like an exercise in helping the rich off the backs of the poor. Worse, it comes out against a gloomy fiscal forecast.

The 'pasty tax' becomes a potent symbol: George Osborne vs. the working man's pie, and the working man's pie wins the day. All the journalists want to know is when George or David last ate 'said pie'. Luckily, David's summers in Cornwall make him something of an aficionado. At least he thinks they do, until the place he claims has sold him his last pasty turns out to have closed down two years earlier.

Of course, it is nothing really to do with pie at all but whether two so-called 'posh boys' are too out of touch to run the country. The 'pasty tax' hits George's Budget because his critics are able to question his motivation ('motivation' being another word for judgement). As a result, the entire package is deemed to be ill thought through.

Over the weeks that follow, he has to back down on many of the smaller tax increases featured in the Budget – on caravans, charities, churches. Our MPs are furious. Although a U-turn is better than sticking to a flawed policy and having to back down

in the face of defeat, George and his team are particularly unpopular with the parliamentary party, who have sent out numerous
letters to their constituents defending the details of the plan, only
to find a few days later that a policy has been changed or, in some
cases, dropped altogether.

Afterwards, David and I talk about what went wrong. We realise
that we spent most of the budget bilaterals talking about one issue
– namely, whether to introduce a type of 'mansion' tax by adding
new council tax bands for higher-value homes. When finally, and
only very much at the last minute, David finally decided against,
we then failed to review the Budget in its new entirety, weighing
it up to see who would gain and who might lose.

The mansion tax would have been the perfect counterweight to
the reduction in top rate tax of 50p, and a good way to tax the
well-off. And George had been keen. Plus, it is hard to argue
against a review of council bands of some sort or another. But the
prospect of introducing what would essentially be a 'new tax', aimed
at the ultimate security of the British family – their home – tipped
the balance. After weeks of deliberation, we argued George down.
I felt completely exhausted by it. From that point, our bilaterals
morphed into an awkward confessional, where each of us were
asked our position in turn. Looking at the floor to avoid eye contact
with George, I sided with David.

And so, the Budget as it stands is politically lopsided. It therefore sinks.

Then, things worsen. There is the threat of a fuel tanker strike
by the trade union Unite. They are saying they will strike over pay
as well as standards on safety and training.

We are more than aware that a fuel tanker strike can bring a
nation to a standstill in a matter of days. No fuel quickly means
no food supplies. Closed schools. Chaos all round. And almost the
same level of pandemonium can be triggered by the mere sugges-
tion of a strike. If people even think petrol might run out, it can
lead to an immediate run on the petrol stations, with queues, traffic
jams, and havoc ensuing.

So, the worst thing to do is to suggest to the public that this is exactly what might be about to happen. Unfortunately, at this point, Francis Maude – Minister for the Cabinet Office, and responsible for civil contingencies – saunters out of the front door of No. 10 and makes a statement to the nation urging people to fill up a jerrycan. It is the wrong message at the wrong time in the wrong place. No one but a prime minister is supposed to speak from outside No. 10, just for a start.

The government looks disorganised at best. On the heels of the botched Budget, the papers declare an 'omnishambles'. Our poll ratings are sinking. The backbenches are jumpy. The economic forecasts are bleak, suggesting that we are in line for the first double-dip recession since the 1970s (only later do we discover that this has been avoided). We are in the doldrums.

'It is time for hard hats,' Ed says to our weekly gathering of No. 10 political staff. And then he warns against loose talk. The comms team are more direct. If you can't keep your mouth shut, don't go out, they say.

The problem with hitting a bad patch in politics is that everything starts to be seen from a negative perspective. Like a run on petrol, it becomes self-perpetuating. Every little mistake is declared a disaster. The No. 10 operation is inadequate. The Prime Minister has lost his way and is too busy 'chillaxing'. The Chancellor should be removed. Nothing is going right – and when it is, it isn't reported.

Against this background you have to work that much harder to keep the show on the road. You need to be on full alert for any mistakes or potential problems. And you cannot simply go quiet and hunker down in the bunker, otherwise the government will be seen to go adrift.

We plough on – with utmost care – aware that we cannot afford another major upset.

THE MAYORAL ELECTION LOOMS as our next big challenge. We know we have to win the London elections in May if we are going to show that we have any prospect of winning the next general election. It will demonstrate that we still have support in key target seats – and the political momentum going forward.

Although Boris has been a popular and successful mayor, the race is tight. London is a left-leaning city anyway, and these elections come right in the middle of the low point of the electoral cycle, when most governments tend to be at their most unpopular. We throw everything at supporting him. And luckily Australian election guru Lynton Crosby has returned to help, as he did for Boris's first election in 2008.

I have known the Johnson family from childhood. Stanley Johnson – father to Rachel, Boris (born Alexander), Jo, and Leo – is an old Foreign Office friend of my father's. All the Johnsons are clever and compelling in their own way. They are also a tribe with an extraordinarily high level of Darwinian survival instincts. This, I am sure, comes from the hostile environment in which they were brought up – in one of the coldest houses in England (the last time I slept there it actually snowed on my head in bed) – along with having to compete with each other on a daily basis. Though to their great credit, instead of turning on one another, they choose to keep close and form a sort of global elite, all their own.

As head of the prestigious Oxford Union Boris was already 'somebody' when I arrived at university. His sister – in the year below him – was his loudest cheerleader. The summer after Boris left Oxford, my family visited them at their family farm in Devon, Boris with his fiancée Allegra. Sitting around, discussing what to do next, Rachel announced that they would write a book together, about how Oxford is a playpen for running the country. The Johnsons had conquered Oxford and were now off to conquer the world. Nothing has changed very much over the years.

A meeting with Boris in David's office does little to allay our fears about the state of his campaign. Boris arrives, his usual bumbling funny self, impossible to settle down. 'What's your key campaign message?' asks David. Boris says it is all about 'driverless trains'. This is not reassuring. David points out that this will surely be unpopular with the train drivers, who will lose their jobs, or the public, who may prefer to have someone at the wheel. 'Everything is great, really,' says Boris, because he has a nine-point plan to go alongside the driverless trains, and he starts reeling off the plan. Only he hesitates after point three. His advisor steps in to reel off the six further points. At least we have Lynton's guile and Boris's charm on our side. We hope for the best.

I am at a birthday party with my son on the Friday evening when the results start coming in. For a while they are going the wrong way. Watching the new Avengers film, I am thinking about what we will need to do if we lose. I will probably have to go back into work later. We will need to rethink the Grid for the next few weeks . . . Then, just as the superheroes seem to finally be hurtling their enemy into outer space, the results finally start to pick up. We just make it: Boris wins with 51.5 per cent of the vote.

The hurdle is jumped. Boris is triumphant and we are still in the doldrums, but at least things have not turned for the worse.

SUMMER 2012 WE HAVE an even bigger challenge looming in the Olympics. We cannot wriggle out of this one – and we know it needs to be a success. But there is a sense that it could turn into a global fiasco. And if it does, we are sure to get the blame. With everything else we have on our plate, it feels like bad timing.

The lead-up is fraught with difficulties. COBR meetings become a near daily occurrence. Then, with just weeks to go, G4S announce they are unable to deliver the security staff we need. We spend hours in COBR with the MOD and Theresa May's team from the Home Office trying to sort things out. In the end, the army is brought in to help. We are again surrounded by men and women in khaki. They welcome me to No. 10 every day with 'Good morning, ma'am'. This is definitely an improvement.

Still more nerve-racking is the security above our heads. We will have a no-fly zone around the Olympic park for the duration of the Games, with our planes on full alert in case it is ever broken. Senior ministers take it in turns to be on duty. The stadium seats 80,000 people; it does not even bear thinking about what would happen if something went wrong.

Hosting the Olympics requires one of the single biggest voluntary surrenders of national sovereignty a country can make. The moment you win the bid, you sign away your right to run your designated host city to the International Olympic Committee (IOC) for the entire duration of the Games – down to the timing of the traffic lights. No one is more horrified than me when Olympic 'fast track' lanes for VIPs, contestants, and IOC officials are put down all over London. Memories of the senior officials-only ZiL lanes, from my childhood in Communist Moscow, flood back. 'Do you know how unpopular these are going to be?' I say to the 8.30 meeting. The thought of David and George driving along in their government cars while London grinds to a halt – our poll ratings plunging still further – is still more disturbing. Liz hands David an Oyster card. We'll being going to the Olympics by Tube.

The press in the days before the opening is unrelentingly bad. Then the Games begin – and the mood changes completely. A tidal wave of warmth spreads throughout the country and seems to draw everyone together. We are a proud nation once again, bowled over by the eccentric creativity of Danny Boyle's opening ceremony, gathering in parks and pubs to cheer on our fabulous athletes. The success of the Olympics and Paralympics gives us a short reprise from the negative press coverage, as the gaze of the media is diverted to London's stadiums and parks, but we know it will not last.

David is caught up in the patriotic mood, and tries to get to as many events as he can in between seeing foreign leaders who are over to support their teams. Putin and he bond over a judo match. In No. 10 we feel literally to be part of the beach volleyball stadium, which has been erected practically in the back garden. Our daily meetings are interrupted by the roars of the crowd. I go with David, Samantha, and the family to one of the matches, marvelling at the strength and power of the bikini-clad women as they do battle in the sand.

However, despite the Olympic fever, the burden of being at a low point in government weighs down on all of us, especially David. It is more than just the challenge of a downturn in political fortune. He has planned his whole life to be Prime Minister and after two years, he is suddenly mindful of his choices. Missing Ivan. Discovering not for the last time that the grief he feels will never leave him. The mood from the flat descends. Ed and I try to keep morale up downstairs. It is tough-going. There are times when the challenges of No. 10 are more bound up in a battle of spirit rather than the battle of politics. I feel relieved to drive myself home at the end of each day, turning on Capital radio as an escape.

George is asked by Sebastian Coe to hand out a medal at the Paralympic Games, but he is booed by the crowds at the park. I see it happen on television and feel horribly protective of him. Even my children are upset. I am cross with George's team for allowing him to give out the medal in the first place. Liz Sugg has been far more cautious with David. Sensing the risk of an unpredictable crowd, she has steered him away from the main stadiums. But George accepts full responsibility.

PARLIAMENT ITSELF IS OFTEN hot and bothered at the end of the summer term, and no more so than in 2012. A plan to introduce a mostly elected House of Lords meets with increasing resistance from amongst our own backbenchers. Although we privately think it unlikely the plan will ever progress past stage one – which envisions 120 elected peers – David feels it is too high-risk to explain the strategy directly to our MPs. It's part of a bargain that we have struck with the Lib Dems in exchange for their support for boundary changes, which will improve our chance of winning in 2015, and David can't risk them pulling out. He hopes that his MPs will hold their noses and trust him. But too many of them are not in a trusting mood.

Originally it been a different bargain: the AV referendum in return for boundary changes. But our highly aggressive and personal campaign during the AV referendum campaign left such a sour taste in the Lib Dems' mouths that we have had to throw them a second bone. None of us can easily forget Nick Clegg arriving at our weekly bilateral looking hurt, one of our more aggressive pamphlets in his hands. 'Did it have to come to this?' he had asked. We didn't reply: 'Well, yes, because for a brief moment we thought we might lose.' So now we are having to make progress with reforming the Lords.

The backbench opposition to reform intensifies – despite the fact that the Lib Dems have indicated publicly they will not sign off the boundary changes if we lose the vote. The truth is that many MPs are sceptical about the real value of the boundary changes to our chance of winning more seats, and don't like having their constituencies meddled with. On 10 July, ninety-one Tory MPs vote against the proposals. Lords reform is a dead duck, and so are the boundary changes. David's colleagues have given him a kicking. And our chances of David securing a majority government in 2015 look a lot weaker.

There is one Conservative whose star is shining brightly, however, and who seems to have managed to personally associate himself with the success of the Olympics, as well as get re-elected, and that is Mayor Boris Johnson. We gaze at him 'hilariously' suspended on a zip wire and wonder whether he will challenge David to a leadership election over the months ahead.

It is well into August when we finally get to leave for our holidays. And by then, we are completely on our knees.

WE COME BACK IN the first week of September determined to hit the ground running. To survive the doldrums you need to first make sure you don't make matters worse; to get out of them altogether, you need to inject some new energy, usually through a relaunch. We decide to start with a strong Cabinet reshuffle, followed by a stronger party conference.

Conference, at least, goes well, and David gives a strong, more personal speech focusing on aspirations – both for the individual and for the country as a whole. He is focused on creating a disciplined, voting battalion out of the 2010 intake of MPs, who are proving to be more independent-minded that the whips would like. We are facing a strong Labour lead in the polls, and a very jumpy party.

A well-off backbench MP, Adam Afriyie, is busy holding dinner parties to whip up opposition to David. Although no one thinks he is a likely leadership contender, his antics do not go unnoticed. 'They can't resist the wine,' David's PPS tells us. But it is more than the wine. There are other issues bubbling beneath the surface. David and George have always been social liberals in a party whose core is more inclined towards social conservatism. Both of them strongly believe in our proposals to allow equal marriage, but it has not gone down well in the grassroots and comes to symbolise a gap between the leadership and the base. So much so that there is a lot of debate as to whether we should postpone the introduction of the Bill.

But we plough on, resolutely, because we believe it is the right thing to do. For David it is a simple equality issue: those who love each other should be allowed to marry whatever their sexuality. Sometimes leaders must lead. Plus, gay marriage has wider support in the country. George writes in support of the Bill in *The Times*. The core goes into meltdown. Graham Brady, chairman of the backbench 1922 Committee comes to see David for one of his regular catch-ups. The letters are pouring in, he tells David. He needs forty-six letters from the MPs to trigger a leadership contest. And because the correspondence is entirely private – between each MP and Brady – no one knows if their letter might be the forty-second. Only Brady himself knows the exactly how near that trigger we really are.

Ed, Olive, and I start to meet very privately to go through the names of the MPs. We need to be prepared. It is frightening how few we can count as true loyalists. All the while the economy

looms like an unhappy cloud over the turbulent political environment.

It is mid-November 2012 and our focus turns to George's autumn
statement. We pray for good figures but they escape us yet again.
Yet by some miracle – and through no lack of talent on George's
behalf – the statement goes off well. George meets the disappointing
figures head on, defiant in his reaffirmation of Plan A. At the same
time, he cleverly softens his targets to make them more manageable,
delaying his objective to have debt falling as a percentage of GDP.
He comes through the whole thing looking stronger – the man
with a plan. And his appointment of Mark Carney as Mervyn
King's replacement at the Bank of England compounds the sense
that George is a determined operator, not a man to be put off his
stride by a few bad headlines. We cannot afford to wimp out now.
However, confronting the grim prospect of a triple dip in early
2013, we begin to feel we are running out of road.

'Don't worry', says Rupert, to the gloomy gathering, 'the economy
will be going gangbusters by the summer.' Ed asks him to write
his prediction down on paper – which he does – and Ed puts it
away in his top drawer for safekeeping. 'I'll hold you to this.'

We are trying to do difficult and often unpopular things for the
long-term good of the country. It is not easy.

IT IS THE FAIR winds of recovery, when they finally come, that
steer us out of the doldrums.

Our minds are drawn to the legacy of a former leader who
famously stuck to her guns when, on 8 April, we receive a call
from Thatcher's office. Lady Thatcher has very sadly died in her
suite at The Ritz.

Britain has lost a 'great Prime Minister, a great leader, a great
Briton,' says David at the door of No. 10. The flag comes down
to half-mast. The Tory party and right-wing press go into deep
mourning. Ed Miliband is gracious though not gushing, feeling
duty-bound to mention the 'deep divisions' of her legacy. Finding
the bright red dress that I had put on in the morning now rather

inappropriate, I sneak upstairs to borrow a black one from Samantha.

Two days before the funeral, David's foreign affairs advisor puts his head around the door. 'Just to let you know, PM, that there are quite a few Americans coming over for the funeral.' Most are from the Bush administrations, with George Shultz and Dick Cheney amongst them. 'The "Neocons" are coming,' George says excitedly.

Later that afternoon we hear that they have hired a plane especially. 'Neocon Air is on its way,' says David. We feel Lady T would have approved and decide to throw a dinner for them. They have made such a valiant effort in coming. And of course we are dying to meet them.

Halfway through dinner, David taps his glass and asks everyone round the table to recall one memory of Lady Thatcher. It is touching to hear these mostly older men, who once ran their country, and who have flown all this way to pay her their respects, recount tales of her strength, and their admiration.

At the funeral, I find myself sitting behind the former Thatcher Cabinet in St Paul's Cathedral. It is strange to see them all here. Their faces evoke memories of my childhood, from my father's time working as a diplomat during the Thatcher years. I think about their era, their battles, and wonder how we will feel about ours in the years ahead.

There is a slight air of frisson as Heseltine takes his seat. Even after all these years, the old battle lines are certainly remembered if not remaining drawn.

Bishop of London Richard Chartres' tribute for Lady T deserves the attention of the cathedral and the nation. It does not buck the issues but leans compassionately into them. 'What, in the end, makes our lives seem valuable after the storm and stress has passed away and there is a great calm? . . . Have I found joy within myself, or am I still looking for it in externals outside myself?' The questions resonate as I look around me. To my right sit David and his Cabinet, in the heart of the intoxicating, adrenaline-filled fast lane of public life. And in front of me, those who once were. Have they found a value in life beyond the storm?

I return to the office to find that the main gossip from the funeral is that George has welled up in tears. 'Where's Sobsborne?' David yells at me through the half open door.

20

RESHUFFLES AND REVENGE

If, as Lyndon Johnson had it, that the first rule of politics is to learn to count, then the second rule must be to figure out why the count stacks up in that way. The answer invariably lies in the MPs. At the heart of politics are people, some of them quite complicated ones, with a range of views, ambitions, flaws, sorrows, foes, and friendships, all of which might be in conflict. Their political journey is wrapped up with our own. And there is no event in politics more likely to bring these to the fore – to make, break, or test loyalties – than a reshuffle.

Inevitably, a resignation (because it nearly always is a 'resignation' in politics, whether imposed or otherwise) leads to a reshuffle of some sort or another. And the reshuffle, whether limited or large, is a strange piece of choreography designed by a small group in relative privacy. However, the outcome is very public and invariably the same: it makes a few people happy (the ones promoted); a small number very angry (the ones fired); and leaves a large number extremely disappointed (the ones who have been passed over yet again). And so the game of musical chairs continues.

Only there is a catch. This is a game where one person, in this story David Cameron, seems to hold all the cards, including one that will ultimately undermine him. Support for a leader is linked inextricably to the parliamentary party's hopes for advancement. In the case of a reshuffle, those returned to the backbenches don't normally feel good about it. The idea that they would thank David for having had a 'good run' and accept the decision in good grace is for the birds. Most politicians never know when it is time to leave, and instead feel furious at being cast aside in their prime (in their eyes it is always their prime). They will join the ranks of the discontented, which grows year after year. It only takes 15 per cent of the parliamentary party to trigger a leadership election. That's forty-six MPs in the 2010 Parliament. It's not hard for us to think who they might be.

Reshuffles themselves are complicated exercises. This is not a straightforward test that allocates the most coveted jobs to the best MPs with the highest grades. Not least because what constitutes the best in politics is a peculiar mixture of talents – charisma, character, intellect, an ability to connect with people – along with a feel for the whole thing. But it is also about what the person brings to the table, what they represent or stand for. Whether they are from the right or the left of the party; represent a northern or southern seat; are socially liberal or from the religious right. Then there are those who are great thinkers but should be kept away from the TV screen, or those who are great communicators but should be kept away from the policy.

Sure, promote the loyal – but leave the disloyal ones on the backbenches at your peril. But promote too many of the disloyal and the loyal ones will begin to falter. A strong team must not just harness the diverse talent the parliamentary party has to offer, but also create a balance, including of gender and ethnicity. You have a narrow pool to choose from as ministers should be sitting members of Parliament (Lords or Commons). This is not like the American system, where you can ring up your favourite academic and ask them to start practising what they preach.

David believes strongly that people should have the chance to bed into their roles so that they might make a real difference. He doesn't want an annual merry-go-round. But on the other hand, you need to keep the water flowing, otherwise the pond will become stagnant. The only way to do this is by creating vacancies – which in practice means moving people up, along, or out.

George is good at channelling a fast-moving stream right through his office, which makes the Treasury a go-to place. Once they've done their time with him, ministers are repositioned across the departments, earning George a reputation as a large octopus whose tentacles cover Whitehall. But the fast stream can drown you if you're not careful. Chloe Smith is sent out to do media on fuel duty, and is devoured by Paxman on *Newsnight*, showing that the Treasury brief is not for everyone.

David likes to try to put people into places where their skills, background, or knowledge naturally fit, but sometimes the deck is moving too fast and you have to ask people to do things they are less obviously suited to. In 2012 we decide to move Patrick McLoughlin from being Chief Whip – a job he had done with huge personal charm and loyalty for nearly seven years. We want to promote him, but to what? We land on Transport, which is currently occupied by Justine Greening. She has been there since Liam Fox's resignation. Moving Justine seems a sensible plan as her Putney seat puts her in an awkward position in relation to the major transport issue of the day: a potential Heathrow expansion. We don't have a huge choice if we don't wish to demote her (which we don't). We decide on the Department for International Development (DFID). Perhaps not the job she most wanted.

We plan the reshuffles meticulously in a tiny group. These are secret meetings, which we even disguise in David's diary. Any indication of a reshuffle will spread like wildfire and is certain to scare the horses. We do the work and then wait for the right moment to strike. The element of surprise is crucial.

George of course wants us to focus on the 'big story' – the most high-profile sacking and the most interesting promotion. It is good to have a strong, wider narrative running alongside it – of more women, of more 'blue collar' Tories.

Everyone comes to these meetings with someone they want to promote and someone they are trying to protect. It is like *Game of Thrones* (still one of our obsessions). George tries to decapitate one of David's friends (not literally; it's not actually Westeros).

David retaliates. George wants to promote his protégé Matt Hancock every time – even though the Chief Whip invariably pushes back.

It is foolhardy to leave the table at such times – a lesson I learn the hard way one year when I get up to take a quick call, returning to find the father of one of my son's friends at school had been fired. 'You can't do that,' I say, 'I'll never be able to appear at the school gate again.' We can't organise the reshuffle around Kate's son, they say. Of course, they make a good point. More seriously, I ask, 'Why does he have to go?' He's a good guy and popular with his colleagues. The answer is simply that the numbers don't add up. There is a strict limit on the number of ministerial posts. You can arrange the chairs a thousand times, but if you are over your number, someone will have to go – and it can be just bad luck.

Later, when the deed is done, I wonder what is the right thing to do. To say nothing, when I know the man and his family, seems uncourageous. But I can't blame it on the others. I send my sympathies to the mother in a carefully worded text that she then tweets to all and sundry. Then I have to explain the situation to my young son.

Once the people have been assigned their new places, the next step is to choreograph the dance itself. This is absolutely vital if you are going to achieve a smooth reshuffle – which speaks to functional and focused government. Unfortunately, this means you must clear the decks, which means doing the firing the night before, well out of the way of the public eye. Because the minute news of the reshuffle is out, the whole media circus will be camped on the doorstep. It is humiliating and utterly disrespectful to ask ministers to walk up Downing Street only to find they are being stood down – with the mug shots to prove it. So, we see those who are being asked to leave Cabinet over in the Prime Minister's parliamentary office beforehand. David always found this to be a terrible task.

* * *

IN THE MIDST OF the doldrums of 2012, we decide to go ahead on our postponed reshuffle. The new Cabinet will be announced on 4 September.

It is late evening the night before. David pours himself a large glass of wine ahead of seeing Cheryl Gillan and Caroline Spelman. They are both extremely nice women who have always tried to do the right thing in politics, and whom I like very much. But the truth is that we need to bring in new talent. David promoted Cheryl from the backbenches in opposition. He had hoped she would be content to have had a good run and pass the baton to someone else. Caroline has had a difficult year, which has seen her back down on her plans to sell off parts of England's forests in the face of public outcry. Both never forgive David for allegedly sipping a glass of wine during their conversation.

The next task is to organise the reshuffle in strict order. You cannot offer someone else's job until they have been told they are vacating it. You need to line your people up. Create a vacancy. Fill the gap, and so on. Keep the show on the road, the cameras clicking, the pictures coming. And there is always the awkward possibility someone might say no. And if they do that is when the whole thing can grind to a halt. Had Justine said no we would have had to think about a replacement in a matter of minutes – and someone who wouldn't blow the rest of the reshuffle off course. Which is why at such times a replacement is often found from amongst the select committee chairs or other grandees who have returned to the backbenches.

We know better than to fall into that trap with Iain Duncan Smith, who we consider moving to Justice. But when David tries the idea out on him in advance, IDS refuses to budge from Welfare. When we offer to bring Liam Fox back into government with a senior role at the Foreign Office and a place on the National Security Council, he refuses because it is not in the Cabinet. We have to do some fast footwork to plug the gap.

From across the Cabinet table, David offers each MP their new role. We catch them as they come out, slightly dizzy, to go through a few details. Even though they might have waited for this moment their whole lives, it can feel overwhelming. Many are about to get into an official car for the first time. Then they will suddenly be in their new department, with only minutes to think about what they are going to say.

Some remain themselves. Others seem to grow a layer of pomposity in the short time it takes them to walk back down the corridor – normally in inverse proportion to the importance of their job. A few feel they need to bring something of themselves 'extra' to the work. Greg Barker brings his absurdly small dog whose cushion needs to be regularly warmed in the microwave. Gavin Williamson brings his pet tarantula to the office when he eventually becomes Chief Whip. Alan Duncan buys a Privy Council uniform, which he wears to Lady Thatcher's funeral.

Michael Gove, with all the best intentions, decides he will avoid as many trappings of government as possible and insists on driving himself to work. This is a very noble gesture, with a slight hitch – Michael is a terrible driver. He has come late to it in adulthood, only passing his driving test after the birth of his first child (and following quite a few attempts). He arrives and is shown the car park, which is accessed via a car lift. Only, Michael takes the angle slightly wrong, and the lift doors close on his car when he is halfway in, then – automatically – the doors go forward and back, forward and back, until the car is crushed with Michael in it.

Mrs Gove is not pleased.

OVER THE YEARS WE are in government, no matter how many reshuffles we do, it always seems to be the role of Chief Whip that is fated to haunt us.

The job of Chief Whip is a tricky one. On the face of it, it is simply a numbers game. The government of the day will have a majority (of sorts). And it is your job to make sure that your army of MPs turn up and vote – the way you want. But this is the complication. Your army is made up of individual people. Worse, they are politicians, with views and aspirations of their own. They also represent (and answer to) another group of people – their constituents. So, they have divided loyalties. However, as the Chief Whip should be quick to point out, you are in fact elected on a party ticket, so your loyalty is to your party. If an MP has lost sight of being promoted, or feels disenfranchised, then the whips' all-important power of patronage lessens over time. The troops can be difficult to handle. There are a group of about twenty MPs during the Coalition years who vote against us in most divisions. Sometimes it gets nasty and personal, as the whips 'remind' colleagues of things they wish had been forgotten in an attempt to bring them into line.

George has argued strongly for a tougher whips operation, which he hopes will help get the party – still feeling edgy and at times even cantankerous – into shape, training the new intake like cadets to obey orders. In George's view, Andrew Mitchell is the man. I have some reservations. I see the sympathetic figure of Andrew Mitchell at DFID, a far cry from the Andrew Mitchell who ruthlessly did the numbers for the David Davis campaign – and wonder which man will turn up to work as Chief Whip? But it is agreed. David goes with George and we give the news to Mitchell, who is not pleased.

For although we think the job of Chief Whip a sought-after position – as part of the hallowed inner team – it turns out this is not everyone else's view. Neither Andrew Mitchell nor Michael Gove ever wanted the job. They like being their own person, running a department, and the status of being a Secretary of State. Andrew reluctantly accepts, but remains unhappy and tense about it. He only wants Ed, as chief of staff, present when he meets with the Prime Minister, until David and Ed have to spell it out: Kate is included. He speaks about his plans for the whips' office – creating 'an officers' mess' – which does not bode well. I am not alone in wondering if we are doing the right thing.

We meet the day before the reshuffle. We have ordered pizzas for George's dining room. Andrew is there, and Ed, George, and me. The flight from Cornwall is late and David doesn't arrive till nine. We put the finishing touches on the reshuffle and press the button. Within two weeks the whole thing will have unravelled.

There is an issue around whether Andrew will have an official car or not. For now he is using his bicycle.

A couple of weeks later, as I am clearing my desk to leave the office, Chris Martin asks for a private word. There's been an unfortunate incident involving Andrew Mitchell and one of the policemen at the front gate. The policeman has refused to open the gate to allow Andrew to wheel his bicycle through – ushering him towards the side gate, which is mostly used by pedestrians. Andrew has lost his temper – and according to the policeman, called him a pleb. It is an ugly, cringe-worthy word to use, full stop – but especially at a policeman. Andrew admits to losing his temper but vehemently denies using the 'P' word, and the policemen equally vehement in saying that he has. It is a very unpleasant, awkward situation, but for now it is entirely a matter for 'the House'. Chris thinks it can all be patched over with the right apologies. We talk to Andrew; Chris talks to the policeman. We all agree we need to get Andrew a car.

But it does not stay a 'House' matter for long. The next thing we know the story is the front-page splash in *The Sun*. And now we have the police and a Cabinet minister in a very public row – with an ugly 'us against them' word at its core. We want to be supportive of Andrew. But this places us in the politically unenviable position of seeming to be looking down our noses at the police, at a time when we are fighting a narrative of a government run by 'out of touch' 'posh boys'. The whole thing is toxic.

I sit for hours in the basement of No. 10 with Olive Dowden and Jeremy Heywood, searching in vain for answers from the silent CCTV footage. Things are complicated still further by a constituent of the very solid and well-liked Deputy Chief Whip, John Randall, coming forward to say he witnessed the whole thing whilst on a visit to London. We ask Jeremy Heywood to formally investigate, but his findings are inconclusive. The idea that there is a conspiracy around this part of the story seems far-fetched – yet in the end turns out to be exactly that.

As we head up to the party conference, Andrew is still in place but told to stay away because he is too much of a distraction. We are literally the last people left supporting him: the parliamentary party makes clear his position is untenable at a highly charged meeting of the 1922. Andrew has no choice but to stand down. Our first major reshuffle has unravelled; our attempts to bring the MPs into line never got off the ground. Our new Chief Whip, Sir George Young – who we bring back from his short, two-week retirement – is charming but not a disciplinarian. We are back to square one.

And the Mitchell saga continues with huge personal pain to him and his family. He attempts to clear his name with mixed results. First – a triumph. Shocking proof that there was a conspiracy around the police at the gate. Then – a rebuke. Andrew sues *The Sun* for libel at the same time the policeman in the actual dispute, furious that MP Mitchell has continued to doubt this word, sues him – and the judge comes down on the policeman's side, ruling that 'at least on the balance of probabilities . . . Mr Mitchell did speak the words alleged, or at least something so close to them as to amount to the same thing, including the politically toxic word pleb'.

So, the slate is never wiped completely clean.

But Mitchell is only part one of our Chief Whip saga.

IN 2014, WITH LESS than a year to go until the next election, we have been contemplating a reshuffle. Now William Hague's decision to leave politics makes it completely unavoidable. Although we have all tried to rationalise keeping him in place we finally accept it is impossible. William, of course, is the first to reach this conclusion. By announcing his resignation, so that his Richmond (Yorkshire) seat can be contested, William will make himself a lame duck Foreign Secretary at the start of the EU negotiations. And worse, rumours that his job is being kept warm for George after the election creates a lame duck Chancellor as well. Our whole mantra – the Long-Term Economic Plan – is based on the premise that the two men who have done so much to fix the economy should be allowed to finish the job – namely, David and George. George, who was partially interested in the move, sees the weakness in all of this and backs off the idea. Anyway, he wants to deliver the post-election Budget if we win the following year. William moves to be a very grand Leader of the House and Philip Hammond becomes Foreign Secretary. But the 'big story' is the new Chief Whip.

In 2010, Michael Gove arrived at the Department for Education – the radical reformer, a Cameron warrior in chief. Education is a big passion for both men: David asked for the education brief under Michael Howard in opposition, and worked hand in hand with Michael Gove on developing the current policy. Michael was ready to fight for what they both believe in – to create a wave of new good schools, improve standards, and a give a better chance to thousands of children. This meant challenging the system and going into battle against the entrenched, vested interests – 'the blob', as Michael liked to call it.

And although Michael struggled to begin with, he was soon in his stride – a rising star of the new government, especially popular on the right of the party and with the commentariat, who applauded his courage, radicalism, and verbosity. During his early struggle, he begged David to allow him to hire his close advisor, Dominic Cummings. But Dominic had had run-ins with Andy Coulson when he worked for IDS in opposition, and we strongly suspected him of being the source of our strategy meeting leaks in 2010. David was cautious; Dominic might have been loyal to Michael, but he was not exactly a team player. But everything was going so well for David, and he was (and is) so fond of Michael, he felt he could afford to give in. Dominic was duly hired.

Trouble was brewing from early 2012, with a flow of briefings allegedly from Michael's operation. People seemed to be picked out for special treatment. Nick Clegg. Nick Clegg's wife's charity.

Theresa May's position on combatting extremism. Pretty soon we were under a barrage of furious complaints from senior Cabinet colleagues on both sides of the Coalition. Surely, they asked, David can put a stop to the briefings? Later, when Dominic turned his fire on David, calling him a 'sphinx without a riddle', and then in 2014 Michael declared the number of Old Etonians in No. 10 'preposterous', our colleagues began to see that we might not be masterminding the briefing operation after all. But we were trying to keep the team together coming into an election year, and none of this was helpful.

And there were other issues. Michael's valiant fight with 'the blob' seemed to have gone into overdrive. Where he skilfully built a consensus of support for the Education Act, which gives schools greater freedom from local education authorities and allows all schools to become academies, there was growing unease around his next wave of reforms, to exams and the national curriculum. Soon there was a wall of noise, and not just from the usual suspects.

David remained supportive of Michael and what he was trying to do – but he also needed him to calm things down. We were coming into a pre-election period, which required 'steady as she goes' as we brought the ship into harbour. Yet David's pleas fell on deaf ears. In fact, the noise got louder. Michael was seen to fall out with the chief inspector of schools, Michael Wilshaw, then even started a row about Blackadder's version of the First World War.

David knows it falls to him to sort things out. Michael is his friend; their families are friends.

We have been mulling over the 2014 reshuffle for a few weeks. In the car, on the way back from a visit, David tells me the good news: Michael has offered to be Chief Whip if we think we need a change at Education. Really? I say. Yes, absolutely, David is positive, and explains how Michael told him that Chief Whip was one of the jobs he would really like to do because he is such a keen observer of people. This is certainly true. Michael is infamous amongst his friends for his character sketches – often around a rather boisterous kitchen table.

The idea is growing on David. This seems a perfect solution. He thinks Michael will thrive as part of the core No. 10 operation and that we will benefit from having him. He envisions a powerful Chief Whip 'plus' role for Michael – with access to papers, people, and committees. 'Hand of the King' is how he puts it to Michael over dinner, knowing that Michael is as obsessed with *Game of Thrones* as he is. Michael says he will do whatever David asks. But then Michael is always very polite – and has not yet spoken to his wife.

It is clear over the next few days that Michael is not at all happy about the job – and perhaps more importantly, neither is his wife. They operate very much as a team. Sarah Vine is a clever, funny, powerful, and forceful woman who is used to proactively managing her brilliant but not very down-to-earth husband. Michael is in touch with George; Sarah with me. Sarah has also been close to Samantha for some time, volunteering to play a strong, supportive role; over the years I have watched her ferrying the Cameron children around, or attending to Samantha, and wondered if she might weary of it.

We are days from the reshuffle itself, so there is still time to talk it over. George and I come to the same conclusion: this is not going to be worth the pain. I feel it is too much like Groundhog Day. When someone doesn't want a job that much – back off. It is only going to head in one direction. Andrew Mitchell was a case in point.

But David is in a different place. He feels completely furious at being let down by the Goves, whom he has promoted and supported through thick and thin. He has made Michael a very good offer, one for which Michael himself volunteered. Above all, he thinks Michael should take one for the team. Just this once. David texts me: 'I've told Michael "you're either a team player or a wanker".' Michael can be promoted again once we are through this difficult patch. David needs his closest friends around him. That means George and it means Michael.

Both David and Michael feel their personal loyalty being stretched to breaking point.

The decision is made. But coming into the reshuffle itself, Michael and Sarah are getting more, not less, wound up. They see the move as a humiliating demotion; they are particularly cross about the pay cut. David suggests that I find out if we can make one of the Admiralty House flats available for them. This way they can rent their house in west London and have more time as a family when Michael is busy working late nights in the Commons. Sarah comes by to have a look round but decides against the move.

On the day of the reshuffle we put a huge effort into presenting Michael's new job as a positive move to beef up the No. 10 operation, but the press is mostly negative. David is criticised for giving up on Michael's reform agenda and punishing Michael for no good reason. Personal resentment remains – and festers. And although the Goves and the Camerons seem to patch things up enough for the Goves to spend New Year at Chequers, the cracks in the friendship are there to stay – and would re-emerge as gaping chasms the following year.

Older, wiser people have warned that political friendships don't last. I thought, *You just don't understand these ones. They are different.* And some were. But I see now the truth in their words. Perhaps there are just too many conflicting priorities. Of loyalty, of belief. Of ambition, of friendship. Politics forces you to choose.

We all laugh to hear that one weekend at Chequers, one of the Gove children, followed by a confused Cameron child, runs into breakfast saying, isn't it true this house will be ours when Dad's prime minister?

21

SCOTLAND

Early on in opposition, I follow David, who is walking down Princes Street in Edinburgh, live on TV. He is surprisingly well-received, given we only have one Tory MP in the whole of Scotland. An unexpected snowfall keeps us in the city overnight. 'Right everyone,' says Liz Sugg. 'I need to know your size so the team can buy you some underwear.' 'I'm an extra small,' I say chirpily. David and George look at their feet, uncomfortable, murmuring theirs. The ops team head back to Princes Street, hunting for underpants.

Over a nightcap we muse over why we still have so little support in Scotland. It wasn't always like this. Thatcher's government had Scottish Tory MPs. But after 1997 they were wiped out. Now Labour, who have been running Scotland and weaning their Cabinet ministers there for years, are being supplanted by the Scottish Nationalists. In May 2011 the SNP gain control of the Scottish Parliament. Their one aim: to deliver an independent Scotland. A Scottish referendum is now on the cards and Alex Salmond is running rings around us.

We feel we cannot refuse a referendum outright; the Scots will simply hold one on their own. Even if this is deemed 'illegal', it is difficult to ignore. It may look like we are turning our back on democracy or worse, fuel their sense of grievance. The nationalists are already questioning our political legitimacy (although, thanks to our Lib Dem allies in the Coalition, the government is at least slightly represented). So, the question is, Do we play for time or do we lean in, and try to take back at least some control over the issue?

George wants to take Salmond on and announce a referendum at a time of our choosing with a question of our own making – namely, a simple decision to stay together or leave. David mulls it over and agrees with George.

The reasons will echo in future discussions around a future referendum. If a Scottish referendum is coming whether we like it or not, we need to do all we can to shape it, so we have the best chance of winning. And David doesn't want to dodge the difficult issues on his watch. He wants Britain to try to resolve them, and hopefully put them to bed for a generation. Ultimately, he thinks, we will come through the process a stronger, more unified nation.

In January 2012 David appears, as usual, on the first Marr programme of the year and surprises everyone by announcing the Scottish referendum: 'We owe the Scottish people something that is fair, legal, and decisive.' We have taken the initiative from Salmond. Everyone is pleased, especially George. Until, that is, we realise that we have to fight the referendum – and win it.

Salmond immediately tries to wrestle back control over as many of the details of the referendum as he can. The date is pushed back to autumn 2014, and Salmond gets his way on including 16- and 17-year-olds in the vote. George's hope of a quick vote is not to be realised, but David is understanding. If the SNP don't consider this a fair referendum, then they will never live with the result. And we know what matters most is the framing of the question – with a clear-cut, yes or no answer. This is what we dig our heels in for.

The deal is signed in Edinburgh. The 'Yes Scotland' and 'Better Together' campaigns are born.

FAST FORWARD TO 2014. We are spending a lot more time in Scotland, and on Scottish issues. Although our excellent special advisor for Scotland, Andrew Dunlop, as well as others are working discreetly under the radar, the message coming loud and clear from Scotland is that the Tories are toxic. Stay away from the campaign and leave it to 'us' we are told – 'us' basically consisting of Scottish Labour, led by Alistair Darling, and a handful of Lib Dems. The unusually talented Ruth Davidson is one of the few Tories allowed anywhere near the campaign trail.

Yet there is also a lot of criticism of the Better Together campaign. The tensions of running a multiparty campaign with conflicting egos, ideas, and allegiances against a united and single-minded adversary quickly emerge. (And will re-emerge as a problem in the next referendum, when parties and their members rally around Leave or Remain.) But our lead in the polls remains steady at around 10 per cent. We are quietly confident of a good result.

Over the summer the politics shifts dramatically. The momentum gathers around Yes, and by September a poll shows Better Together's lead has halved. David is beginning to look a bit green – not least because he is about to head off for his annual weekend with the Queen at Balmoral. Normally a happy experience, this time the visit only adds to the pressure, reminding him of the enormous stakes at hand. Over the weekend a poll published in *The Sunday Times* puts Yes in the lead – 51 to 49 per cent. The future of the Union looks seriously at risk, as does our future in Downing Street. I feel a bit sick flipping through my copy of the paper, thinking of David awkwardly flipping through his at Balmoral.

At the political Cabinet meeting the following Tuesday, the table erupts in panic. Question after question is fired at Andrew Dunlop, whom most of them never really clocked before, about an issue they have barely given two seconds' thought to. To his enormous credit, Andrew remains as cool as a cucumber in the full-beam headlights of these panicking MPs, politely answering their questions one by one and advising everyone to hold their nerve. He predicts a result of around 10 per cent for No.

Behind closed doors we are anxious.

Hours of deliberations later, we decide to launch three major offensives – David (good cop) takes to the Scottish Borders to make a heartfelt speech about the value of the Union. George (bad cop) tells them they can't keep the pound and might not get to join the euro. And coming into the final week, the 'vow' is rolled out, promising a new settlement for Scotland if the No camp wins. We are trying to win hearts, appeal to heads, and address their yearning for more freedom all at once.

We also need reinforcements.

The question is, Where's Gordon? Does he not exemplify the Union as a Scottish British former prime minister? After a series of email exchanges – he promises to do his bit but will have nothing to do with the Better Together campaign. By the time he gives his barnstorming address, the day before polling, we simply don't care what he does and how he does it; we are just truly grateful. 'Go Gordon!' is the mantra of the day. Not something we have heard in the Cameron No. 10 before.

The final run into the referendum feels precarious and unpredictable. The polls are all over the place. Everyone is tense. The SNP have been aggressive campaigners, so no one knows if there might be a hidden group of 'shy' Unionists. Even less is known about the new group of 16- and 17-year-olds who are allowed to vote for the first time – not least, how many of them will actually turn up to the ballot box. We throw love at the Scots as the Scottish Nationalists hurl abuse back over the border, giving a head of steam to the English nationalists who are muttering under their breaths about English votes for English laws.

We face the very real and ugly possibility of being responsible for the break up of our Union – David, the Lord North of the twenty-first century. David reassures everyone that he will stay if the result goes the wrong way, but we know this could change. We are less than a year from a general election we might not even get the chance to fight.

We do what we always do when it feels like we are approaching disaster: a small group of us meet to discuss what a pickle we are in and what to do if it goes wrong. Behind closed doors we know the game is up if we lose. We draft the two speeches – the 'if we win' and the 'if we lose'. It is best to be prepared.

Chris Martin and I discuss what precautions we should put in place for 'the House' for the night of the referendum. The core team will need to be here, and a fully staffed press office. Then there is what happens if the result goes the wrong way and we have a sliding pound and wobbly banks. We will need a team from the Treasury and Cabinet Office too. The list of people who need to be on hand grows longer.

An email is sent round to what looks to me like a small army setting out the plans for the night. It appears 'the House' is arranging a giant sleepover. There are blow-up beds being erected (so it says) in every corner – from the Thatcher study to the state dining room. If this email were to be leaked, it will not be a good look, I tell Chris unhappily. Think, 'No. 10 prepares for poll disaster with giant pyjama party'. Chris quickly follows up the email with a 'please delete' and tells 'the House' to allocate the beds offline. I am quietly smug as David says I can stay in their spare room in his flat. It will be a real bed for me.

It is Thursday, 18 September. We meet up for a late supper in the No. 11 dining room, a beautiful though somewhat austere wood-panelled room designed by Sir John Soane. Word on the street is that there has been a high turnout – as high as 84.59 per cent – which makes us nervous. A high turnout for change or the status quo? Who knows. Everyone tucks into Indian takeaway; it promises to be a long night.

A YouGov poll after the ten o'clock news puts No on 54 per cent and Yes on 46 per cent. This lifts the mood. After hours glued to the television screen, and with no results expected until 3 or 4 a.m., we decide to try to get a few hours' sleep. I follow David to the lift. 'Oh, about the spare room . . . ' he says. Samantha thinks he'll be pacing round the room all night, so he may end up in it himself. 'Sorry.'

I say how I completely understand, etc., etc., though quietly I am rather crestfallen. Worse, I am bedless. I bump into Chris Martin and tell him, laughing, how my carefully prepared plan has blown up in my face. Chris sets off to see what might still be on offer. It turns out every bed and sofa has been taken – that is, except those in the No. 11 study. For some reason, George's rooms have been considered out of bounds. Within five minutes the rather wide and soft purple sofa in the study is made up with a sheet and blanket by the front of house team, a pillow placed beguilingly at one end. At 1.30 a.m., this looks extremely attractive to me and I am beyond grateful.

But my night on George's purple sofa is not a comfortable one. I cannot breathe for the smell of curry that has pervaded every part of the room. I try but fail to open the window. I opt for the door to the dining room itself, which leads out to the terrace. Only a storm has erupted of Shakespearean pathetic fallacy proportions and the door starts blowing open and shut – open and shut – and rain pours through. I feel at one with this hurricane.

I have set my alarm for 3 a.m. and have not yet slept a wink. A quick check of the news reveals a series of regional results heading in the right direction. Feeling that disaster might have been averted I decide to give myself another half-hour's sleep and rest my alarm – not realising that 3.30 is the magical hour at which the Treasury team have been told to arrive. These are not George's close team who I know well, but a group of rather serious and tired civil servants who find the sight of me fast asleep on the sofa hard to compute. I decide to ignore them – treating the whole thing as a common occurrence. (Didn't you know? I sleep here every night!) I set off to have a shower, wash bag in hand. Just before 4 a.m. I am dressed and all evidence that the study has been used as a bedroom has been removed. I go to find David. He is glued to one of the large televisions in the packed press room.

It is another moment that will seal our fate. Win, and life goes back to normal. Lose, and it's all over: job, reputation, place in history marked forever by the break-up of our country. We await our fate.

In the end, it is a win for No and Better Together. And a good decisive win of over 10 per cent – enough to put the question away for a generation (or so we hope). As Dumfries and Galloway, Perth and Kinross, and Edinburgh come in decidedly for No, we celebrate with more tea and croissants. Nancy and Elwen run down from the flat in their onesies. They have set an early alarm, worried because they sense their Dad is. David gathers them in his arms, a relieved man.

With our early morning victory in hand we gather in the study to prepare a statement for the morning broadcasts. We sense there has a been a build-up of resentment on the English side that we have been bending over backwards to appease the Scots, and we need to rebalance and lean a little way back. So, we give a nod towards those English sentiments by announcing a review into English votes for English laws (EVEL). David's statement is designed to bring the country together. But in retrospect we wonder at the wisdom of this. We should, perhaps, have said less – and closed the chapter on a good result.

Statement delivered, it already feels like a long day's work. At 7.30 a.m., David goes off to have breakfast with Samantha. Ed, Rupert, Craig, and I decide to follow suit, crossing the road to have porridge in St James's Park – a nod to our Scottish cousins.

Watching the birds flock to the lake I feel an enormous sense of relief. But also, a sense that we have saved a life we had not meant to risk in the first place.

22

PROTECT AND DEFEND

The next election looms. Just like last time, it comes back to the old question: is it time for change? But now we're arguing: you can't afford change. We have a plan we're halfway through implementing. Don't give up on us.

Approaching a general election as the incumbent feels totally different. Whereas in 2010 we were on the offensive, taking risks, we are now risk-averse – all protect and defend. Emotionally, we are at a disadvantage; like most incumbents, we have much more to lose than the challengers.

This time, though, we know exactly when the next election will be, because we have already set the date: May 2015. The Coalition agreement has committed us to fixed-term parliaments of five years. We veered between four and five during the Coalition negotiations, with the enormity of the task ahead weighing in favour of buying more time. Time to give out the unpalatable medicine *and* see the patient recover.

We had been secretly discussing hiring Aussie election guru Lynton Crosby for a while, knowing him since he worked on Michael Howard's general election campaign and Boris's London Mayoral campaigns, but he is not an easy man to land. David quickly tires of the long courtship, complaining that he spent less time wooing his wife. However, in 2012 Lynton finally agrees to come on board, and we head off to Christmas hoping for a brighter new year.

Early in 2013 we gather for dinner at Chequers with Lynton

for the first time. It is a small group – just David, George, Ed, Lynton, and me. Lynton has asked to keep it as private as possible so he can tell David what he really thinks. I look down at my plate of offal and I realise I have lost my battle with the menu yet again. It seems to me that the Chequers chef like to take people out of their comfort zone. Lynton eyes his food suspiciously.

At this rate, you can win but you might well not, says Lynton, pulling no punches. He tells us that we are doing far too much, have no central message, and have to stop fighting our base. 'You've gotta get the barnacles off the boat,' he adds. By this, he means getting rid of the smaller things that are undermining our overall message. Together they are sinking the boat. He is particularly cross about gay marriage. He doesn't care if we are wrong or right. You can't win a war if you are battling with your own troops, full stop.

'Pass the beer nuts,' he says, often. None of us knows what this means. After a while, worried that his advice is being lost in trans-lation, I finally ask, 'What does "Pass the beer nuts" mean?'

'It means, "So what?"' he explains.

'Aussie for "whatevs",' says David, who refers to Lynton from then on as PTBN.

Lynton is a strange paradox: an alpha control freak leader of men with very thin skin who is devoted to his family and knows every word to every song of *The Sound of Music*. He has his own name on Google Alerts and goes into a meltdown every time anyone says anything nasty about him, firing angry emails into the night with his signature opening line – 'FFS'.

Over time, David and Lynton begin to get used to each other, and the relationship works. But I always have the impression that Lynton prefers working with more needy 'high-maintenance' candi-dates – the desperate incumbent PM who rings him first thing in the morning and last thing at night. This is just not how David is wired. If he sought advice during the weekend (which he doesn't very often, preferring to reflect whilst he tends his vegetable patch), George would get the first call.

With Lynton on board, our operation is far more organized. But he is still worried our message is not focused enough. What you need is an economic plan, says Lynton. We have one, says George. It's called Plan A. This is not what Lynton means. 'That's Westminster talk,' he says.

IN AUTUMN 2014 LYNTON urges us to find a formulation which speaks to the country, which is how the Long-Term Economic Plan is born. The LTEP, as it is fondly known in No. 10, contains all the central planks of our policy: cut the deficit, cut taxes, create more jobs, cap welfare, reduce immigration, deliver the best schools and skills for young people. People may not remember the details of the plan but they know we have one, and that the two men who have delivered it so far – David and George – will finish the job if they are given the chance.

As important as the plan is the motivation behind it. 'People *know* if you mean it,' says Lynton. And it is here where Lynton directs his firepower at George, urging him to spend less time trying to destroy Labour and more time on trying to help people. George wants to do both, of course. And anyway, you can't help people if you lose. Winning means being intellectually ahead of your opponents – boxing them in where you can.

This matters because the 2015 election is not just about David in the way that the 2010 election was. This time it is very much a double act. David and George are the two men who have turned Britain around. By the time the economy is picking up at the end of 2014, George has won the respect of the nation for standing by his plan for the economy – even though it has been tough. This has given him the confidence to relax and soften in the public's eyes.

But over the months that follow there is a wall of criticism that our messaging is too stark, too male. Lynton's response: 'Pig's bum'. His ears are tuned to the focus groups around the country, while ours pick up the noise from the Westminster village. Ignore them, he says. People will go into the ballot box focused on their own prospects, putting their trust in these two men to continue their work. And Lynton sticks by this, despite the criticism. So, although we are already all bored to death of talking about the Long-Term Economic Plan, the message resonates with the public, bringing discomfort to the opposition. The Tories align coming into the election year.

Over the summer, my twin sister Mel is diagnosed with cancer and begins her difficult journey to recovery. Once every three weeks she comes to stay after a gruelling dose of chemotherapy. 'Yum,' say my children, 'it's a chemo weekend,' as our home is deluged with delicious food from supportive friends dropping by – a slither of a silver lining. Heading into the election period my weekends feel stretched between my BlackBerry, the children, and caring for my sick sister. Especially when our Sunday night meetings begin again in January. Making my way over to No. 10 for the meeting, I wonder anxiously, and not for the first time, whether enough of my energy is going into supporting those closest to me.

Our strategy is in place and there is no question of reopening it. We gather in the No. 11 flat for our weekly election planning sessions, with a slightly different group this time. The core is Lynton, David, George, Ed, and me. Ameet Gill is on the Grid. Liz Sugg remains on ops. Stephen Gilbert is covering the party's operation on the ground. Plus, we have Rupert Harrison, George's chief of staff. The Sunday night meetings are set for 7 p.m. if David has spent the weekend at Chequers and 8 p.m. if he has been in Dean. This allows him to leave home at the same time he always has, so the family is not disrupted. We dispute the pros and cons of each time at my home. Seven means I will be back by 9 or 9.30, in time to catch the end of a favourite Sunday night TV show and have a late supper. But it means leaving at 6 p.m., shortening the afternoon. Eight means the evening is a write-off but our afternoon is left intact.

When we have our first Sunday meeting at 8 p.m., I feel I should offer the team a drink, and as it's been a 'chemo weekend' I certainly need one. Michael from front of house duly appears at David's flat with a tray of drinks. He is firmly sent away. 'This is not a drinks party, it's a meeting,' he is told. I bump into Michael wandering down the corridor, disgraced tray in hand. This is solved the following week by the relocation of the drinks tray. We sit in the den, in our jeans, discussing the weekend media over a beer or a glass of wine waiting for the summons to the flat. 'PM's ready for you,' says the duty clerk. We put down our drinks and up we go.

A small group of us start to meet on Thursday afternoons in the Thatcher study to kick off the manifesto process. I can see why she chose this room to work from, with its shelves stuffed with beautiful vintage books and views over St James's Park. Her portrait hangs over the fireplace. The Blairs have left their own mark on the room – a series of bees carved into the bookshelves. I look round, trying to locate them all. Oliver Letwin begins. This time the process is going to be different. We are keeping things focused and tight. It all looks promising until the papers start complaining that only Old Etonians are writing this manifesto.

Oliver and Jo Johnson guide us through paper after paper on every conceivable issue under the sun. One afternoon I have lost the will to live when I hear Oliver cancelling his evening engagements. My heart sinks. It is 7 p.m. and we have been at it for hours already. 'Isn't it better to do this in shorter bursts?' I suggest, as a sort of darkness descends.

In amongst the manifesto's big-ticket items are lots of smaller ones. I personally think that Jo's efforts to think out of the box are very commendable – like his programme of lidos for seaside towns. Or his plans to build a new forest in the North of England, or introduce a ban on circus animals. George is less convinced. Why would you need a swimming pool by the sea? Or a new forest in a land of trees? And his kids like the hungry-looking lions. Surely we shouldn't even be wasting time on this small stuff anyway. What is the big message we are trying to convey? The misfit between Jo and George intensifies when Jo ventures, unwisely, into matters fiscal. A volcanic eruption from George sends most of the private office under their desks and Jo into an orbit from which it is possible he has never entirely returned.

But of course, our biggest offer in the manifesto is not fiscal. It is to reaffirm a promise David made in a speech, back in January 2013, to hold an 'in/out' referendum, after Britain's terms of membership in the European Union have been renegotiated.

LIKE LAST TIME, THE question of TV debates is in the air. Every time Craig brings them up David changes the subject. David – ostrich – sand. Everyone agrees that debates are a risk for the incumbent and frontrunner – but not doing them may be worse. Appearing to be 'too chicken' to face his rivals would be a gift to our opponents. Lynton is largely against, thinking, on balance, they are a gamble not worth taking. David is reluctant but fatalistic. He knows they're coming, not least because Craig insists.

So, the question turns to how and when to have them. On this David is clear: the debates should not dominate the short campaign; they cannot go ahead on the same basis as last time. Politics has changed too much. The Lib Dems are polling less than UKIP. The SNP are resurgent. It is now nonsense to focus on just the three party leaders. What about Farage and Sturgeon? He sends Craig in to negotiate on our behalf. Keep it complicated, is David's message. Secretly he is hoping they will run out of time. Craig and I think he is kidding himself. There will be debates. No doubt about it.

The deliberations drag on. Suddenly it is early March and nothing has been agreed. It is just weeks before the election is to be called when Craig brings us a final offer. There are three proposed debates or, more precisely, 'television events'. Firstly, a Paxman interview, followed by questions from a live studio audience, for potential prime ministers only (David Cameron and Ed Miliband). Secondly, a debate for party leaders – all seven of them. And finally, a *Question Time* special with Dimbleby, to which Nick Clegg, Ed Miliband, and David are invited. 'This is the best deal you are going to get,' says Craig – and we agree.

We have ten days until the first 'debate' and have done nothing to prepare. 'Help,' I say to Bill Knapp, currently sitting in Washington, DC. He jumps on a plane and I clear David's diary. We need lots of time and are fast running out of it.

Nothing more brings home to me the reality of the election being upon us than Bill walking through the door of No. 10. 'Here we all are again,' he says, smiling. We get straight down to work, bringing Bill up to speed with the issues; where our weaknesses are, and where are our opponents'. But it really comes down to an assessment of what this election is all about – and what we would like it to be about, which are not always the same thing.

'You can't still be talking about austerity,' he says, incredulously. He is a Democrat, after all, and they prefer to throw money at problems. 'I know it worked for you last time, but are you sure you guys want a rerun?' It's not exactly a rerun, Craig and I explain, our message is more, We have a plan and it's working . . . Don't ruin what we've worked so hard together to achieve. 'OK,' he says with that American slant that suggests otherwise, 'what's your top line?' Eager Adam Atashzai, from the political team answers, 'That's simple: it's LTEP.' 'Which is what, exactly, in English?' asks Bill, looking mystified. 'Or American?' 'The Long-Term Economic Plan,' Adam chants. 'OK,' Bill says again, though this time he is silent for a while. 'That trips off the tongue . . .'

Bill's point is two-fold. One, you cannot run a second election on austerity. It must be austerity plus hope; austerity for a reason – to create a country that is safe and secure because we live within our means. Two, the Long-Term Economic Plan must be translated into 'real talk'. Real talk means explaining what the plan will mean for normal people, in language they understand. It's not about lower unemployment, it's about more jobs for families. It's not about debt and deficit, but about not going on a spending spree you can't afford and then leaving your overdraft to your kids. We go through our arguments, phrase by phrase, translating LTEP into real talk.

We also need to talk about our record. We have had five years in government. We have lots of positive things to say about what we have done. We are now one of the fastest-growing economies in the Western world creating record numbers of jobs. But as the incumbents, we also have our fair share of vulnerabilities. Running the country requires making tough decisions.

It's time for our first rehearsal. Bill is unyielding: we must again role play; reciting lines to the shaving mirror is not good enough. Bill wants to start with the most difficult – the party leaders' debate – which means there are a lot of people to cast (not an unenjoyable task). Craig and I sidle up to Olive Dowden, who has been avoiding us all day. 'I know you're going to ask me to play Farage,' he says and sighs. You guessed right, we say. Farage, we know, will be the most difficult. He loves to play to the gallery and likes to take risks. He will be toughest on immigration. Olive accepts – on one condition: that it does not leak. He is fighting his first election as an MP. Of course, the whole thing appears in the weekend papers.

Our arch-feminist, punchy researcher Meg Powell-Chandler is cast as Natalie Bennett, leader of the Green Party. Laura Trott from the Policy Unit has perfected her Welsh accent and takes on Leanne Wood of Plaid Cymru. Our Scottish expert Andrew Dunlop bravely agrees to be Nicola Sturgeon. Rupert is Ed Miliband – because only he can fathom his economic policy. And by popular demand, Jeremy Hunt returns as Nick Clegg. Former 'X Factor' debate victor Nick Clegg is now one of the most unpopular politicians in the country – a bit unfairly, I think.

We set up the seven podiums in the rehearsal room. We work out there will only be time for five questions max, given the number of people. Our guess is there will be one each on the economy, immigration, security, and public services – health or schools. Plus, one more on something like climate change or equality issues.

In the rehearsal, everyone is talking over everyone else. It feels like chaos; it will be chaos. The women are strident and ganging up against the men. 'Don't patronise us!' Meg screeches, finger wagging. 'We all know David Cameron can't handle women,' Laura says, flicking her hair. Andrew jumps on the bandwagon on behalf of Nicola. 'Oh, put a wig on,' says Olive, on behalf of Farage. It is getting out of hand.

David just stands there, watching in horror. But out of the carnage comes a valuable lesson. He will be facing a very formidable group of women. Since his infamous 'Calm down, dear' in the Commons, he has been perceived to have a 'woman' problem. So, his demeanour will be particularly important. He must at all costs avoid any Flashman-style put-downs.

'Can I go now?' asks David.

'Here's the thing,' says Bill. 'You're gonna have to stay for the full two hours.' David looks at the scene and sighs.

Now 'purdah' is upon us. This is the moment when the election officially begins and we must resign our roles as quasi-officials to join the party campaign. In just a few days' time, we will be thrown out of No. 10 – BlackBerries handed back, email accounts frozen, desks cleared. Our offices are being renovated so I am not able to see my desk, and I wonder if I will ever again. And somehow it is not really mine just at this moment, but a desk between owners, waiting for the outcome of the election. Waiting just like the Civil Service, who are busy preparing for whichever outcome faces them.

I place a large box of my personal items into the boot of my car. We are only allowed in the building to visit David's flat or George's rooms in No. 11. For now, our time at No. 10 is up. And if we don't win, it will be forever.

23

HAPPY WARRIOR

Lynton is adamant that I go out on the road with David every day for the 2015 election. At least I don't have to move into a hotel this time. I am safely ensconced at home in west London with my children, radio alarm set to 5.30 a.m., just ahead of *Farming Today*. If there is a big problem with the headlines at six o'clock, there will be a quick conference call with David and George. Otherwise, I am in the car at 6.10, on my way to CCHQ in Matthew Parker Street, for our morning meeting at 6.30. I have timed it to a tee – it takes precisely twenty minutes, door to door, at this hour of the morning.

There are times when the calls and the meetings seem to merge. It can be hard to get out of the house as phone calls interrupt morning routines. I have heard people brushing their teeth on the line. On one occasion Craig complains someone can be heard peeing.

My first meeting of the day is with Lynton, Ed, Craig, Ameet, Liz, Rupert, and Stephen Gilbert. George and David will arrive at CCHQ for a briefing at 7.30. If I'm lucky I'll grab a coffee before we hit the road. From then on my life is entirely in the hands of the ops team, under Liz's direction; a day of rallies, visits, interviews, trains, planes, and automobiles. Most days we return to London for an evening catch-up, courtesy of a helicopter. Other days we stay out on the road, spending the night in a hotel.

On day one, I call Lynton from the back of the battle bus,

assuming one of my duties will be to go through the main points with him, ahead of David's interviews.

'What do you need?' he asks.

'I'm just checking in – is there anything in particular you want David to say or steer off?'

'Not really.'

That ends the conversation. After a few days, it occurs to me that Lynton just wants the 'on the road' team to get on with it. Although we see David as the epicentre of the campaign, for Lynton we are a small (though significant) part. He wants us out there – but he doesn't want us rocking the boat. Lynton is very busy masterminding a tweet campaign, orchestrating some offensive on Labour, and doing a million other things, which (we hope) will all add up to a brilliant campaign. One of his priorities: micromanaging target seats.

Lynton identifies the seats we could lose – mounting a defensive campaign – and then the seats we need to win – mounting an offensive one. MPs who are not working hard enough get a bollocking. Coming into the campaign the battleground shifts, as some seats come within our reach and others drift away. We are very careful not to let anyone know. These are the secrets that a campaign must hold close. Yes, let the other side know you have an eye on a new seat, so they will put more resources into defending it. But if you show you have concerns about a seat you hold, suddenly your campaign looks weak and floundering.

Lynton works twenty hours a day, every day. He's the man you want at the helm of your ship on a stormy night, the sort of guy people will take a bullet for. He knows how to create a sense of belonging and unity of purpose. If you win the cuddly kangaroo he throws at you for being 'campaigner of the day', you feel like it really matters.

The first TV interview with Jeremy Paxman is coming up, and David is getting nervous. Bill is puzzled. It's just an ordinary interview, right? Paxman has form with David, we explain. 'He's worried about the pink pussy,' I add, and then realise this is not very illuminating for Bill. He wasn't there in 2005 to witness the curve ball from Paxman on 'pink pussies' – a highly intoxicating cocktail sold in a bar owned by a company David was on the board of – during the Tory leadership interviews. It is possible David has not fully recovered from the experience, I think.

The hour-long programme is split evenly between David and Ed Miliband. It opens with a one-to-one with Paxman, followed by questions from the live studio audience. Paxman is his usual vicious self. This is not an interview aimed at bringing out the best in someone. Or about helping the nation form a well-rounded opinion about these men seeking to be their future prime minister. This is all about Paxman, the predator. Will he eat or be eaten?

This feels slightly ironic given that we were recently in discussions with Paxman about whether he should stand for the Tory seat of Kensington, now that Malcolm Rifkind has announced he is standing down. I have been speaking to Paxman for a while. It is hard work pulling in a big fish on your own, so I ask for reinforcements in the form of George. But at the last minute, Paxman changes his mind.

The interview begins with a difficult question on food banks from which David never never fully regains his composure. He remains slightly stiff for the rest of the interview, forgetting to relax and talk to the 'folks' at home. After the one-to-one David takes to the front of the stage for his live Q & A session. Now he is a different man – relaxed, and in his element.

Next up is Miliband, who has clearly been schooled in the Nick Clegg interview style. His gaze is fixed on a point past Jeremy Paxman, where he clearly hopes there is a camera, and he is smiling his wide, toothy smile. Paxman looks behind him as if to ask, Is there a third person in this interview? Ed is unfazed. He's ready with an armoury of macho language, for which he wins plaudits. For example, 'Am I tough enough? Hell, yes' – when asked if he would stand up to the likes of Putin.

Only Paxman emerges from the event looking like he has had a good time. To me, it feels at best a draw. The commentariat largely declare for Miliband, but a snap ICM poll calls it for David. Who am I to complain? We know David can do better. And that the first debate is always the worst.

The next show is in Manchester in two weeks' time. The taxi driver who drives Lynton and me to the hotel takes us by the posh part of town. This is where the footballers and George Osborne live, he tells us. This is not actually true, as George lives somewhere quite different, but we don't say anything. 'At least they know who he is,' says Lynton cheerily.

The next day we arrive at the Midland Hotel in Manchester. It feels strange to be there outside of conference time, the lobby devoid of alcohol-infused activists drowning out the sound of angry demonstrations out on the street. On the way, we have swept past the Salford studios to check out the set. The seven podiums look like something out of *Star Trek*. David's is on the far side; they have drawn lots and he's thankfully not next to Farage. Afterwards, David takes to his room to go through his notes in private and we head off to meet George for a bowl of pasta at the Carluccio's in the city centre. A friendly group approach George for selfies, which pleases him – until they announce they are voting Labour. 'Nothing personal.'

Later, the studios are full to bursting. The seven candidates have each brought with them their own small army of supporters. We are directed towards our allocated green room, where Samantha and I sit eating peanuts and drinking warm white wine to dampen our nerves. The debate begins, and only then, seeing all seven of them standing in a row – Natalie Bennett, Nick Clegg, Nigel Farage, Ed Miliband, Leanne Wood, Nicola Sturgeon, and David – does the sheer spectacle of it hit home. It is a wonder to behold. How is anyone going to get a word in?

David is slightly aloof standing at the side of the stage, landing his answers at the audience and trying his best to ignore his neighbours. Nigel Farage's answers don't seem to be resonating with the audience as we had expected. The real drama is around the women. Like in *The Hunger Games*, they seem to be working as a pack to take out one of the contenders – and it isn't David they are after, it's Ed Miliband. For the SNP and Plaid Cymru, Labour are the main rival for seats, not the Tories. And the leader of the Greens is cross at Ed for not being hard-line enough. Ed Miliband is still smiling his wide smile as the pride go in for the kill.

Once we are sure David is doing well, Samantha and I relax, sit back, and enjoy the show. Soon we only have eyes for one contender: Leanne Wood. We are mesmerised by her high hair, red dress, and Welsh Valleys' lilt. Above all, we love that she speaks her mind. She's a far cry from the political machine next door (Nicola), but that is precisely what we like about her. 'We love Leanne,' we chant happily when David returns. 'But you're supposed to be supporting me,' he says, mystified.

David is declared the winner against Ed Miliband. But most of the coverage is around the women – that is, until someone discovers Ed has left prep notes urging him to be a 'happy warrior' in his dressing room. (We greet each other with 'Happy warrior!' for days afterwards.) Miliband looks faintly absurd, but not drastically so. This is not a Gordon Brown 'bigot' moment, or a Neil Kinnock 'We're all right'. Those moments were singularly damaging, like a light bulb went on and – suddenly seeing – the voters simultaneously moved their hand away from the box on the ballot paper by the candidate's name.

It is no coincidence that so many of these fateful moments befall the frontrunners as they reach the end of the campaign. The most lethal enemy is not your opponent but yourself, in the form of hubris. Candidates become unable to see the bad idea right in front of their nose. 'Happy warrior' is not such a moment for Miliband, but then he presents his 'Ed Stone' to a baffled country days before polling day. The edifice, with Labour's key election promises carved in stone, is to be mounted in the No. 10 garden if he becomes prime minister. The press will relentlessly mock Ed for this all the way till polling day.

We make two big calls on our own campaign. Seeing the uncomfortable possibility of Labour doing a deal with the SNP, Lynton drives this prospect ruthlessly through the last two weeks. The image of Miliband perched in Salmond's pocket resonates with the public. The second call is down to David's own performance. Our 'play it safe' strategy seems to underwhelm in an increasingly close campaign. David responds by turning up the energy big-time, with a series of speeches and rallies.

All of this goes to show that although the best campaigns will be planned meticulously, they must remain responsive in battle. Whether something comes at you from left field, or a weakness emerges in your campaign (or theirs), you need to be agile enough to either mend your problems, or take advantage of theirs.

THE FINAL DEBATE, THE special edition of *Question Time* with David Dimbleby at Leeds Town Hall, has finally arrived. This time David is up against just Nick and Ed. We arrive in Leeds and Craig and I decide to get some lunch. We have been on the road all week and are dying for some peace and decent food. But so infantilised have we become by the ops team dictating our every move that we find ourselves barely able to order. It's called a 'campaign' for a reason: elections are like miltary ops. The ops team are the sergeant majors and you're not supposed to argue. 'Do you think we're allowed pudding?' I ask Craig, tentatively.

Later, David wants some fresh air, so I head off with him and the protection team along the canals, which fan out along the back streets of Leeds. A few dog walkers seem surprised to share their path with us. It is good to be outside and to talk. Each day the momentum seems to be with Miliband. The press is relentless in their criticism of us. It is a hard slog.

The *Question Time* audience look ready for the kill. One wonders where on earth the BBC find these so called 'normal' – but in fact highly politicised – people. Labour are making some headway criticising some of our welfare cuts. David survives the mauling and gets into the swing, the audience slowly but surely warming to him. He comes back to the green room upbeat, pretty sure he has nailed it. Ed Miliband is up next. He starts well but is a bit defensive, and the whole performance ends on a bad note when he trips on the tail of the 'Q' of *Question Time* as he leaves the stage.

We find Lynton and Mark Textor – his polling geek, known to all as Tex, disguised as Crocodile Dundee – in the room where we left them, conducting an alcohol-fuelled post-debate tweet operation. 'It's a clear win, mate,' they say, cheerily pouring themselves more large glasses of wine. 'Happy warrior!' we chant and go to find some dinner.

'To my last debate,' Dave says, raising a glass.

Craig grimaces, 'I wouldn't be too sure about that.'

At first I am confused. David has said he will not stand for a third election, so this must be his last – categorically. But then I remember the promised EU referendum.

24

THE SWEETEST
VICTORY OF ALL

I swear I will never do an 'all nighter' on the bus again. But I am drawn in out of a sense of duty to David. Things are not going so well. The pressure is enormous as we draw into the final days of the campaign. We are neck and neck with Labour, and although we are relatively confident about winning the largest number of seats, we are not sure it will be enough to form a government.

I bump into Chris Martin. We find a quiet room to chat about how everything is going. Towards the end of our discussion, Chris moves into more sensitive territory. He wants to know what plans the Camerons have made to 'move out' if the result goes the wrong way. We have, in fact, given this some thought. A removal van has been booked under another name. The children have put their school uniforms, a few summer clothes, and their favourite toys to one side of their bedrooms. I tell Chris all this – and emphasise that it is top secret.

It has been a long and difficult campaign. We have never had the wind at our back. If we lose, all that we and the country have worked so hard to achieve will be discarded. Five years of hard grind, trying to turn things around – it's all hanging in the balance. I leave by the back gate into Horse Guards, glancing up at the building that has been so much part of my life for the past five years, and wonder if I will return.

* * *

WE FLY DOWN TO Cornwall in heavy winds, arriving at St Ives for the first rally at the start of our seventy-two-hour-long final campaign journey. I have always had a soft spot for the beautiful painted houses, windy streets, and white beaches of St Ives – a place of happy family holidays. I suddenly wish I were eating an ice cream with my children. David gives a strong rallying speech and we feel in good spirits when we get on the bus, first stop done. From St Ives we head up the tail of the West Country, jumping off to do visits and interviews, watching the rolling news as we go.

We stop for dinner in a pub, the journalists all desperate to get a bit of David. He handles them with ease and dignity – cracking jokes, giving them a bit of colour, but not too much. No one at the dinner thinks we are going to win outright. It is bets on whether he will be prime minister in a day. Liz hands him a large glass of red wine. You would never guess he was a man on trial by the nation.

We drive on into the night. At midnight Liz takes us off to a hotel. We have decided to break with tradition and stop for a few hours. We'll have another sleepless night ahead of us after we get off the bus, as we wait for the election results, and we need David to have his wits about him. I set my alarm for 4 a.m. hoping that a shower and a cup of coffee will trick my body into thinking it has had a normal night's sleep.

We set off a few hours later in the pitch black, up in the helicopter into a gale-force wind. Samantha has begged David not to fly today but here we are, flying – sort of. We are literally thrown across the Bristol Channel and up over the Brecon Beacons. The countryside beneath us is stunning. David gives me an 'Oh god, I'm in a helicopter with Kate' look; we have had a few near misses in the past. We land in a field to have a cup of tea with a farmer and his family. The press corps is massing in their barn. It is less than twenty-four hours before polling stations open.

We spend the rest of the day in the bus stopping and starting on our way up the country. We are tired and I can sense David's mood darkening in the privacy of the back of the bus. He has calculated that the most likely outcome is for us to win the most seats, but not be in a position to form a government. So, we could win but lose – similar to last time, but without the momentum of a swing in our favour, winning us new seats. So, he is preparing himself for the humiliation of defeat. Although we are a team, at this moment I can see that he feels very much alone; we will all share the pain, but it is he who will face the public music. I try to be optimistic. Between naps I awake with new theories about why it's really going to be OK. 'Take another nap and try and come up with a better one,' David says. Gallows humour is descending.

I emerge from my final catnap with a message of optimism: the mood of the country has not felt against us on the ground, even if the polls do not show it. Even David concedes I may finally have a point. He calls it the 'look me in the eye test' – his theory that people who avoid eye contact with him will not vote for him – and on the whole, he thinks more people have looked him in the eye than not. And it's not just us: MPs are texting us with anecdotes from their campaigns, and most say it feels good on the ground.

This time I have remembered to organise a postal vote and so I have come prepared to spend the final hours out on the road. My daughter has helped me pack. Jeans for polling day. Something for the evening. And the day after that? Who knows. Olivia picked out a light blue cotton dress covered in bees. This, she says, is in the case of victory. We put it in the bottom of the bag.

I head back to Dean from the rally in the helicopter with David, Samantha, and Liz. Whatever happens, in just over twenty-four hours' time the all-consuming thing that is an election – which forces itself into every moment of your life – will be over. I look down over Merseyside and thank god I have come through it. In a year when had to care for a sister with cancer and had two children at home doing exams, it will be nice to regain a semblance of normality again.

We cover ourselves with blankets and open a bottle of wine. Then, over the two-hour journey to Dean, we reminisce about all the good times we have had over our years together in politics and reflect on the privilege of our five years in Downing Street. We have not accepted defeat – but we feel prepared for it if it comes. Now it is up to the British people to give their judgement.

WE WAKE TO THE anxious stillness of polling day. The broadcasts are saying it's too close to call. We set off early so David and Samantha can vote. David is nervous. The village is heaving with press.

David wants a small group of us to meet to discuss the options. However, we have to be very careful. The last thing we want is for images of William Hague, George, and others arriving to appear on every news website, alongside the headline, 'Emergency summit as Cameron prepares for disaster poll'. This could affect the outcome. So, gathering at David's house in Dean is out of the question. It already resembles a film set, with a camera for every tree. We are offered the use of a beautiful and rather obscure set of farm buildings, courtesy of Samantha's cousin. After voting, David and I head off to our secret location.

William turns up, looking slightly out of place by one of the barns. George bumps into a Sikh wedding party going into another. It seems the buildings are used as a full-time events venue. We wonder if the others will ever find us, but they eventually track us down. George, David, Oliver, William, Lynton, Ed, and I settle into comfortable leather chairs, coffee in hand. A door suddenly opens on the far side of the room and everyone leaps up from their seats. We arrange for someone to stand guard at the door.

David begins. He is matter-of-fact and the mood is sombre. Let's start with the numbers, they will dictate the options. We concentrate on that magic number of 323 again. We were on 306 MPs last time but have lost a few over the Parliament – 2 to UKIP. Lib Dems are on 57 and Labour 259. There is no question of gaining seats, in our minds, and nothing in the polls to suggest it. Incumbent governments don't tend to increase their share of the vote, anyway. And although we have felt some warmth on the ground during the campaign, we are not basking in it.

The best scenario, we imagine, is if we stay where we are, but we are more likely to lose some MPs. We have felt a shift towards Labour, especially in the North. However, some Lib-Dem-held seats in the West and London suburbs seem to be coming our way. Although we would love to form another coalition with the Lib Dems, it might be that we are victims of our own success and have made gains at the expense of our former political partners. If we don't have the numbers between us, we will try to attempt a minority government. And if the scales begin to slide still further from us, Labour's prospects of forming a government – possibly supported by a large bank of SNP MPs – could be a real runner.

Nearly all of these scenarios are going to be tough. Even if we are capable of forming a second coalition, the Conservative Party will be pretty unforgiving. Some might simply refuse. Minority government will most likely lead to a leadership election, possibly even another general election. If Labour hooks up with the SNP to form a majority, the game is over. 'It might well be curtains for our dear friend David,' Oliver Letwin admits, and then laughs his high-pitched, slightly hysterical laugh, reserved for his most anxious moments.

After lunch, Lynton, William, and Oliver disappear. George, David, Ed, and I head back to the Camerons' house in Dean.

Clare Foges, David's speechwriter, is waiting for us when we get there. David wants to be ready for every eventuality. 'Let's prepare two scripts,' he says. Clare goes off to write the 'win' version; David will write the other version himself. We all go to find a place to rest for an hour but, just like last time, I am too restless to sleep. I lie on the bed in the spare room, looking at the large tree outside the window.

I feel somehow that the party will fare well enough tonight, but I am less sure about David – and I feel horribly protective of him. He has worked so hard to do what is right for his country, and achieved so much. But it has been a tough few years for everyone. And who knows what will really drive people's vote, in the end, at the ballot box.

I make my way downstairs to make myself a cup of tea, and then walk out into the garden. David is restless and wants to go for a walk. Samantha lends me an old pair of slightly-too-large trainers. There is a path leading from the back of the garden up through the forest to a clearing at the end. We set off – David, Samantha, Ed, George, and I. It is a relief to be outside in the spring evening, the bluebells briefly lifting our spirits.

On the way back, David asks us to indulge him in what a future Conservative-only Cabinet might look like. It's not going to happen, says Ed.

'Go on, make a middle-aged man happy,' says David. So, we plan our reshuffle trudging home.

It is time to say goodbye to George. Again, there is a helicopter waiting for him in a nearby field. There is nothing to say. We all know the drill now.

We turn to the speeches. Andy Parsons, our friendly photographer, is with us. David reads out the draft of the 'win' speech – *Snap* (happy group). David reads out his draft of a resignation speech – *Snap* (sad group).

In the zone of election night, I give no thought to what I will do if we don't make it, other than that if we win, I will be busy; and if we lose, I'll have plenty of time to think about it. But I am concerned that my children will be upset. I don't want them to wake up to bad news without a close relative on hand. So, I have asked my twin sister, who is like a second mother to them, to stay the night. I ring her in London. She is on her way to one of the election parties – feeling a bit apprehensive. No one thinks David is going to win, and there are a lot of ugly predictions and criticism in the air. Boris's allies are circling. 'Just stick by Andrew Feldman and everything will be OK.' I tell her. 'And don't say anything, even if someone is rude!'

'Is it going to be OK?' the children ask. They are older now and know what is going on. 'I am sure David will still be prime minister tomorrow,' I say, choosing my words carefully. But they sound anxious. 'Auntie Mel's going out,' they say, unimpressed. 'We've told her she should be here with us.' They are like a small trade union of two, demanding their rights. Mel gets back on the phone. 'I'm only going out for a few hours,' she reassures them, as she speaks with me.

As late afternoon gives way to evening, there is a visible change in mood. Samantha is sorting dinner, complaining that she has a nervous stomach ache. 'I look like I'm expecting twins,' she says, pointing to what looks like a pretty flat stomach to me. Isabel, who is pregnant, is trying to keep Samantha calm. *Snap* – Andy takes a picture of Isabel and me on the sofa. She looks the picture of radiant, maternal beauty; I look gaunt and exhausted after weeks on the road.

David is outside building a small bonfire. He has convinced himself all is lost, and is close to losing the plot. I look round for the rest of the team. Ed and Craig are glued to their phones. Ed is getting some positive feedback from MPs on the ground, Craig less so.

Just before we eat, Craig takes Ed and me aside. He has just had a report from a pollster and former colleague called Andrew Cooper. It is not good news. He says there has been a high turnout for UKIP and Labour. We're stuffed if that's true. We agree not to tell David. 'What is the point?' I say. He'll know soon enough.

We sit down to dinner, refilling our glasses regularly over the meal. The conversation comes and goes; everyone is checking their phones. Ten o'clock looms – but this time with a worse sense of destiny than five years before. Craig, who edited the *News at Ten* for the 2010 election, tells us the exit polls are pretty accurate, so prepare to take the news head on.

Just like last time, we cannot help but be both drawn to and repelled from the messenger of our fate. As ten o'clock approaches, we take our seats in front of the TV. Everyone is silent. We know better than to let our emotions cascade around the sitting room. Andy Parsons sits with his camera on his lap. We are so used to him by now we don't notice he is even taking pictures. For what and for whom? We have long forgotten. *Bong* – the first chime of

Big Ben – and countdown to our destiny. Then the announcement is made: the evening goes to the Tories. They are set to be the largest party, the clear victors, the broadcasters say. A blue line streams across the screen. There is a Pinteresque pause and then pandemonium.

We hug each other in turn, and then we do it again. George calls in, then Lynton.

Ed tries to calm us down. This is just a poll, we have not won, he reminds us. We might still not be able to form a government. There is no talk of a majority. Ed is right – although we are not really in the mood to listen. We settle down to watch the results come in. It is a slow start, but they are mostly all in the right direction. We let the good news run over us in warm waves.

At around 1 a.m. we leave for David's count in Witney – arriving, as it turns out, way ahead of schedule. We are parked in front of a large television in the upstairs section of a vast, freezing, and very smelly sports hall. At any other moment in time, this would be an agony, but tonight it is a delight.

At about 2 a.m. we hear of an unexpected hold and swing to us in Nuneaton. David turns around to us and says, 'We're headed for a majority.' Are you sure? I ask. 'Yes, I really think we are.' Craig and I look at each other. Then I look back at David. He looks different, transforming in the last few hours from condemned man to leader of men. The weight of these moments falls on the shoulders of those who lead their parties. It is they who largely embody a sense of victory (or of failure), they who feel responsible for it. This is a very personal triumph for David – and it shows. Power has a way of expanding someone.

I can see quite quickly that he is right about where the result is heading. The unexpected, quirky wins, which start coming through, speak of a historic victory. David is the first prime minister since Lord Salisbury in 1900 to increase his party's vote share after a term of longer than two years. We will end up with twenty-four more seats, opening up a full 7 per cent lead over Labour, who lose twenty-six MPs. We win seats in London and the North that we thought were a long shot. Our Coalition partners have been reduced to a mere handful – just eight MPs. And with this come some high-profile and slightly ugly losses: Ed Balls, Vince Cable. I am too soft to enjoy these public humiliations of people who have tried hard to do the right thing by their country. I leave the crowing to others.

Our exhausted if elated reverie is interrupted around 5 a.m. with news that the Witney count is finally to be called. Suddenly we realise this will be a very public moment – the first words from a now victorious David Cameron – and we have about two minutes to think about what he should say. David is writing some notes on the back of an envelope. Craig suggests revisiting the 'One Nation' theme. It is a good thought: the nation, coming together to enjoy better times, after hard years of austerity. It gives form to the second Cameron term right from the start – and is authentically 'David'. He does not believe in a winner-takes-all democracy. Instead, he believes that as prime minister you preside over the whole nation – those who voted for you as well as those who didn't.

Samantha, Isabel, and I stand side by side trying to keep out of the way of the cameras in the hall. I think back fourteen years, to when I helped David fight his Witney seat whilst very pregnant with my second child. It was our first victory together. It is hard not to feel rather emotional standing there so many years later, watching him win an all-out general election victory. The eyes of the nation are on us in the gym. 'We will govern as a party of one nation, one United Kingdom,' says David.

We head off to London in a convoy of cars, helicopters following our progress overhead. Ed rings me from CCHQ: 'This is incredible! Every time we gain another seat Lynton gets up on one of the desks and blows a trumpet.' I can hear the toots in the background.

'We'll be with you soon,' I say.

Dawn is breaking as we come into the city. The cars sweep in to Matthew Parker Street and stop outside CCHQ. We come up the stairs into the reception, where three extremely proud and exhausted men are waiting to greet the Prime Minister: Lynton, Tex, and Andrew Feldman. Although we know the entire election team is waiting next door, it is an important moment. We do not rush it.

Then Lynton opens the door into the floor of the campaign headquarters – to a roar from the near-hysterical team. I watch from the back as David is mobbed. 'This is the sweetest victory of all,' he tells them.

25

STORM CLOUDS

Ed and I follow David through the door of No. 10 to find Chris Martin waiting to greet us in the front hall. It is amazing to be back – the enormity of the privilege of working in Downing Street is brought home yet again. It has been a long, hard slog. Chris hands me back my old phone and Lara Moreno-Pérez, David's diary secretary, has a coffee for me. I sit down at my desk and turn on my computer – it feels too good to be true, like finding something you have treasured and lost. Note to self: try not to lose it again.

I ring my children. They are in a huge state of excitement and want to have the day off school (which I refuse). Olivia gets on the phone. 'Are you wearing the victory dress?' *The what?* I can't think what she is talking about. 'You know – the bee dress!' And then I remember that I have been wearing the same thing for about forty-eight hours, though, lurking at the bottom of my overnight bag, is the 'in case of victory' dress she selected for me.

Lucy – a highly efficient and absurdly beautiful duty clerk – takes matters in hand. She finds me a towel and directs me up to the top of the building where there is a rather nice bathroom – completely unknown to me, even after five years here. I probably use the entire rations of SW1's water supply and reappear a while later, rejuvenated and reclothed.

We get straight down to business. David will have to make a speech outside No. 10 after he returns from seeing the Queen. We gather in the den. Clare arrives clutching the 'win' draft (the other is kept for posterity). We know that the moment will be lost if we don't stamp our mark on what a second Cameron administration will look and feel like right from the start. And this is not just a second term. It is the first term of the first Conservative government since 1997. It needs to feel different.

Over the years, there have been many things we wanted to do but couldn't, either because we have had to make concessions to the Lib Dems or because austerity has so dominated the political landscape. This is political liberty. And we know exactly what to do with it: return to the themes of the pre-financial crisis David Cameron, whose time has finally come. Social problems that need mending. Prison reform. Creating more good schools. Tackling the sensitivities around cohesion – of a divided nation who, in some parts of the country, live parallel lives. Helping more people back to work. This is our 'Life Chances' agenda. Not that we think we have fixed the economy – far from it. At just under 5 per cent of GDP, the deficit is still one of the largest in the developed world. But now we want to move beyond it dominating everything we do. It has been a long haul to get Britain growing again – and we want everyone to feel the benefits.

There is also a collective sigh of relief from 'the House'. It cannot be easy to see out an old boss, and see in a new, in a matter of an hour – especially if you have grown fond of the old one. That day will come, but it is not today. Even Larry seems pleased to see us. This time when David and Samantha are clapped in, it all takes much longer, as now they know the staff and stop to talk to them on their way down the corridor. I go down to the canteen. 'You're back!' say Marg and Alison cheerfully, making me a cup of tea.

Our next task is to form a government. Chris Martin is ready with the lists. This is the bit of his job he loves the most. With no Lib Dems to take up key roles we should be able to make a lot more people happy in the party.

There is some talk about a big generational clear-out. After all, we have kept a lot of the same people in the same places for a long time. But we decide against it at this point. With a bruising election campaign behind us, and a European negotiation coming, we feel the need to have our loyal big hitters around us. And we have just lost William Hague, who has stood down from public life.

We announce the top security team first. In addition to being Chancellor, George becomes First Secretary of State, taking over William's former role as David's effective deputy. His new nickname: Mr Secretary. We have thought about Theresa as Foreign Secretary, a job which we think she would do well. But we need someone who can work on the renegotiation of our terms of membership of the EU and being a team player is not her strongest point – nor are her advisors very easy to work with. Plus, if we ever want to do the swap with George later, this puts Theresa in the Treasury, and we fear a return of the wars of old between No. 10 and No. 11. So, we decide it is safer to keep her as Home Secretary, at least for now. David tells her, and Theresa leaves the Cabinet room clearly disappointed. But there was little choice. Anything else is a demotion.

So, Philip Hammond stays in situ as Foreign Secretary. We all like his sweet, dry charm, and the fact that he doesn't play games. He is a get-what-you-see type of person. He likes to move with caution and 'check in' before doing anything radical. Apart, that is, from when he's driving his car, which he clearly likes to do at great speed.

The next big decision centres around whether we keep Michael Gove on as Chief Whip, a job which he hates and is not particularly good at. We are agreed that it would be best to move him to Justice where he can put his considerable creative intellect to reforming prisons. And there is another reason for the move. Michael brings much to our team at No. 10 – not least his brilliance and charm. But although in many ways he fits in as an ultra moderniser, he is also of a very different political mindset – more radical than conservative. David once branded him as a bit of a Maoist, someone who believes progression only comes through creative destruction

(Gove himself being the force of creative destruction, of course). Sometimes, this approach to government is refreshing; it is important to be challenged, especially now we are entering our eleventh year working together, and there are many places where a bit of radicalism is just what is needed. But sometimes David and Michael just don't agree. Although he has asked Michael to be the 'Hand of the King', but where the hand thinks differently from the king, it sows confusion. And if there's one thing No. 10 can't cope with, it's confusion. At the end of the day, prisons need reforming, Justice is a big promotion for Michael, and we are all pleased to think he (as well as Mrs Gove) will be pleased.

As for Iain Duncan Smith, David believes he should behave honourably towards him, as a previous party leader, and let him decide when he wants to leave front-line politics. It turns out that IDS doesn't. But his decision to stay prolongs the battle between him and George on welfare. George is looking for cuts, as he tries to bring fairness in line with sound finance, while IDS stands firmly by Universal Credit – his baby. Ultimately, this gives IDS a platform from which he will make a high-profile resignation down the line – perhaps another example of where David's trusting loyalty to his colleagues was misjudged.

We all have our concerns about Universal Credit. Yes, it looks good on paper, and it's built on the strong and simple premise that it should always pay to work. It also makes sense in theory to merge six separate means-tested benefits and tax credits into one payment. But in practice we are worried about whether this 'grand project' will actually work – and about the losers. It means moving some of the most vulnerable in our society to a monthly payment from a weekly one. And what about the efficiency of the transition? There also appears to be a lack of real statistics about what the project will cost – from a department (and Secretary of State) who view their project with almost religious zeal. The welfare of vulnerable people will be reliant on a huge computer programme that is already proving challenging. The project keeps getting postponed, year after year. There is a sense in some quarters – especially from

George, who opposes it – that the project is unmanageable and ultimately will never happen.

Then there's the question of what to do about Boris – by no means a new one. We want to bring Boris into the Cabinet. He is still Mayor of London, but his time is nearly up. David discusses the Department for Digital, Culture, Media and Sport, with a view to something more senior when he retires from the mayoralty. DCMS might sit well with him whilst also being in charge of the nation's capital. And it is a good first step. But Boris turns it down. He is nervous of joining the team – and nervous of not – always trying to gauge the political advantage. But the money weighs hardest with him. He would need to give up all of his outside interests – including his weekly column with the *Daily Telegraph* – to join. And he thinks, on balance, it is not worth it for now. So, he stays away – except that he will attend political cabinet, which meets once a week, as Mayor. It is strange to see him there, sitting alongside other members of the Cabinet, after having been an outsider for so long. We brace ourselves for his motivational 'Churchillian interventions', but they never seem to materialise.

This Cabinet will be one-third women, with Amber Rudd, Priti Patel, Nicky Morgan, Anna Soubry, Liz Truss, Tina Stowell, Theresa Villiers, and Joyce Anelay joining. Of these, Amber is the most natural and able. It has been a decade-long struggle to get more women onto the Tory benches. We have come a long way from the days of being stuck on a tiny group of under twenty to reaching 20 per cent female MPs. But we still have a long way to go, especially if we compare ourselves to Labour, who are near to parity. I feel proud to hear strong female voices resonate around the Cabinet table.

Late on Saturday afternoon, with most of the government appointments decided and plans in place for our first full week back, we call it a day. I head home to enjoy the remains of the weekend. I open the door to a trail of presents from my children: wine, cake, bath oil. We celebrate together. And then it's time to sleep.

The weekend papers are glorious, the sort you throw away too carelessly, thinking the good times might last. Every major poll brings with it a changed political landscape – and this one is no exception. The bodies of the defeated lie around us. Ed Miliband resigns and calls a leadership election for Labour. Nick Clegg does the same for the Lib Dems. Boris has retreated to his cave and his friends are brooding. Only David and George remain – looking around them at the carnage, seemingly having conquered all.

Yet, perhaps sown in our unexpected victory, lies the seed of our undoing. Had we not won an election by vanquishing our centrist Coalition partners, would we have pressed our foot firmly on the gas towards the EU referendum and ultimate defeat? Yet David had always been clear that he wouldn't form a second coalition without an in/out referendum. And I am pretty sure the party would not have let him wriggle out of it. We shall never know if the Lib Dems would have agreed to join a government under these circumstances – though it is worth remembering that they went into the 2015 election reconfirming their pledge for a referendum in the event of more power passing to the EU. Which, given the pressure on the Eurozone, might well have been triggered, with or without the Tory pledge.

But where all the attention should be on David – as the victorious prime minister – it shortly turns to rest on George. It is David's own fault, of course. He has let slip in an interview with James Landale that he will not fight another election, and so in his moment of glory he has already made himself a partial lame duck. Only partial, because he has been careful to say he will serve a full five years, and that is a long time in politics. But still – George is the coming man. Just now, after a decade of David dominating politics, people want to focus on someone new.

And there are other changes. George's loyal ally and wise advisor Rupert Harrison leaves for a new career in finance. He has always been such a big part of the intellectual fabric of our joint teams – a level head, and a great friend – so his leaving is a great loss to us all. Olive Dowden won his seat, and so has been sacrificed to

Parliament. His sunny optimism and brilliant political mind is hard to replace, though we are able to give very deserved promotions to Liz Sugg, Ameet Gill, and Laurence Mann as a result. We bring in Camilla Cavendish from *The Times* to be the new head of the Policy Unit. She is a formidable senior female voice, and I only wish she had joined us years before. And in George's team, the talented duo of Thea Rogers and James Chapman step forward.

Ed Llewellyn and I remain in charge of No. 10, but Ed is now restless, contemplating his departure. He has served David for so long, so well – but his heart is in foreign affairs and a career in the Foreign Office. The perfect resting place for 'Mini Metternich', as David is fond of calling him. We cross St James's Park to get some lunch. He is torn between his loyalty to David and the team and his opportunity to leverage this moment to leave. I cannot imagine doing the job without him; we have been a partnership for a decade. In the end his loyalty grounds him and he decides to stay, to see the negotiation and EU referendum through.

WE WANT TO FOCUS the start of our second term on the Life Chances agenda, but two other issues are impossible to ignore, and will set the stage for the coming year. First, the summer Budget. Second, the timing of the referendum.

Although we have put much of our house in order – we are now the fastest growing of all the advanced economies – we still have a deficit. David and George want to tackle it and aim for a surplus. At the same time, we don't want to lose the sense of a national unity of purpose that Plan A had. Going for 'shining black numbers' may be seen as overly ideological or, worse, blind to the human cost. But David and George are emphatic that it is responsible thing to do. It makes no sense to be enjoying a recovery and not address our mounting debts, only to find next time we hit a rough patch we have nothing to fall back on and must hand the problem down to our children. If we are about anything, we are about putting the economy back on the straight and narrow. 'Fixing the roof while the sun is shining.' A country living within our means.

Of course, in practice, Plan A was always both a firm and a flexible strategy. More 'Plan A and a Half' – as George had the political agility to both stick to the plan and move a little from it when he needed to. For example, the target to eliminate the structural deficit during the life of the previous Parliament was extended to soften the impact of the cuts. Keynesian investment projects like Crossrail, HS2, and a full-scale road building exercise were snuck in under the fiscal conservatives' radar. Likewise, Northern Powerhouse and Tech City were added, to boost entrepreneurialism and growth.

We went into the election promising a further round of cuts amounting to £30 billion over two years – £13 billion from departmental savings, £12 billion from welfare, and £5 billion from cracking down on tax evasion and avoidance. However, the departmental savings are not that easy on the back of previous cuts in the last Parliament, with quite a few areas considered to be a no-go, like overseas aid, health (where we pledge to spend more), and schools. Any hint of cuts to the defence budget will cause a stink, especially as we are not quite meeting the 2 per cent required by summer 2015 as members of NATO. We are increasingly of the view that this is not a worthwhile row to have.

So many of the cuts will have to fall across other departments: the Home Office, Business, Innovation and Skills, local governments. At best, this requires creative thinking about government. More decentralisation. Less waste. Less interference. It's the perfect challenge for the refreshed Policy Unit. Camilla is given her marching orders and looks rather faint. This is a massive operation and a difficult transition for her – to come from years of journalism, where your role is to critique everything, to government, when you actually have to make choices and do things.

And then there is welfare. We have pledged £12 billion of further welfare cuts on top of the billions from our first term, when we made changes to housing benefits, introduced a household benefit cap, reformed our disability support scheme, cut child benefit for higher rate taxpayers, and started rolling out Universal Credit.

Some cuts have proven more acceptable than others. Where a policy earns a damning nickname, needless to say it generally means it hasn't gone down well. The 'bedroom tax' is judged harshly – especially in Scotland, where it is harder to find alternative accommodation nearby.

But overall, our national thinking about welfare has been revolutionised. David has taken an issue that was once deemed politically 'untouchable' and encouraged a national conversation about it. Now everyone is talking about what sort of system they want. What they think is fair – for the people who need support and for the people who are paying for it. Caretaker Labour leader Harriet Harman urges her party to listen to the public and not to vote against the Welfare Bill in July 2015.

A small group of us gather to look at the options for further cuts for the Budget. All low-hanging fruit is long gone. There are no Lib Dems here to argue our numbers down. Looking round the room, the new reality comes home: the Quad, with its role of providing checks and balances, is a thing of the past. It is just us. The question about whether the nation has a stomach for another round of cuts of this size lands solely on our plate.

It is a rare moment when David and George don't see exactly eye to eye. But George is now more determined. He has an eye on the electoral cycle too. If we are going to make tough decisions they should be at the beginning of the Parliament, he says. David is not against further cuts but he senses the nation is quite near saturation point. We are aware of the growing numbers of people using food banks. Our majority is tiny. Only a few worried MPs might topple the apple cart. We agree to proceed, but with the utmost caution.

The next question is where exactly to make the remaining cuts. IDS is guarding his vast Universal Credit budget at the Department for Work and Pensions (DWP). So, we are forced to look elsewhere for savings, turning to the tax credits that became hugely bloated during Brown's time at Treasury.

In the lead up to the budget the relationship between IDS and

George reaches a new low – their spads are at each other's throats. It is in the 'ether' that George does not rate IDS intellectually, which does not help. Camilla Cavendish and I sit down with both sides in an attempt to keep the warring factions at bay and work towards a solution. Our discussions are leaking into the newspapers, so we don't dare tell IDS's spads about our plans to introduce a National Living Wage. This means we have no sweetener to put on the table. Nothing to show them that, while we still want to make some cuts, we are also thinking carefully about how to alleviate some of the pain.

And we are. George, proud of his record of increasing the minimum wage, wants to go further and introduce a National Living Wage. David readily agrees. The National Living Wage doubles down on our narrative that it should pay to work. But more importantly, it tries to address stubbornly sluggish wages, which have meant that many people still feel the pinch despite the recovery. We want the recovery to be felt by everyone. When the policy is finally announced, it is received to great acclaim in the Commons – even IDS is pleased, punching the air – and elsewhere.

But we are not out of the woods. A few months later, when the MPs' mailbags fill up with letters pushing back on the cuts to tax credits, we cannot escape the growing sense of unease. A thorough whips' operation delivers the legislation on tax credits, in the form of Statutory Instruments, through to the Lords, but in the Lords it comes unstuck at the hands of two feisty baronesses. George decides to accept defeat and move on.

It has been a damaging exercise for us and for him. There's a sense that we have misplayed the politics, and not listened enough. That Parliament does not have the stomach for more welfare cuts. And that George has created a restless enemy in IDS, and a situation that has not yet run its full course.

Exhausted but in good spirits, we gather at Chequers after the post-election Budget. It is a beautiful, long, and light summer's evening, and we will soon be getting ready to leave for the holidays.

Over the last five years, Chequers has become a place where we have gone to talk properly – in private – often late into the night. Where our mobiles don't ring because they don't work. A place of relative peace. And I feel happy to be back.

We are contemplating our next years in government, all the things we want to do. But it wouldn't be true to say there wasn't a cloud in the sky. There was. It was called Europe.

Over dinner our conversation turns to the timing of the EU referendum. Andrew Feldman is convinced it will mark the end game for David – win or lose. But our eyes are fixed far from our departure. We feel in tune with the party and in step with a country who has just voted David back into office for another five years. We are optimistic for the future.

PART 3

Europe

26

JOURNEY TO BLOOMBERG

On 23 January 2013, David made a speech at the European headquarters of Bloomberg in the City of London, in which he committed to holding an in/out referendum on Britain's membership of the EU before the end of 2017. The speech – in which he talked about Britain's place in Europe and his aspirations for its future based on a renewed mandate – was a long time in the making. It reflected years of an issue growing in the heartlands of the party and of the country. And it came from hours of vexed conversations.

But first, some background. As a nation, we have never aligned ourselves with Europe. Rather we saw it as an organisation whose coexistence with our own nation-state requires constant vigilance, even just in standing our ground. The United Kingdom was not an original signatory of the Treaty of Rome in 1957, which first created the European Economic Community – a 'free trade area'. We turned up late to the party, in 1973. Two years later, the British people were asked in a referendum whether they wanted to stay in. They said yes by an overwhelming margin.

The French and Germans, who were there at the start (at least West Germany was), have on the whole always identified with 'Project Europe', seeing their national interest naturally bound up with it, and are generally happy to make sacrifices to keep this project on track. Their presidents and chancellors return home after summits with tales of grandiose leadership. Ours tend to return home with tales of scalps won, or reports of what dastardly euro plan we have scuppered – from Thatcher's rebate, to John Major's opt-out from the social chapter, to more recent fights over Eurozone bailouts or even the banning of straight bananas.

As the political dimensions to the economic community grew and there was a move towards a more integrated union, including towards a single currency, tensions increased. In 1979, the European Monetary System was established with the aim of preventing large exchange rate fluctuations between the member countries' currencies. Britain's brief experiment in joining the Exchange Rate Mechanism ended disastrously with Black Wednesday 1992, when the sterling's value plummeted and the UK withdrew. It was an experiment unlikely to be attempted again.

Britain, nervous of integration, preferred to concentrate on the economic benefits of being part of a huge single market. When the Iron Curtain fell, we championed extending it to our new democratic neighbours in Eastern and Central Europe. We were, for the most part, 'wideners not deepeners' – we believed in creating a Europe that was a vast market of independent nation-states and a long way from a unified federal state.

But Europe continued to 'deepen' as well as 'widen'. It was never really heading in our direction – it was heading in theirs – and this seemed to grate at the soul of the British people. Over decades an atmosphere of antagonism grew on a steady diet of negative headlines, especially as Brussels tried to bring common rules to the single market that were perceived to be interfering and often ridiculous.

On the whole, British politicians were defensive from day one. Defensive abroad – fighting our ground – and defensive at home – defending our reasons for being in Europe at all. And amusing their constituents on the weekends with stories of glory battles in Europe.

Europe's evolution from an economic community to a more complex European Union was encapsulated in the 1992 Maastricht Treaty, which caused friction as it came before Parliament. Around this time, the Conservative Party divided loosely into three groups: a not inconsiderable number of pro-Europeans; a small group of very staunch anti-Europeans, who in time will publicly declare their goal to take Britain out of the EU and define their entire political careers by it; and a growing number of moderately Eurosceptic MPs (with a small 'e') in the middle. This last group believed that Europe must reform and change to survive; they hated regulation and were vehemently against the euro but at the same time see that Europe has benefits – mostly as a huge market, but also as a group of free democratic nations who believe in free trade and Western values. This was where most of the MPs were.

John Major's government was undermined by a group of Eurosceptic 'bastards', as he famously called them, who used his small majority to thwart him at every turn over Europe, especially as he tried to get Maastricht through the Commons. A perfect case study of how not to handle Europe came in early 1996, when BSE spread through our livestock and the Europeans moved to ban our beef. Our farmers were up in arms – along with the British press and public. Major decided to hold Europe to ransom, refusing to cooperate until the beef ban was lifted. He had started a full-frontal battle he was unable to win and which, despite his best efforts, did nothing to help the farmers. It only resulted in undermining his leadership.

The government was under siege. I was working at the Conservative Research Department at this time, with the responsibility for the European brief as well as agriculture and animals. In my mostly urban life I had hitherto barely encountered a cow, and yet found myself at the centre of a department in meltdown over meat exports. An emergency debate was called in the Commons and it was my job to write the brief for the MPs. I rang George: what on earth should I write? The problem, he said, was that there was no agreed policy – yet. But he promised to come round with the details as soon as they emerged from the Ministry of Agriculture, Fisheries and Food, where he was a special advisor to Douglas Hogg. It was late that evening when he finally appeared, sheet of paper in hand (this was pre-email). The phone on my desk was ringing non-stop with calls from the public – mostly farmers, screaming at me over the government's handling of the crisis. I wrote my brief while George fended off the calls, and delivered it to the whips' office just in time.

The Major years came crashing to an end with the massive Blair victory in 1997 – a New Labour dawn, soundtrack Blur and Oasis. John Major was left with the indignity of having to reply to the man who swept him out of office on a landslide – fresh-faced, brand-new Prime Minister Blair – when Blair made his first EU Council statement on the follow-up to Maastricht, the Treaty of Amsterdam. There was no one around to brief Major on it, save the former Europe Minister, David Davis, and the CRD Europe desk officer – me. The three of us sat in Major's Commons office, helping him devise the questions. It would be his last appearance in the Commons.

Over the following years in opposition, the Conservative Party spent a lot of time talking about Europe, under a succession of strongly Eurosceptic leaders against the Europhile Blair. This was seen to be a 'wedge' issue – one which is both divisive and carries weight in terms of how a person might vote. William Hague made his stand against the single currency the centrepiece of his 2001 campaign. Under the subsequent leadership of IDS and then Michael Howard, Euroscepticism became even more entrenched.

WHEN DAVID WAS ELECTED party leader in 2005, he was very much in step with the party on Europe. A self-confessed Eurosceptic, he was strongly anti-euro and pro-reform. He was never an 'outer' Eurosceptic, however; there were still not many of those around at that time. In those days, small 'e' Euroscepticism did not translate as Leave. David believed that being in Europe was better for Britain than being out – but that we should do more to find a comfortable place for us to be. Why should we pretend that we want to march with our fellow Europeans to 'ever closer union' when we don't? And we had to find a way to stop the endless ratchet of powers to Brussels without any accountability to the British people. These sentiments echoed the views of the mainstream of the party.

Most of all, David just wanted the party to stop 'banging on about Europe' – which he spelled out very clearly in his first party conference as leader. The sense that the party had been talking to itself for well over a decade, whilst Labour was talking to people about things that mattered to their daily lives, weighed heavily. In his early years as Conservative leader, David's main achievement in terms of Europe was that he didn't talk about it for the most part.

But we didn't neglect the issue entirely. Aware that we had not earned the party's trust on Europe (and may never), we wanted to put someone in charge who had, and identified that person in William Hague. But us wanting William was not the same as him wanting us. It was a big decision for him to come back. Fortunately for us he did, believing his political life had not quite run its course.

As soon as he became party leader, David wanted to 'do something' that showed we were serious about our direction of travel on the question of Europe. For example, if we didn't believe in creating an integrated European state, then we should not sit with the right-wing federalist grouping in the European Parliament who do. Leaving the European People's Party would be quite a wrench though, as it would mean removing ourselves from our natural centre-right allies in Europe, like Nicolas Sarkozy's Union for a Popular Movement (UMP) and Angela Merkel's Christian Democratic Union. We may have shared similar views on the economy with our 'sister' parties, but on Europe, we wanted different things.

Forming a new group was not so straightforward. We were hardly spoilt for choice. If there had been a deluge of other right-wing, Eurosceptic, anti-federalist parties in Europe, things might have worked out rather differently. Some of these parties would emerge, but not for a while. Luckily we found solid friends in the Polish Law and Justice Party (PiS) and the Czech Civic Democratic Party (ODS).

In 2006 we headed off to Poland and the Czech Republic to

shore up our new allies with a series of speeches and rallies, flying first to Prague to campaign for Mirek Topolánek, the leader of our new sister party, the ODS, in the upcoming Czech general election. And then on we went to Warsaw to see the Kaczyñski twins – one of whom was president, the other of whom was leading the new right-wing Eurosceptic party PiS. The twins were absolutely identical and impossible to tell apart – save one had a cat and the other didn't. 'Look out for cat hair,' David said. When David shared a platform with Jarosław Kaczynski, the party leader, Liz moved him slightly to one side of the sign saying PiS. (Tragically, his twin, Lech, the president, died along with half of Poland's ruling elite on a plane crash a few years later.)

We needed more parties from more countries to form a real group in the European Parliament. William's Europe advisor, a fastidious man called Denzil Davidson who has a distinctive badger-like grey streak running through his otherwise dark hair, arrived with his list of candidates, which made for interesting reading. One group apparently took the view that women should not work but stay at home to tend to domestic tasks such as baking bread. 'We're not having them,' I said. But Denzil thought I should be more open-minded, given the limited choice of parties we had.

The European Conservatives and Reformists (ECR) was finally born in 2009. The next question was how to put a stop to what felt like a constant flow of power to Brussels without the consent of the British people.

The European Constitution, which was repackaged as the Treaty of Lisbon in 2007, had been a step-change towards a more federalist approach. It formed the constitutional basis for the European Union, with its own foreign policy and more qualified majority voting. This meant fewer vetoes, and therefore less control, for member states. David wrote for *The Sun* promising a 'cast-iron guarantee of a referendum' on Lisbon under a Conservative government, with one crucial caveat: 'should it be signed but not ratified'. In other words, if Lisbon was already law by the time we got to government, we wouldn't reopen it.

The wording had been toughened up by Andy Coulson. It was significant because it was the first time we offered a referendum on Europe – of any sort. Elsewhere in Europe, it was not unusual for a new treaty to be put to a referendum, most commonly in Ireland and Denmark, but also in France in 2005 to ratify the European Constitution. And perhaps had we done this right from the start, the British people would have felt more in control and less minded to press the nuclear button when they were finally given the chance. Lisbon was ratified before we got to government, so the pledge of a referendum was no longer on the table. But this would come back to bite us.

The Eurosceptics felt betrayed. There was a sense in some quarters that by not reopening the ratification of the Lisbon Treaty, David had dodged the issue – and possibly always would. And now he had no solution on offer to address the apparent flow of power to Brussels without the British public's consent. Soon UKIP was looming in the background, polling second in the European elections in summer 2009.

We mulled things over and decided we needed a more substantial offer on Europe coming into the next general election. In autumn 2009, David announced the 'referendum lock', which guaranteed that the Lisbon episode would never be repeated. Under the policy a British government could only transfer more power to the EU with consent from the British people given through a referendum. And the speech went further than this, talking more broadly about reforming the EU and returning powers to Britain.

With the economy and recovery from the financial crisis taking centre stage, we got through the 2010 general election campaign without talking much about Europe. UKIP did not poll particularly well. Then we found ourselves in government with the most pro-European party in British politics. It did not look like the moment for a radical reshaping of our relationship with the EU. The Lib Dems agreed to our referendum lock as part of the Coalition agreement. Yet there were strong factors in play that would bring Europe back to centre stage – most especially, the ongoing crisis in the Eurozone. The financial crisis was still making its mark, driving the euro countries into further integration as they tried to shore up the single currency.

The euro was never an economic vision; it was a political one. So, each time when it fell ill, Europe's leaders went through the motions of delivering a dose of strict economic medicine – but really, they were coddling it with political will and a lot of German money. Showing, not for the last time, that the Europeans are happy to sacrifice the most economically literate solution in the name of a greater political goal.

When Greece looked like it would fall out of the Eurozone time and time again, pressure piled on Britain to help financially. George dug in his heels and we negotiated our way out of the European Stability Mechanism. We are not part of the Eurozone, so why should we be bailing them out?

AS A NEW PRIME minister, David naturally worked hard to build relationships with fellow European leaders. The German Chancellor was unarguably the most important of these. David liked Angela Merkel, and they spent quite a bit of time together. She was far from a show-pony politician; she was clever, considered, and liked to mull things over, a characteristic that drew her to Obama, who was similarly deliberating. They might have been academics in another life. Over time, she earned the respect of the German people, and the world. She has a personal sparkle too.

She came to Chequers with her husband. They were relaxed and good company, though David took her on a country walk and nearly got her stuck on some barbed wire. Given our differences of opinion on matters European, there could be awkward moments. But she remained our most important relationship in Europe, and David invested a great deal in it – maybe putting too much weight on what she could deliver for him. For she was to let him down badly – once, twice, three times.

Of course, there were other European allies. Nicolas Sarkozy and David bonded over Libya, and pushed through a major Franco-

British defence treaty together, signed at Lancaster House. And we were all excited when the glamorous Carla Bruni visited with her husband. But Sarkozy proved to be a difficult ally to pin down, and the Franco-German axis took precedent, even though it was in one of its cooler stages – Sarkozy and Merkel are worlds apart in personality.

David was particularly fond of his northern colleagues. Sweden's Fredrik Reinfeldt, the Netherlands' Mark Rutte, and Denmark's Helle Thorning-Schmidt were leaders who, like David, took a more pragmatic view of Europe. We tried to develop this cultural alignment into something more substantial. It was Steve Hilton's idea to host a 'northern gathering' each year. The prospect of steam baths and log cabins made it a popular trip as well as a strategic one – though Liz nearly resigned when David joined his colleagues in a canoe, wearing a bright orange life jacket. 'You look a total idiot,' she told him. But David insisted he would do whatever was needed.

Ultimately, while these relationships paid dividends over the years, none of the other leaders faced the same degree of angst over their relationship with the EU at home as did David. The rise of Eurosceptic parties across Europe was still some way off. Though it was coming, even to Germany.

IT IS IN OUR second year in government when the temperature really begins to rise.

In autumn 2011 a petition on the government's e-petition website calling for a referendum on British membership of the EU gets 100,000 signatures, which qualifies it to be debated by Parliament. It soon appears as a motion. We now face a vote and have to decide what to do about it.

There is no easy answer. Supporting the motion is out of the question. There is no mandate for an EU referendum either in our manifesto or the Coalition agreement. Imposing a three-line whip on a popular motion – especially one on Europe – is going to be tricky. We are sure to have a rebellion, making the government look weak. But if we reduce the whip then the MPs of Eurosceptic constituencies have no excuse for not supporting the motion. We could end up facing a bigger rebellion, with the government looking even weaker. We are damned either way.

Later, we learn to ignore these sorts of motions as much as we can. Reduce the whip. Send everyone home and take the heat out of the whole thing. But this time we fall straight into the trap and launch a massive whips' operation – with disastrous consequences. Eighty-one Tory MPs defy the three-line whip – including two parliamentary private secretaries, who have to resign. Our Chief Whip, Patrick McLoughlin, is crestfallen.

During the Coalition, there are a core of about twenty-five Tory MPs who consistently vote against us at every turn. This number often rises to eighty in any Europe-related vote. Many of eighty defied this three-line whip. And they would form the basis for the Leave campaign in the parliamentary party.

The campaign to leave Europe is gathering momentum. At the same time, Europe is feeling poorer – and less stable. In autumn 2011, driven by France and Germany, the Eurozone countries say they want to urgently push through some new fiscal rules to steady their economies, and once again we find ourselves at odds with their objectives. David puts his foot down: you cannot expect Britain – who is out of the euro – to have to abide by new regulations that are designed for shoring it up. Especially where financial services are concerned, as this is such an important part of our economy. Attempts to amend the new proposals or devise an opt-out are ignored.

Coming into the December meeting, David warns that he will have to veto if the European Council continue to push the package through. They pay no attention – perhaps thinking, not for the last time, that David is bluffing.

The drama unfolds in Brussels in the early hours of the morning. Most EU councils don't get really started until well after an alcohol-fuelled dinner. Whether this is a good way to do business is questionable. Our EU team hovers outside, feeding off emails from David, trying to catch a bit of sleep in their chairs whilst they wait for white smoke. In the end, David is left with no choice but to use the veto.

Ultimately, though, it makes no difference whatsoever, as the European Council leaders go ahead with their plans anyway, acting outside the treaty structure which requires British support. It looks a lot like a classic (and well-prepared) Franco–German stitch-up. Merkel does what she had to do to shore up her own position at home. German public opinion is bristling over the cost of constantly bailing out Greece.

This is the first time we were let down by Angela Merkel.

Nick Clegg is very unhappy. He believes David wielded the veto without his final consent. David reminds him that they spoke right up until the council began. He claims to have had Nick's support for the negotiating strategy.

The following week, Nick arrives for the weekly bilateral bruised and brooding, having been screamed at by his party grandees all weekend. David and I watch him licking his wounds on the sofa. From then on, Nick insists that we have a number of his team accompany David to Brussels – presumably to stop David rushing into another veto. David happily agrees. But the opportunity never arises again.

For everyone else, David is the hero of the hour; for once even the *Daily Mail* like him. He returns home covered in glory, though some of his more Europhile officials look down at their feet. 'I warned you David wouldn't put up with any nonsense in Brussels,' I say. I can hardly hear myself think as we stand at the back of the 1922 Committee for the banging of desks from delighted Conservative MPs.

And yet it all feels a bit ominous. For I am sure the victory will be short-lived, knowing as I do the insatiable appetite for all things anti-European in parts of the party. To celebrate this frenzy around the veto misses the point – that Europe is hellbent on going in one direction to prop up its currency, whilst we strive to carve out a different relationship with them. And all this against the backdrop of a strained mandate, and the drumbeat from those in the party who wish to renew. The discomfort intensifies.

This is when the realisation that we couldn't go on like this indefinitely begins to dawn on David. At some point, we will have to call out Britain's place in Europe and ask the British people if they are happy with it.

The case for a referendum on our membership of the EU is built around strong democratic arguments. There is a sense that it is time to renew our mandate with Europe and put to bed an issue that is a growing poison in our national life. The British people have only been asked once, in 1975, about our membership, and the EU then was a very different organization. But the question of the terms of our membership is difficult to address by simply adding it, like something of an adjunct, to a general election manifesto; general elections are fought on a range of issues. And David believes in confronting political demons and trying to resolve them, which means allowing the country to discuss and debate, and then to choose. He is not one to dodge a difficult issue, leaving it to another leader's watch. He also believes there are inherent dangers in not addressing people's concerns: issues which are brushed under the carpet have a way of re-emerging in their own fashion, in politics as in life. There is a strong sense that the referendum is coming, whether we want it to or not.

Then there is the party to consider. The issue of Europe is becoming impossible to ignore. William – who is more pragmatic about these things – thinks we would never be able to keep the party together, marching unified into another election, without a commitment for an in/out referendum. In his quietly determined way, he drives forward the case for the referendum. And had David stood down before calling a referendum, it is hard to imagine any future Tory leader winning a leadership election without committing to one. Then we would likely have had a referendum with a prime minister arguing to leave rather than one arguing to stay.

But there are strong arguments against, voiced most convincingly by George, who believes a referendum is all downside – potentially devastating for our country. Whatever the outcome, he says, it may very well split the party for a generation. It is foolhardy to solve a problem today by creating a bigger one down the line. We must dodge it – keep throwing meat at the Eurosceptics, just enough to keep them from devouring us. We should certainly not have an in/out referendum to save the Conservative Party.

The question of whether to remain in the European Union is of course much bigger than a one-party issue. There is a history of broken promises, of offering referendums and not holding them, on both sides of the political divide. Blair was twice guilty, promising referendums both on the euro and on signing the European Constitution (which morphed into the Lisbon Treaty), but then dropping the pledge. And we followed suit by seemingly offering a referendum on Lisbon, which was ratified before we were in government.

Ironically, it was the most pro-European party, the Lib Dems, who were the first to break cover, offering an in/out referendum in their 2010 manifesto: 'The European Union has evolved significantly since the last public vote on membership over thirty years ago. Liberal Democrats therefore remain committed to an in/out referendum the next time a British government signs up for a fundamental change in the relationship.' They would stick to this line in their 2015 manifesto. Labour would try to match them in their own 2015 manifesto, pledging that 'no powers will be transferred to Brussels without an in/out referendum' – probably with an eye to the growing UKIP vote in their northern heartlands. In the end, all three parties would go into the 2015 election pledging an in/out referendum in one form or another.

UNUSUALLY, IT IS ED who is sent away to write David's speech calling out Europe, which we plan to give at Bloomberg HQ in mid-January 2013. Ed's diary is cleared. 'Why so much time?' I ask, teasing. 'There is only one line that anyone will notice.'

For the most part, it is a measured speech about reform in Europe and renegotiating Britain's terms of membership. The thrust is the three Rs. Renegotiate. Reform. And, only when these two are done, will we ask the British people to decide whether they still want to be members of Europe or not – Referendum. The third and final R.

The speech is delayed as we pour over drafts and 'roll the pitch' – which means preparing the ground in advance by discussing the speech with the senior Cabinet, senior parliamentarians, and key allies. It is amazing the whole thing doesn't leak in advance, so many people are brought in to read it. But we want the party to have a sense of ownership over what David will be saying.

We put together a team to reach out to the business community as soon as the announcement is made, and another to talk to the European capitals. It is a huge operation. The moment David gets up to speak at Bloomberg HQ – the date has finally been set for 23 January – we will fan out to make hundreds of calls.

Afterwards, David is more convinced than ever that we had done the right thing. We have faced up to the big constitutional issue of our time – one that has preoccupied the country for years – and given the British people the chance to make a choice. Most of all, David wants Britain to feel happy in its skin with its relationship with Europe. He has an innate trust of his fellow countrymen and women.

27

SPITZENKANDIDATEN

We are clear: the referendum promise has not been made to appease UKIP. Which is a good thing too, because the Bloomberg speech makes no difference whatsoever to our polling. UKIP continue to gain ground – still polling 13 per cent in April 2013, three months after the announcement.

David famously described UKIP as being full of 'fruitcakes, loonies, and closet racists' in 2006. Over the years, they have had their ups and downs, polling highest at European elections and then falling away at general elections. They began life as a single-issue party but developed into something with a much wider appeal, attracting people across party divides – people who are dissatisfied with the mainstream parties for a variety of reasons. Angry about rising levels of immigration. Angry that they paid a hefty price for a recession caused by rich bankers. Nostalgic for a bygone era. Issues like gay marriage were a popular recruiting agent.

Nigel Farage's leadership of the party gives UKIP a notoriety and personality they lacked in their early days. And although they started by predominately taking votes off us, they begin to attract a strong Labour vote too, especially in the North.

With UKIP polling steadily in the teens, a lot of MPs are becoming nervous of their seats. Some look over their shoulders at UKIP, who seem to say a lot of things they agree with in private. The whole thing is destabilising, especially at the grassroots. It's compounded by a view that we, the 'out-of-touch liberal elite' leadership of the party are at odds with our core, seeing our own activists as 'swivel eyed loons' – an alleged remark by Andrew Feldman which he vehemently denies.

The debate rages about the best strategy to deal with UKIP. Over the years we come under constant pressure to tack right to win back disaffected Tories who are said to be falling under Farage's sway. Instead, we resist the temptation and stand our ground.

And yet it is difficult not to feel uncomfortable as UKIP's vote share rises, and rises – coming close to 30 per cent in some European polls. Whispers of defections rebound round the Commons tea room. We profess in public that we are right to dig in, but sometimes lie awake at night, each of us sharing private doubts with our pillow.

Lynton Crosby brings with him a different perspective: David's colourful language has done huge damage. 'You aren't going to win any voters back if you call them names. You can criticise UKIP the party, but you must respect their supporters. Stop kicking your core.'

We are increasingly nervous coming into the 2014 European elections. 'It's all going to be fine,' says Craig ironically at the 4 p.m. meeting when we get the news: Nick Clegg has challenged Farage to two televised debates. Nick to the rescue! We all know this is going to be a car crash, and David tries to talk him out of it to no avail. Watching him battling it out on television I can't help but respect him for having the guts to take on Farage. But after a while I can't take any more, as his meticulously prepared arguments are swept aside and ridiculed by a merciless Farage, who is brilliantly playing to the gallery. I switch the TV off. A bullfight is a kinder sport.

UKIP win the 2014 European elections, polling nearly 27 per cent of the vote and winning twenty-four MEPs. Luckily for us, our pitiful third place looks good next to the Lib Dems, who are virtually annihilated, losing all but one of their twelve MEPs. It is a bad night for us, but a disastrous one for Nick, who wanders forlornly round his palatial Whitehall office in the following weeks.

Our European woes are far from over for the summer. There is the small matter of who should be the next President of the Commission. This would be important at any time, but it is particularly so as we contemplate a renegotiation on our terms of membership.

David is adamant that he does not want it to be a man called Juncker, who is an unreformed, old-fashioned federalist – a gift to the tabloid press. Jean-Claude Juncker's chief of staff, Martin Selmayr, is almost viciously anti-British. Not since arch-federalist Jacques Delors ran Europe would an appointment be more of an own goal. Especially in the lead-up to a referendum on Europe.

David starts lobbying other leaders to oppose Juncker – in particular Angela Merkel, who is not a huge fan either. They plan to build support around an alternative candidate. With Merkel's heft behind our cause, we feel increasingly confident that Juncker won't make it. Mostly the Germans get what they want in Europe, which is why having Merkel onside matters. And why it matters too, when her support falls away.

Coming into the critical council meeting, the British press are true to form: the job they do on Juncker is absolute and thorough. Juncker is deemed a drunk ('Junck the drunk') with dodgy family links to the Nazis (though to be fair, his father was forcibly conscripted during Germany's occupation of Luxembourg). Juncker is appalled, and complains that his elderly father is more appalled still. It is difficult to explain in a rather awkward conversation why we are not responsible for the *Daily Mail*. There is always a sense amongst foreign leaders that we egg on our press. It took them decades to recover from the infamous *Sun* headline, 'Up Yours Delors'.

Our foreign affairs team at No. 10 are mumbling about some unpronounceable 'process' and sighing, which is not greatly re-assuring. When I finally find someone to translate, it turns out they are right to be worried. The success of the 'right' in the European elections means the presidential nomination favours a right-wing candidate. The process is called *Spitzenkandidaten*. The chosen candidate should reflect the election result. And Juncker is from the right.

David would far prefer an affable socialist over a hard-line, right-wing federalist, but this is not a view shared by his colleagues on the right. As we approach the date for the council, Merkel, under pressure from her party, is also changing her tune. We have underestimated how buffeted she is by her party dynamics, making her a less reliable ally than we had assumed.

Ahead of the council, David calls around to other EU leaders. Everyone has a worst-case candidate in mind – but they are not the same. They all want a right-wing candidate, and there are not many of those. David finds himself high and dry – with not even his northern boating companions, Rutte and Reinfeldt, onside. The last man standing for President of the Commission is the now unstoppable Juncker.

So, a year from our general election, Europe ignores David's pleas and picks a leader to oversee our membership negotiations who David has very publicly implied he can't stand. We're the second biggest economy in Europe, and our requests are being ignored. David is furious. Jean-Claude Juncker symbolises not only our powerlessness in Brussels, but a type of European controller who sits so uneasily with Britain. Worst of all, we have set up a fight against Juncker, a man who just might have been managed better with a bit of stroking.

The appointment darkens the long summer days but is soon forgotten in the busy early autumn weeks. This is an election year, and we have a conference to plan. We gather at Chequers, meeting in the upstairs dining room. This room is always freezing, no matter the weather. I learn to bring a sweater and a large shawl to wrap myself in. David sits next to me wearing his favourite blue short-sleeved polo shirt – opening the windows because he thinks it is stuffy. There is no democracy in the running of the Prime Minister's house.

Lynton is giving a presentation with Stephen Gilbert on the election battleground. There are important strategic decisions to be made. David has threatened to send the next person out who is caught playing with their BlackBerry, so everyone is attentive

– for a while. However, Craig must have his in his lap, because halfway through Stephen's presentation he turns a bit red and says, 'Sorry to interrupt – and I don't know if this is a spoof – but Douglas Carswell has just popped up on my screen. He seems to be in the middle of defecting.'

There is a pause whilst we briefly wonder if Craig is going to get a huge bollocking for breaking the BlackBerry ban. I suggest we go and find a television. We can't get the one in the long gallery to work, so we pile into the small office downstairs where the garden room girls and duty clerk work. There he is – Douglas Carswell sharing a platform with Nigel Farage. He has announced not just that he is defecting, but that he is standing down to fight his seat as the UKIP candidate, offering us the further headache of managing a by-election. During the press conference, UKIP boast that this is just the beginning. A season of defections seems to beckon. This would not be a good start to any political year, let alone one with a general election looming.

I travel back to London in the car with Lynton and Olive. We know this will have a terrible effect on the morale of the MPs. They are already worried enough about UKIP, whose support in their constituencies make them nervous. And a colleague crossing the floor always hurts. Friendships are broken. It's personal. We call Gavin Williamson, our parliamentary private secretary, and arrange to meet as soon as we're all back in Westminster. We need a whips operation in place quickly, to steady the ship. And we also need a candidate to put up against Carswell. Boris? A quick text gives us a firm reply: fuck off.

A few weeks go by and there are no more defections. We focus on organising our pre-election conference and hope for the best.

IT IS THE SATURDAY of conference, always the most challenging day of the year for work/life balance. Every year I make the same mistake, imagining a nice morning with the children before I depart for the best part of a week. The chances of not being interrupted are near to nil. In all likelihood, I will have my phone glued to my ear dealing with some story that has gone pear-shaped in the morning papers.

This Saturday is no different. I was feeling quite sorted (relatively speaking). I had packed, seen the children off. Then my phone bleeps with a news alert: Mark Reckless has defected.

Ed rings as I jump in a cab to Euston. *Shit. This is bad.* And worse than Reckless going is the threat of more still to come. We are contemplating a conference week with a stream of defections, the stability of the party gathering completely undermined. Our credibility on the eve of an election conference – blown apart.

We find Craig on the train, phone to ear. 'Reckless!' we mouth at him, trying to get him to end his call. We need to have a discussion immediately, probably somewhere between the carriages, out of earshot of the numerous journalists and activists on the train.

But Craig is preoccupied with another story. 'Dick pics!' he mouths.

'What did he say?' I ask, looking incredulously at Ed.

We leave Craig to sort out the press frenzy around Brooks Newmark's leaked pictures. Brooks had waited years to be a minister, and then, just two months after his appointment, this.

Ed and I spend the rest of the journey on our phones. Up in Birmingham, we all gather in David's hotel suite in the Hyatt. Michael Gove, Gavin, George, Ed, and I focus on managing the parliamentary party. We make lists of MPs we think could be UKIP material and then allocate the calls out amongst us. These are not easy conversations to have. 'Er, hello – were you thinking of jumping ship?' And will they even tell us the truth? Some are understanding when we ask. Some are furious. You can't really blame them.

With this counter-operation in place, we manage to navigate our way through the week with no more defections. This is helped by the backlash from the party, who unite in their condemnation against such disloyalty.

I breathe a sigh of relief to be back in London. I collapse at home just in time to watch the semi-final of *The Great British Bake Off* with my children, finding the Victoria sponge to have an oddly soothing effect. But although a party meltdown has been averted, we are not out of trouble, with two by-elections to fight against UKIP in the next weeks. These will require a huge amount of resources at a time when we should be gearing up for a general election.

October brings a resounding victory for Carswell in Clacton; November, a lesser though decisive victory for Reckless in Rochester. The party is shaken. We now have two UKIP MPs in Parliament, a year and a half *after* we committed ourselves to an in/out referendum.

The very wearing effect UKIP had on the Conservative Party over this period should not be underestimated. That we prevented it pushing us to the right was thanks to our stubborn political determination, and it turned out to be the correct call, even though it felt pretty uncomfortable at times. We certainly learnt our lesson not to speak disparagingly about the people who supported them. But sticking to our guns did not stop UKIP from making their mark on the political landscape. They ground down the morale of our MPs. They destabilised our core. They kept Europe in the limelight. And they ensured other, related issues came to the forefront of public debate.

One of those was immigration.

IMMIGRATION IS ONE OF those uncomfortable issues which politicians have often liked to shy away from. But we know we need to find a way to have a grown-up discussion about it. Ideally, in a way that takes into account the economic necessity of immigration – filling vital jobs across a wide range of jobs in our economy, especially in the NHS – but also addresses the fact that the British public understandably want to feel they have control over the numbers of people who come into their country.

When David said on *The Andrew Marr Show* in January 2010 that he would like to see net immigration fall to the tens of thousands from the hundreds of thousands, it seemed like a reasonable objective. Immigration figures are divided into two main clumps: non-EU and intra-EU. The government has control, in principle, over non-EU migration, but it was clearly finding this number difficult to manage – or at times, had not tried to. Then there is intra-EU immigration, where there are no limits at all. This emanates from the 'freedom of movement of labour', one of the core four freedoms that lie at the heart of the single market, along with freedom of movement of goods, capital, and services. Experience so far had shown European immigration tended to ebb and flow, creating a natural stream of workers. For the most part, the EU figures were not the problem.

David is steadfast in his promise to exert some sort of control over immigration after the free-fall of the Labour years. As Prime Minister, he is determined to deliver, waging a war against bogus colleges, forced marriages, and lax visa rules. He finds a keen ally in his new Home Secretary, Theresa May.

An immigration target seems a sensible way to offer reassurance, whilst also maintaining our commitment to the EU. But this target would soon come to haunt us. As we fail to reach it year after year, there is a growing sense of us being less, not more, in control of our country's borders. And the more we talk about our missed targets, the more we feed into a narrative that immigration is a bad thing.

Just as we are starting to get non-EU levels of migration under some sort of control in government, intra-EU migration takes off, especially in the second half of the Parliament. This is largely thanks to the fact that our economy is bursting back to life whilst the Eurozone is limping from crisis to crisis, with disturbingly high levels of unemployment, especially amongst the young. Britain looks like a safe bet for a job – and if you can't get one, there is a generous benefits system to plug into, which, for the most part, is not based on the number of years worked. Unlike in the rest of Europe, our benefits system is non-contributory.

Our immigration target seems further and further beyond our

reach. Amongst our team, a division opens between those who believe immigration is a force for good – so why not be bold and say so (and drop the target) – and those who believe we must address growing anxieties around the rising numbers and the uncomfortable questions being raised – including crowding out on jobs, sluggish wages, and strains on some community services.

Underlying all of this is a sense that hard-working people have taken the brunt of the financial crisis and are the last to be feeling the benefits of the recovery. That the political class is not listening – and in some cases patronising them. There is a growing feeling of political alienation amongst the public.

Perhaps we missed our moment to steer the conversation. Had we focused less on picking up the pieces of Labour's open-door policy, we might have spent more time building a progressive argument around immigration, as we had on welfare and schools, right from the start of David's leadership. We might have been able to encourage a national debate about what is both tough but fair – a debate that embodied the British values of generosity, kindness, and tolerance. We might have instilled in this debate our pragmatism about what would be best for our economy. And showed that there is truth to both sides of the argument – that immigration can bring enormous benefits, but also raises problems that need to be addressed.

David faces the growing unease in his 2014 conference speech. 'We know the bigger issue today is migration from within the EU. Immediate access to our welfare system. Paying benefits to families back home. Employment agencies signing people up from overseas and not recruiting here. Numbers that have increased faster than we in this country wanted . . . at a level that was too much for our communities, for our labour markets,' he says. 'All this has to change – and it will be at the very heart of my renegotiation strategy for Europe . . . I will go to Brussels, I will not take no for an answer, and when it comes to free movement – I will get what Britain needs.'

The grassroots seem happy. But as members of the EU, we

cannot exert control over intra-EU migration. What can we feasibly do? We set to work.

First, we look at the so-called 'pull' factors, trying to find ways to make Britain less of a honey pot for large flows of European immigrants. We try to make it fairer to UK citizens by stopping people being able to claim in-work benefits such as tax credits until they have lived and worked in the UK for four years. But the crunch issue is whether to have a cap of some sort, or an 'emergency brake', for when the numbers seem overwhelming. We somehow doubt that the European 'founding fathers' envisioned the sort of mass exodus of young people we are seeing, which causes havoc in the host country as well as devastation in the home country. It must surely make sense that a nation-state can sometimes say 'Sorry, we need a pause – for now'. An annual limit of some sort, which is reviewed each year.

This is where David wants to head. And it is over this ground where we now clash with the EU, whose attachment to the four fundamental freedoms, including that of free movement of people, is almost a religion. We are once again at loggerheads. British pragmatism vs. European idealism.

We pencil in a day for early November 2014 to make a speech on immigration, and the latest draft is sent round with the emergency brake in the text – at which point, all hell breaks out. An emergency meeting about the emergency brake is called. It's tense. The Euro-pragmatists argue that the policy floated in the speech will never be accepted in Europe, so why ask for it? David will lose all credibility. Water this down, and you're going to shoot yourself in the foot, warn the likes of Olive Dowden. Ratchet this up, and you'll regret it abroad, the other side responds. We need to try to build a consensus but can't seem to find the common ground amongst ourselves. An initial talk with Angela Merkel is disappointing too. She is largely unsympathetic. Germany has a falling population, after all.

'We're making the speech this Friday, no ifs, ands or buts,' announces David at the 8.30 meeting on Monday, 24 November.

'We haven't sorted the policy yet,' Ed says.

'You've got till Friday,' says David.

We still have the emergency brake in the speech. Many of the Cabinet have seen the draft with it in. But now Tom Scholar, Ivan Rogers, and Ed are talking to their 'oppos' – their opposite numbers in European governments. They are more sure than ever: this will never get through. More importantly, Merkel is against it and some of our team question whether the idea will work in practice. At the last minute, the emergency brake is removed from the speech, but David adds a line warning that he has not finished with this issue. 'If our concerns [about freedom of movement] fall on deaf ears . . . then of course, I rule nothing out,' he tells an audience gathered at JCB's factory in Staffordshire.

We seem to have settled for the worst of both worlds. We have ratcheted up the argument and watered down the offer.

With summer 2015, the climate gets more toxic, as well as tragic. The horrifying image of a small Syrian boy with a red shirt washed up on a beach shakes us to the core. Refugees are risking their lives and those of their children, piling into overcrowded boats in search of a better life in Europe. Day after day, they are making the journey, barely afloat, not always succeeding. The Mediterranean – once associated with relaxing, sun-kissed beach holidays – has become a scene of death and despair.

And no one has bargained on Merkel's next move, which intensifies things still further. Driven by compassion, and possibly her own experiences having come from East Germany, she opens Germany's doors to Syrian asylum seekers – suspending the 1990 protocol which forces refugees to seek asylum in the first European country in which they set foot. With this executive decision, she welcomes another million refugees to her country – numbers that seem to surprise everyone, including the Chancellor. Pressure mounts. Things feel like they are spinning out of control. Europe is reeling from a refugee crisis it cannot even begin to get its head round. Schengen countries shut their borders; the Hungarians are building a fence. Meanwhile, Brussels looks on – seemingly unresponsive. The refugee crisis and our own immigration issues are conflated in most people's minds, building up more pressure.

Our target to see annual net immigration fall to the tens of thousands looks increasingly unrealistic. Coming into the 2015 general election, George tries to persuade David to drop it, but David insists: we will keep the target.

28

STARTING GUN

Summer 2015. A new Tory dawn, and an unexpected one at that. We have promised to renegotiate Britain's membership of the EU and then hold a referendum before the end of 2017, and now we have to decide exactly when it is going to be. We have time on our side – but not that much. There are external issues at play, which affect the date for doing the renegotiation, like the French elections (in April/May 2017) and the German elections (September 2017). During the run-up to these contests, the two pairs of eyes that matter most will be looking elsewhere.

For David, the sooner he holds the referendum, the sooner he can turn to other things. Leave it, he thinks, and the landscape of his second term will be entirely dominated by Europe. Off the back of our election victory he feels in step with the country. George, though still uncomfortable with the whole idea, sees the attraction of an early vote for different reasons. He is worried the economy might turn against us if we wait, and that the government at mid-term might, as history predicts, be more unpopular. And there is that other, more personal reason. An early referendum would give him time to rebuild his relationship with the party membership, who are 80 per cent for 'Brexit', before he takes his own shot at the leadership, after David stands down.

Most of all, the timing is dictated by when we think we are most likely to win. Sitting on a strong economy and a clear election victory, we wonder if that moment might just be now.

As usual we argue furiously amongst ourselves. In the end, David and George decide over a curry in St James's. The lightness of summer and a beguiling victory entices them back to the battlefield. They are both at the top of their game.

However, I sense the beginning of a friction between our teams – something that has not been present before. After his election victory, David has morphed into a sort of king, looking affectionately at George – his bumptious, ambitious heir apparent. There's a feeling that George's team think they are the future whilst the No. 10 team are the past. They fight over column inches. At the party conference George is adulated, which amuses David and me, but others in No. 10 are less sanguine.

And it's not just friction between Nos. 10 and 11. Straight after David delivers his conference speech, Boris follows David and me to the lift, begging us not to give way to George on the third runway at Heathrow. Boris sees everything through the prism of how George plans to torture him next. This is all great fun for the media who – thanks to David's announcement that he will not run again – see they have a full-blown beauty contest on their hands. George vs. Boris vs. May. They have years to build them up and pull them down again. What fun it will be.

SO, AN EARLY REFERENDUM has been decided, but as yet no date has been announced, as we have to get cracking with the first R: Renegotiation.

The negotiations to deliver a new deal for Britain in Europe engulf all and everything – including my diary, which fills up with meetings. The most important of these is a weekly session, chaired by George, in the No. 11 dining room, where we thrash out what will form the guts of the package. We must make choices about what we want – and what we think we can get. Every choice is underpinned by whether it will deliver enough to persuade the British people to renew their mandate with the European Union.

The dining room is filled with members of the senior teams from both No. 10 and the Treasury, along with the chief European negotiators – Ivan Rogers and Tom Scholar, as well as Jeremy Heywood. There is a huge amount to cover. The political side ask for more, trying to extract the most appealing offer; the Euro pragmatists push back with an eye on what the Europeans might agree. It's a push-me-pull-me process. Ivan sits at the far end of the table, with the political team at the other. I sit in the middle, opposite George, as if by a geographical force we can manoeuvre the opposing sides into some sort of reasonable place. And George is a dexterous chairman. Tough but pragmatic.

We try to organise our thoughts around what a new deal for Britain would look like. Top of the agenda is the economy. We want to keep our lead in financial services whilst steering clear of the stuff we don't want to do, which is aimed at shoring up the euro. We want to maximise the benefits of trading in the single market – a huge free trade area of 550 million people – which means protecting jobs, aggressively promoting our competitiveness agenda, and pushing back on unnecessary regulation. Then there are issues around sovereignty: our national power versus Europe's. We want to shift more power from Europe to Westminster and other national parliaments. And we want to be the first EU country not to pursue 'ever closer union' – in other words, to openly and officially say that we do not share the common goal to create a 'United States of Europe'.

And really, we are building on a special status that others have worked hard to achieve before us, from Thatcher's budget rebate to later opt-outs from the euro and Schengen Area. Bit by bit, over time, Britain has carved out a distinct niche for itself in Europe. Now we want to encapsulate this in a different type of membership. One that does not aim to create a federal state.

But just as we are attempting to reinforce our special status in Europe, Europe are driving towards further integration, propelled by the necessity of supporting their wobbly common currency. We are poles apart.

Then there is the question of immigration – again. We take another look at the factors that make Britain such an attractive destination for people across Europe. We come back to the policies set out in our manifesto that intra-EU migrants who want to claim British tax credits and child benefit must have lived here, and contributed to our country's system, for a minimum of four years. We also want them to leave the country after six months if they haven't found a job.

And once more, we return to the vexed issue of whether or not to have an emergency brake on immigration from Europe. We get another firm set of 'nos' from our officials. The view over the Channel is that David Cameron is going to win this referendum – and so they are not going to budge an inch more than they have to in order to help him. Once more, they consider our call for help on immigration a giant bluff.

The negotiation begins to take form. The clock is ticking. The idea is for David to test the water with other leaders by outlining his 'asks' in time for the December council, at the very latest, and then to secure the deal at the council after that. We are all well aware that if we miss the winter councils, then the referendum may have to be pushed back by months. We need a proper lead time to run an effective referendum campaign, and we cannot possibly hold the vote in the middle of the summer holidays. If we wait until the autumn we'll smash straight into party conference season, with the difficult conversations that are bound to go on within the party hijacking the agenda. It will be 'Tory Party at War – the Musical', in full glare of the media. And with every day, there are more disturbing reports of the boats crossing the Mediterranean. This too will have an impact.

David outlines his plans for a new settlement to the Cabinet. The 'asks' fall into 'four buckets', as he likes to think of them: financial protection, competitiveness, more powers for Parliament (in particular exempting Britain from 'ever closer union'), and restrictions on intra-EU immigration. A letter is duly sent to Donald Tusk, the President of the European Council, which will be discussed at the December meeting.

David hopes to achieve a 'new deal' for Britain and, off the back of it, recommend to the British people that we remain in the EU. But he is careful to say that if he doesn't get what he wants, he may have to make another recommendation. The Cabinet is still united behind this policy at this point – to renegotiate Britain's relationship in Europe first, and to hold an in/out referendum afterwards. The decision on whether we come down for staying or leaving depends on the outcome of the renegotiation. Even well-known 'outers' like IDS are not expected to say publicly what side they will take, until we know the outcome.

It is still undecided whether or not, when the time comes, there will be a free vote, allowing all MPs including the Cabinet to choose which side they support in the referendum. There are strong arguments on either side. Those who favour a free vote (David, me, others) do so mostly because we believe the referendum should, in part, be a cathartic exercise for the nation and the party. Have a fair fight and the issue can be laid to rest for generations, and we can regroup as a party afterwards. Hobble the horse and the issue will remain an open sore. And there is a practical argument about how even to achieve a three-line whip on the question. There will definitely be Cabinet and other ministerial resignations if they are not allowed to campaign as they wish. Then, there would be a danger of the government looking a shambles.

George disagrees. He thinks a free vote enables and therefore encourages people who would otherwise stay loyal to the leadership to take the opposite side. It could become a test of Tory 'virility' to vote Brexit. If you whip the referendum, of course there will be resignations – but in the end, not as many as you think. Surely this is more advisable than allowing the party to divide down the middle. He strongly believes a free vote is the wrong call.

We decide to put off the decision on a free vote, aware that if we leave it too long, we may be pushed into one.

In the meantime, the Eurosceptics are busy working on a 'Leave' campaign. We are totally hamstrung because we cannot be seen to take sides. In theory, we are committed to both options – remain or leave – until we know the outcome of the renegotiations.

But someone needs make a start with a 'Remain' campaign. If it cannot be us, then who? The Remain campaign begins to take form, mostly driven by the old Blairite faction of the Labour Party, led by Peter Mandelson. This puts it at odds with the new Corbyn leadership, and creates a dilemma for us. Is this a campaign we will join at a later point? It is cross-party, but it's also full of people we don't normally do business with. Should we instead form an entirely separate operation when the time comes?

Every day, we head slowly and cautiously into the storm that lies ahead. And then we are hit with a significant personal loss.

Chris Martin, David's senior official at No. 10, has been battling with cancer for the last two years. He had determinedly worked through the chemo with extraordinary bravery. Work is hope for Chris. By summer 2014, the treatment behind him, he was beginning to enjoy life again. But this is to be short-lived. The cancer returns, if it had indeed ever left. But Chris is still positive, and determined to enjoy life to its full until the end.

He sets off with the Camerons for the annual weekend at Balmoral accompanied by his new girlfriend, Zoe Conway. The Monday of his return, feeling a little unwell, he leaves work early to check in with his doctors. He never comes back.

Chris was a charming, clever, and well-loved man. He thrived in his No. 10 role and was devoted to David. Above all, he was a highly professional civil servant who believed it was his duty to serve Queen and country, which for Chris meant doing the Prime Minister's 'intent' to the best of his ability. He loved to make 'the System' work, and had particular reverence for the intelligence community, which we called the 'deep state'.

One of the last time I see him is with David, in Chris's flat in Islington. Over a cup of tea we chat over things in a relaxed, everyday fashion, as if we have years of friendship in front of us, but all knowing in our hearts that we have come to say farewell.

In late November, Chris dies. He is just 42 years old. A few weeks before he had married the wonderful Zoe, who rings me to break the sad news. It is a Wednesday morning, and David has

left for the House of Commons ahead of PMQs. We are all shattered, but we gather our strength and fan out to share the news
as best we can with the rest of 'the House'. I wander from room
to room, hugging friends and comforting colleagues. David races
back from the Commons to address his devastated staff. His words
of sadness and love for Chris fill the room. I cannot bear to look
up at him, for I know he too is crying.

A saddened David returns to the Commons and gives a personal
tribute to Chris. Alluding to *Yes Minister*, he says, 'I have lost my
Bernard today.'

No. 10 goes into mourning. Chris's funeral is an amazing tribute
to him. Andrew Parker, Director General of MI5, gives the address.
The church is packed full of senior officials and politicians. As we
kneel in our pews it feels as if the deep state is truly at prayer.
Chris would have approved.

29

BATTLE LINES

We collapse into Christmas. We all need a break, especially David – the months ahead are going to be tough. Normally the Camerons are in Dean for the New Year, preferring the informality of their own house and the company of nearby friends. But this year they choose to stay at Chequers, and ask the Goves to join them. Which is good, I think. They must finally have put their differences behind them.

The main thing that comes out of this New Year gathering is that Michael is going to do the 'right thing' on Europe, says David, when I catch up with him after the break. Really? I ask. David nods. Sarah Vine says it will be fine.

I am relieved. We need our closest and most talented allies around us at this time. Michael may not be a fan of the European Union but he is above all a loyalist and an ultra moderniser, who had urged David against holding the referendum in the first place.

On our first day back in the office, Ed and I both have a missed call from Chris Grayling. We look at each other, smelling a large rat. 'Let's not jump to conclusions,' says Ed, and rings him back. Chris Grayling wants an urgent word with the PM. Never a good sign.

Just as we suspect, Chris wants to resign – to fight for Leave. Our sense is that he has mused over his career during the Christmas break and decided (rightly) that it's not going in an upward trajectory. There will certainly be a reshuffle after the referendum. And his calculation is that in making himself the senior 'outer', he will be near impossible to leave out of a post-referendum Cabinet, which will need to be balanced between Leave and Remain supporters as we try to heal party rifts. It is clever thinking from him. But there is a flaw. We have decided, on balance, to go for a free vote, so he is going to look a bit foolish resigning for nothing.

Pulling Chris Grayling back from the brink is difficult – like stopping a JCB digger heading over a field. But he sees the sense in our argument and says he will come to a decision as he goes out to walk about St James's Park. We gather in David's office. Though we had all but decided on a free vote, if Grayling stays on this basis, we are now stuck with it. But George still thinks it is a mistake . . . A text comes from Chris: he's in. David announces on 5 January that the party will have a free vote.

Chris Grayling isn't the only person who has been musing over the Christmas break. In his wakeful moments in the early hours, David has come to the conclusion that our immigration ask is not strong enough. He wants to go round the houses one last time.

David, George, Theresa, Philip Hammond, Ed, Craig, Jeremy Heywood, Tom Scholar, and I sit round the enormous mahogany table in David's office in the House of Commons. The room is nearly large enough to hold a full Cabinet. It's not a very cosy place; the most elaborate of Pugin wallpaper is hung alongside dark wooden panelling. There is a more comfortable annex, with a few sofas and a television, where we watch PMQs each week as the press team wage their silent Twitter battles for public opinion. In another life, Churchill used this space as a bedroom.

'This is an informal meeting,' says David, the Pugin wallpaper notwithstanding. He wants to make sure we haven't missed our chance to get this absolutely right. We are already pursuing a set of Home Office asks, but should we be asking for more in the renegotiation, specifically on immigration?

Round the table we go, confessional-style. It is a strange division. In a rare moment I find myself agreeing with Theresa. Our proposals on immigration are constructive – but however worthy, they feel more like tinkering than topline stuff. I am with David (and Theresa): we should go back to the idea of an emergency brake of some sort. But the others push back. Whether we are right or not, we haven't a cat's chance in hell of getting it, they say. This is not a realpolitik solution.

Realpolitik wins the day.

THE JANUARY COUNCIL OF the European Union is hijacked by the Syrian refugee crisis, and so the British renegotiation is moved back to February.

If a deal is reached, it will mark the start of the referendum campaign. The week itself will require careful choreographing. We should have the nation's attention, and must make the most of it.

There goes half-term, I think gloomily, looking at the council dates, which sit right bang in the middle of it. This was time I'd planned to spend with my children, who have had nearly a year of missed holidays since the 2015 general election. Another year, another poll, taking its toll on family life.

We are confronted with the full realisation that we have set ourselves an enormous challenge in having to pivot immediately from negotiating for change in Europe into arguing for Britain to stay in. After decades of battling with Europe, is it going to be too much of a stretch to turn around in a day and say, 'It's all for the best'?

Craig's plan is to give the deal its moment in the sun, but then move on as swiftly as possible to the bigger arguments around why we should stay in the EU. He thinks that no deal, however good, will be well received by the sceptical British press. But his media plan is blown apart by Tusk, who releases a draft negotiation package two weeks ahead of the council itself. Two weeks for the press to savage it. Two weeks for the other European leaders to try to water it down. Two weeks for our MPs to get jumpy. We feel on the back foot.

We turn to trying to work out how the MPs are likely to divide. Gavin Williamson is our lead on this, working with Nick Herbert (who heads up the Conservatives Party's campaign for Remain) and Ed and me. George takes charge of Priti Patel, Sajid Javid, and Liz Truss. David is man-marking Michael and Boris. All initial signs show Boris as being pretty supportive.

Boris made his name as a younger man feeding the nation a daily dose of euro-bashing pieces while writing for the *Telegraph* in Brussels. He has always been a critic of the EU, but also a strong European. The grit in the oyster – but very much at home in the oyster. His family, with whom he is very close, are passionately pro-European. His father, Stanley, was an MEP; his sister and brothers are mostly pro-Europe and pro-immigration. Now that Boris is coming near to the end of his mayoralty, he is interested in doing a job in government. So, David is dangling a 'senior' Cabinet role. We talk quite a lot about what this should be – Defence probably. George thinks this will simply be a showcase for him: all uniforms and no tough decisions. 'What about Health?' he jokes.

All the signs show Michael is going the other way. Texts, calls, and suggested family dinners are just making him clam up. In a difficult meeting with David and George in David's flat, Michael seems to be heading for one of his 'infarctions', as his wife is fond of calling them – a sort of intellectual, emotional paralysis brought on by stressful situations. We are all increasingly worried about him as the council looms. A few days before, I send him a text: 'This has got to be your choice Michael – but promise whatever you do – you'll tell Dave your decision first.'

I know Michael, and above all, he is a polite and honourable person.

THE LARGER THAN USUAL team are nervous as they head off for the European Council, aware that history is watching them. I volunteer to head up the 'home' team. We know that David will need to address Cabinet as soon as he returns, and we discuss whether to convene a special Cabinet on Friday or even Saturday morning. 'Weekend Cabinets are for war', says David. But we are concerned. Once the renegotiation is done, that's the end of collective responsibility. So, if Cabinet doesn't meet until Monday, the worry is that everyone will declare themselves for either Leave or Remain on the weekend news programmes, and that will become the story. We will have lost control of the narrative from the beginning. We will not have had a moment of unity before the starting gun is fired.

I am working away in No. 10, anxiously waiting for news from Brussels. Word comes through to quickly line up Cabinet for Friday afternoon. Then there is a delay, and we have to stand everyone down. I finally head home late to await further instructions.

Ed texts just before the 10 o'clock news. A deal has been struck. We have delivered most of what we wanted from the 'four buckets', including financial protection for countries outside the Eurozone and commitments towards delivering a more competitive Europe. On migration, a brake on in-work benefits for EU citizens working in the UK, as well as child benefit payments indexed to the cost of living for children living outside the UK has been agreed. And we have a pledge that 'Britain will never be part of a European super state' – namely, no 'ever closer union' for us. Together, these agreements entrench Britain's special status within the European Union.

There is a mad rush to get David's press conference started, so his words can be carried live into the ten o'clock broadcasts. I switch on the television to see him speaking from Brussels: 'That is why I will be campaigning with all my heart and soul to persuade the British people to remain in the reformed European Union that we have secured today.' The race has begun.

I am about to turn the TV off and then, just at the end of the package, comes more news: Michael Gove has just announced that he is supporting Leave. No warning – no text to me, David, or George. *Splat* – a spoiler, right into David's big moment, his first chance to stamp a mark on his 'new deal' and make the case for Britain staying in Europe. It is the worst, most damaging time for this announcement.

Later, Michael's friends tell me they believe it was a malicious leak from Craig to embarrass Michael. Which is curious, because I am pretty certain this is not true. Not because Craig doesn't leak stuff – of course he does, he is head of comms! – but because it would be entirely against our interests to leak this story at such a time. I can only assume that someone has spun this line to Michael, possibly to cover up their own actions. Whatever the truth, the damage is done. Both sides feel undermined and hurt.

WE ARE BACK IN the office early the next morning, getting ready for a ten o'clock Cabinet. David's script is written. Loyal allies are in place. The tone is always set by the first interventions, so it is important to call on supportive members first. David is pleased with the outcome of the council, but clearly nervous. We do not know exactly how the Cabinet will divide. And Michael's announcement has unnerved him.

I sit behind David, between Simon Case, Chris Martin's successor, and Ed. I glance over at Michael, who is studiously looking down at his papers, and wonder how he is feeling this morning. The meeting begins in hushed silence as David outlines the conclusions of the agreement. Based on his renegotiation, he now makes the case for Britain staying in a reformed EU, arguing that this gives Britain the best of both worlds. The Cabinet pile in. Each and every member speaks, which takes just over two hours. All praise David's leadership and congratulate him on his deal. Most row in behind him – but some don't, declaring long-held views that Britain should leave the EU, deal or no deal. Six out of the twenty-four declare for Leave. There are no surprises (apart from Michael): IDS, Chris Grayling, Theresa Villiers, Priti Patel, John Whittingdale.

David thanks everyone for the constructive and respectful nature of the meeting, and asks that the tone be taken into the battle ahead. There is real hope that we will finally lay these divisions to rest after a fair and honest campaign.

As I leave the Cabinet room I see the six Leave ministers have gathered outside. 'Are we going ahead with the plan?' I hear one ask, and they scuttle off together. An hour later they launch their campaign, holding a poster for Leave. It comes as a shock. Suddenly we are split, campaigning openly against each other.

David goes outside the door of No. 10 to make a statement proposing Thursday, 23 June as the referendum date. 'The choice is in your hands,' he tells the country. The House of Commons vote overwhelming to hold the referendum by 544 to 53. On the issue itself, the Tory MPs divide: 185 for Remain to 138 for Leave. It is closer than we would have liked. The other parties are more united, with the entire SNP, all the Lib Dems, and all but ten Labour MPs supporting Remain.

Michael's decision is a massive blow to David – both profession-ally and personally. Even though we try to persuade him that Michael is an adult politician who has to be left to follow his beliefs, he cannot get away from the very deep sense of personal betrayal. Over the decade that David has led the party, he has been supported by and supportive to a few close friends who he trusts and respects. They have risen with him. Yes, they might have done well enough with someone else, but they happened to have done well with him. No one else – other than George – could have landed him such a blow as Michael Gove.

Perhaps it is naive of David to think that Michael, who was always anti-EU, would be prepared to sacrifice his political beliefs for personal loyalty. But then David believed Michael had committed, in private, to just that.

The sense of betrayal intensifies over the weeks that follow. Some of it is the tone of the campaign. Some is more personal. Mutual friends whisper in David's ear that this is a well thought-through act of revenge. That the Goves have never forgiven him for the Chief Whip affair. That all the dinners, weekends, and shared school runs since then have meant nothing. That they have been like a brood of cuckoos in the Cameron family nest. This is very unhelpful for everyone. I try as much as possible to shut the chatter down.

Michael's leaving is also a big professional headache for us. He gives the Leave campaign huge intellectual credibility and a vocal leadership; he is a powerful persuader. But the campaign still lacks a leader with wider popular appeal. This is what they seek from Boris.

But Boris is more in our camp than theirs. His regular text exchanges with David are reassuring – until suddenly they are less so. Coming into decision time, Boris seems to be revolving like a hotel lobby door. We are aware that Boris is talking to Michael – and a picture comes out of the Goves and the Johnsons having dinner, which lingers.

Boris is weighing up his beliefs on Europe and his desire to lead the party, trying to calculate how they come together to best promote his interests going forward. It is impossible to say what Boris really believes about Europe. Of one thing I am certain: that Boris is convinced that, had he been prime minister, his bravado would have delivered a better deal for Britain than David has done.

At heart, I believe Boris is more for staying and pushing for reform in Europe than for leaving. It is the leadership issue that complicates matters for him. Less than a year ago, poised to take his chance at the leadership after what looked increasingly like a career-ending election for David, Boris was sorely disappointed by David's unexpected victory. A bruised Boris was banished into exile, and teased by his adversary, George, who has been hailed as the coming man. Now Boris has a unique chance to rebalance the scales in his favour. And it is just too tempting.

Opting for Leave looks like a win–win for him. They win – and David resigns, with Boris the hero of the day. They lose – and he is still the hero of the day to the party whose membership is 80 per cent for Leave. This will give him the advantage over George. And he won't have the added problem of needing to sort out Brexit. We wonder often if this was not Boris's preferred outcome – that we win the referendum and he wins the leadership. Crucially, had David never said that he would not stand again, Boris might have had more incentive to row in behind him. The thought of five more years and possibly a third election under David – with Boris exiled to the wilderness – might just have swung the balance.

Boris tells us he plans to make his decision in time for the publication of his regular Monday column in the *Telegraph*. He starts drafting over the weekend following the announcement of the referendum date – one version for Remain, another for Leave. He and David are in touch throughout. And then – *Bleep* – Sunday afternoon the news hits our phones. Boris is gone.

Where once we faced IDS and Chris Grayling, now we have Michael and Boris to contend with. It is a whole different ball game.

But although Boris's decision is a huge professional blow for David, it is not the personal one that Michael's was. Boris was always a friend, but Michael a very close one.

Against the febrile background of a European referendum campaign we head into the 2016 Budget. With IDS leading the charge for Britain to leave the EU, we are wary of touching welfare again, but in an early bilateral George says IDS has volunteered to make changes to PIP – the Personal Independence Payment. This is the replacement for the disability living allowance, and it has had some teething problems. Some of the 'gateways' are not quite right, making the new system even more expensive than the last. IDS says he wants to adjust it – carefully. It sounds too good to be true.

George announces it as part of his budget speech and soon meets a barrage of opposition from the MPs. He asks IDS for help; it is his policy and his idea, after all. Instead, IDS resigns, landing the whole thing in George's lap. And once again we face an unravelling Budget and a high-level resignation.

WHERE DOES THERESA MAY stand in all of this?

David asks her, politely, as they eye each other up from opposite sides of the den. She sits very still and straight, allowing the question mark to hang awkwardly in the air, with no apparent embarrassment. It seems she hasn't made up her mind yet. This goes on for weeks. When finally she opts for Remain, it's because she believes it is marginally the better option.

Once declared, we can't get her to engage with the campaign, save making one speech in which she takes great care to spell out that she thinks both sides have a point. It is interesting that on the most pressing issue of our time, Theresa seems to have no particularly strong view, either way. She chooses instead to sit out the campaign on the fence – which turns out to be a brilliant strategic move – while George, the so-called ruthless strategist, commits political kamikaze for his beliefs, and for the team.

Michael has told George that he decided to go with Leave because he could not go against his own beliefs, but he plans to be as passive as possible during the campaign. This way he will protect his integrity and his personal loyalties. But this is not actually what happens. Michael is, in fact, placed in charge of the campaign.

At a drinks party a few weeks later, out of the corner of my eye I see Sarah Vine making her way towards me. She suggests we go outside to have a chat. I brace myself. Sarah is always so compelling. Even if you profoundly disagree with her, she has a way of wrapping her narrative round you like the coils of a python, until the way of least resistance (her way) seems the only sensible option.

She says that David and Samantha are not acting like grown-ups. This is not personal; it's politics. Let's put all the hurt to one side and have a huge argument and make up over dinner. She wants me to broker this rapprochement, of course. I promise that I will talk to the Camerons.

Which I do.

Only my efforts are made futile by the Sunday papers, which carry an open letter from Michael to David, saying he is undermining public trust in politicians. It is a deeply personal attack – the sort we would have thought twice about before deploying it against even an opposition party leader. David is furious and still more hurt.

The starting gun to the campaign has been fired against the

ominous background of shattered friendships and collapsed loyalty. We now have the intellectual force of Michael Gove and the undeniable though unpredictable charm of Boris Johnson against us, along with a larger-than-hoped-for proportion of the parliamentary party. The Tory family is split – though just for a while, we hope, whilst we lay the issue of Europe to rest, once and for all, so that we all can move on.

30

THERE IS MORE
THAT UNITES US

Less than a year after the general election, and less than two after the Scottish referendum, we find ourselves preparing for yet another seminal poll. Same planning. Same meetings. Same preparation for 'purdah', when we must relinquish our official roles at No. 10 if we wish to take up positions on the referendum campaign. And though the No. 10 team are on top of our game – we have just won a general election, after all – there is a fatigue. A sense that, less than a year ago, we all put our lives on hold to go out and convince the British people that our vision for the country is the right one, and that we have not had the time to recover or rebuild.

The official Remain campaign – now called Britain Stronger in Europe – is quartered along the river at Tower Hill. This cross-party team, which we will join up with when the campaign proper begins on 15 April, tend towards collective and collaborative decisions, making it less agile than it otherwise might be. This is a handicap against Leave, who are a small unit of guerrilla warriors.

Craig has been talking about the referendum debates since the New Year. 'You might not want to discuss them, but they're inevitable,' he says.

The negotiations around the TV debate make those for the 2015 election look like child's play. There are so many moving parts. Devolved leaders who want a say. Tory, Lib Dem, and Labour leaders who each feel only they speak for their supporters. Farage challenging Michael and Boris to be the voice of Leave. Large egos competing for floor space. Our nation's future is on trial. The stakes could not be higher.

David is adamant that he will not debate against someone from his own party. Facing Michael or Boris would look too much like Tory wars. This is damage limitation. We aim to win the referendum without destroying the party in the process.

We finally agree the format. This time there will be no debates at all for David, but a series of interviews and question times with a live TV audience. 'Do we need Bill?' Yes, definitely.

'I thought I sorted you guys for the next five years,' Bill says when he arrives. We give him a studied look and get down to work, briefing him, as we did before, on our strategy, working through the messaging. Our argument is around the simple belief that we think people will be safer and better off in Europe.

At the end of a long day Bill takes me aside. 'I gotta be honest with you . . . You're never going to win this one unless you have an emotional argument for Remain. And you've gotta have a better answer on immigration.' Of course, Bill has zoomed in straight away on our two core problems – problems we never resolve.

The emotions for staying are bound in with a vision for our country of free trade, of tolerance, of embracing the world. Of accepting that multinational relationships can be trying but are worth it. But this is a practical, hard-headed argument by those of us who think staying in Europe is the better option for our country and the people who inhabit it, by making us better off and safer. It is not a very emotive one. No one is pretending the EU is a perfect institution. Quite the opposite. We have spent many years arguing how we would like it to change. Arguing for reform. Securing our special status.

Essentially, we are stuck arguing for a marriage we have just taken to mediation. Saying, it is about more than just the relationship; it is about the kids – and their kids. The house, the car, the holidays, our social life. About our lifestyle. But still, at the core, we are having to mount an argument for what appears to be a soured relationship – and this is hard. All the emotional energy is with the other side, the side that chants for liberty, freedom, a fresh start. A free heart.

We are doing all this from a standing start. On the heels of a negotiation which, perhaps, fell short of being the whole new deal for Britain that was promised. Off the back of all those years that preceded, when we were always doing battle with Europe – pushing back against Franco–German hegemony, fighting our corner. We never rolled the pitch for Britain staying in Europe.

And everywhere you look, people are looking at their feet. Labour are nowhere to be seen. Business just wants it all to be over. There are lots of people who want us to win – but few who want to help us. Some think David should leave the campaigning to others too. That the Prime Minister should sit it out. Leaving who, exactly, to put the case for staying?

David is anxious that if he says he will leave in the event we lose the referendum, he might inadvertently encourage some people to vote for Leave in an attempt dislodge him. There is too much at stake to allow this referendum to become about him. So, he commits to stay on as prime minister, whatever happens. He has learnt this lesson from his experience with James Landale. On the whole, leaders should never say they are going to leave until the moment they do.

SOON IT IS TIME to unleash David on a series of TV shows. First, with Sky News – David is up first; Michael Gove follows the next day. Then it's ITV's turn. Finally, there is *Question Time* with Dimbleby – a full hour of Q & A with a live audience. Again, David is up first with Michael the day after.

The audiences in these studios are intelligent and focused. On both sides, many of them are angry and persistent. It is a true clash of cultures – a nation divided, battling for its future. And although we knew Europe was an emotive issue, perhaps no one had foreseen how intense and at times vitriolic the debate would become. Passions run high, sometimes boiling over on both sides. Friends are falling out. So are families.

Bill has sent over a page of thoughts for David. Try to engage emotionally. Keep talking about what is at stake, in a way that matters to people. We wait in the green room tucked away in the corner of a vast empty football stadium in Milton Keynes ahead of David's final appearance.

An hour is a long time to be the single focus of an entire audience's questions. David negotiates his way through the minefield. There is a moment in the middle where he feels he has lost his way. It comes during his response to a question on immigration. Afterwards, he goes over and over it. Despite our reassurances, he is still unhappy. David puts his finger in the air and senses the mood. Things are not coming together quite as they should.

We watch the huge gathering at Wembley – Ruth Davidson and Amber Rudd on our side against Boris and Labour's Gisela Stuart on the other. In footage of the spin room, we catch the sight of a familiar bald head bobbing up and down. It's Steve Hilton. Doesn't Steve live in California?

Steve's role in the campaign is a mystery. A few months ago, he had emailed David and me saying he will be back in England to launch the paperback of his book. We'd all gathered earlier in the year to wish him well with his hardback. Steve warns us that before he arrives he will state his position on Europe – but he doesn't intend to get drawn in to the campaign. David and I are well aware of Steve's views on Europe. His Hungarian heritage has given him an intense dislike of empires. Communists, the European Union – they are all the same to him. We thank Steve for giving us the heads-up. We had heard he had returned home to California. But not for long, it seems.

Steve must have had a good response, as he returns a few weeks later to continue campaigning for Leave. This time he emerges from the shadows, making a number of high-profile interventions. I wake up to a Steve-devised story in the *Today* programme headlines – a report from him that David was warned four years ago by officials that his immigration target was impossible. This is followed by another, saying that David is at heart a Leaver and went soft once in government.

A picture of Steve and Boris in Norwich in front of the Vote Leave bus symbolises another friendship strained by a sense of betrayal. In some ways, this seems even more personal: Steve, not being an elected politician, was under no pressure to throw himself into the campaign. Perhaps we had underestimated his anger as he left Downing Street, feeling that David should have done more to keep him there. Or maybe we had simply not understood that Steve, above all, wanted some limelight for himself. There is a moment in politics when some who serve grow tired of the back-room and want to be number one.

Coming into the end of the campaign, there is just one issue that is cutting through for Remain – it's the economy. And while we hone in on this, our one strength – protecting our country's wealth, people's jobs, and their standard of living – everyone accuses us of launching 'project fear'. When George sets out the measures we would need to take as part of an 'emergency budget' in the event of a Leave win, it is seen to be a step too far.

Leave hone in on their strengths too. They drive a bus around promising £350 million more a week for the NHS. When people question the validity of their figures, they launch an attack against 'experts'. Leave also talk about sovereignty and taking back control. They lean in to the growing unease around immigration – and the sense that London 'elites' aren't listening. They talk up the possi-bility of a future Turkish accession, claiming in an advert that 'Turkey (population 76 million) is joining the EU' – despite the fact that we have a veto on any future membership, and this particular membership isn't even on the horizon. They fight a brilliant, agile, ruthless campaign – playing on fear of immigration and making promises around a windfall for the NHS. We focus on how Britain would be poorer and less safe outside the EU.

This was project fear versus project fear. Only their campaign was scarier.

* * *

OVER THE PENULTIMATE WEEKEND before the vote, David decides he wants to go back to Angela Merkel on the immigration issue. He was right all along. We haven't got enough to win. Merkel needs to cut us some slack on freedom of movement, otherwise we're heading over the cliff. He talks to George over the weekend, and to Ed and me.

A call to Merkel is a high-risk strategy. It will certainly leak and it smells of panic. On the other hand, if we are really losing, surely it's worth a try? The polls are not giving us any clues. Craig gets wind of our musings and storms down the corridor. He is strongly against. Have faith. Stay calm. But David is not sure.

Ed is asked to set up a call with Chancellor Merkel on the pretence of official business of some sort. The call goes through. Minutes before, David decides, on balance, that it's too risky. He speaks to Merkel about something else. Had Merkel or her team given any indication that they would have responded positively he would certainly have taken the risk. But after years of interaction, he is sure she won't. She has let him down twice before. Once in forcing him to use the veto to protect British interests, then again on the selection of Juncker. This counts as the third time, in making it clear she would never give us an inch on immigration, even if we had asked one final time.

WE ARE NOW DOWN to the final week of the campaign, planning the last days and hours in all the detail we do for a general election. There is a huge operation to try to get all the former prime ministers to speak together outside No. 10 which never transpires.

Although the old Blair wing of the party are supportive, the Labour leadership is doing little to pull its weight. We are relying on Labour to get their vote out on the day, but we are not clear whether or not the party is really organising on the ground. The Labour members of the Remain campaign seem to have long lost control of the levers of their party machine – but are hopeful they will be pulled by someone else. They aren't. And the fact that they aren't is another important reason we lose.

Coming into the final PMQs, we hear rumours that Leave have organised a flotilla of 'Fishermen for Leave'. The sight of boats on the Thames outside Parliament is sure to draw huge interest. We need a counterstrategy, and fast – but what? I ring Daniel Korski, deputy head of the Policy Unit, who is one of our blue-sky thinkers at No. 10. He tells me he has a plan but he's not going to tell me what it is. 'Believe me,' he says, 'it's best you don't know.' This makes me nervous on so many levels.

It is late morning on Wednesday, 15 June. From our offices we hear a huge din. It seems to be emerging from the river. Our hearts sink. Without doubt it is the Leave flotilla in all its glory. Then up on our television screen pops the familiar face of Bob Geldof with what looks a lot like a counter-flotilla. Not since the Armada has there been so much political heat on British waters. But at least there is noise on both sides – to Daniel's credit. And smiling from the side of one rib are two young children who are about to lose their mother.

THERE IS NO PLACE in the United Kingdom more likely to gather a tumultuous patriotic crowd for Remain than on the peninsula of Gibraltar. And that is where David is heading on 16 June, going into the last week of the campaign.

Tensions are mounting. Farage launches his anti-migrant poster – 'Breaking Point' – showing a queue of so-called 'migrants' trying to enter the country. The people in the poster look a lot more like refugees fleeing their countries in a desperate state. They are mostly men and mostly not white. It is not nice politics. It's an image that the Gove 'outers' strongly disassociate themselves from – and rightly so. But their campaign has been built in part around an anti-immigration message.

Just when I think things can't get any uglier I am asked to get over to No. 10 as soon as I can. Simon Case has just had a call from the police. A Labour MP called Jo Cox has been stabbed outside her constituency surgery. She is on her way to hospital.

I have never heard of Jo Cox – but after a quick search on my phone I see a picture of an attractive, rather determined-looking young woman and feel glad that she is in politics. I say a prayer on the way over. I have also seen on her profile that she is a mum to two small children. She'll be OK, I am sure of it.

But looking at Simon, I am less certain. Less than an hour later, the heavies from the Cabinet Office appear – always a sure sign of bad news. And it is. Jo is dead. They don't want to say this out loud, for good reason. Barely anyone knows yet. And it stays that way for hours, as her husband makes the terrible journey to her constituency with their two small children to say their farewells. He posts a beautiful picture of Jo, smiling on her houseboat, with no comment – a silent and dignified tribute. The awful truth is that a young woman MP has been murdered in cold blood doing her duty.

Tom Watson is ringing in tears. The Labour Party seem to be collapsing in a heap. I have to get to the team who are with David on their way to Gibraltar. They're on the Queen's flight, and we have to call the cockpit before they land. We tell them to lower the shutters on landing and call in straightaway. 'Do not, on any account, leave the plane.'

The guard of honour is sent away and the rally cancelled. Campaigning is suspended until further notice.

When the team return, we gather in the den. Except for when Ivan died, I have never seen David so broken. It is such a tragedy. Such a waste. Such an ugly act. Many MPs, especially the female ones, are worried for their safety. And there is already the haunting question – was it politically motivated? We think of the children on the boat just two days before. It is dreadful to contemplate.

We are paralysed by the horror of it all but we also need to make some decisions around how best to honour her. We decide on a visit from David to pay his respects, but with the other party leaders. There must be no politics. Calls are made to Corbyn and to the Speaker. Calls will be made to the family – but only if they want to talk. Ed and I talk to the Chief Whip about how to coordinate Parliament.

The days pass in a flood of grief. Tributes are made in Parliament, with Jo's small children looking on. Commons is united in sorrow and praise for her. I sit in the box, listening to her colleagues on the Labour benches paying tribute to their lost friend.

'We are far more united and have far more in common with each other than things that divide us', Jo Cox said in her maiden speech. Yet here we are – a country at loggerheads, seemingly with no time for each other's views; no compassion for our neighbours' plight. Jo comes to symbolise a sense of the best of Britain. Our generosity of spirit and tolerance seems to have been forgotten somewhere in these weeks. We have become a nation divided, living under a shadow of loss and fear.

31

REFERENDUM

Referendum day is in sight, and the polling inconclusive. I go out to get a coffee with Ed. Crossing Horse Guards, all we can talk about is how it will land – avoiding mention of what will happen if it goes wrong. We both know the answer to that.

Tensions are rising. Sunday night – less than four days before the polls open – David sits in the garden of No. 10 with George, a glass of wine in hand, mulling over the options.

David is resolute: if we lose, he will go. There is no alternative. He has staked his premiership on one future for the country, given his 'heart and soul' to the argument to remain, which will have been rejected fair and square by the British people, it must fall to someone else to lead the country, to take it where he has said it is best not to go. To stay would be a bit like refusing to leave Downing Street after a general election. And even if he wanted to, he will have all the Brexit press and at least half of the parliamentary party campaigning to get rid of him. He will have no authority, no mandate to rule, and a tiny majority in Parliament. He will be witch-hunted out of No. 10 in months if not weeks. It will be game over.

'But what happens if we lose by a very (very) small margin?' I ask. Picture the country divided and destabilised, in need of strong leadership. Is there is a case for David to remain and steady the ship? Might he even have a duty to do so? We examine this option for a while, but are increasingly coming to the realisation that it's win or lose; stay or go. The grey area is in our imagination.

George, looking to history, is more sympathetic. There is no reason to think David can't or shouldn't continue he argues. In fact, he may well be criticised for throwing in the towel and leaving the country in a mess. After all, it was he who called the referendum in the first place. George thinks it could well be David's duty to stay – but only if it's close. We deliberate for hours, knowing in the end the decision will be made fast, and intuitively, in the moment.

On polling day, the weather takes a turn for the worse. It feels judgemental in its fury, this rain pouring down. Many commuters in the South miss their trains home. We are anxious it will keep them from voting.

The plan is to meet for a late dinner in No. 10 and watch the results come through. We gather round the television in the Thatcher study, the sword of Damocles hanging. On the ten o'clock news, pollsters are predicting defeat for Leave by 48 to 52. By 11 p.m., Nigel Farage seems to have conceded. The relief in the room is palpable. The pound rallies.

But we are wary. The results are not due in for another few hours. I can't take another one of these results nights, Samantha says to me. I agree. 'This will be our last one. David isn't going to stand again, remember.' We take the seats around the table we had made up for the G8. Nancy, who has insisted on staying up, is perched between David and me, George on the other side. We have set up the computer on the table, which breaks down the results we need to get, area by area.

Newcastle upon Tyne declares first – a win for us, but not a big one, making us slightly nervous. This is followed by a decisive victory for Leave in Sunderland (61 per cent to 39 per cent). More results start trickling through. Most just miss the mark for a Remain win. It is beginning to look like a trend. We remain positive though, hoping that the worm will turn when the results come through for the southern cities – especially London. Nancy is marking them off. 'Another bad result, Dad,' she says. And another. John Curtice says Brexit now looks the most likely result. Morale plummets.

'Dad, we're losing,' says Nancy. David is tense but maintaining total calm. Finally, defeated by exhaustion, Nancy slips in to her sleeping bag, which she has positioned under the table. But she can't sleep without her childhood cuddly toy, which is duly fetched from upstairs.

There is some good news from Wandsworth. But some more very bad. Sheffield has voted to leave by 51 per cent. We sit exhausted and shell-shocked, watching the results like a slow-motion car crash. Nothing is coming to stem the tide. There is an agonised hush in the room. We all know it is lost, that it has slipped from our hands, but no one wants to say it out loud – at least not just yet.

In the end, Leave win 52 to 48 per cent – seventeen million for to sixteen million against – with a turnout of 72 per cent.

Around three in the morning David suggests a small council of war. George, Ed, and I follow him down the stairs, past the pictures of past prime ministers, into his den.

'It's over,' says David. 'We've lost. I'll stand down first thing.'

We look at each other, knowing that this is the only course left. David's hopes of all he wanted to achieve in a second term – and the dignity of leaving on his own terms – are over. George's dreams of replacing him are over too – at least for now. And worst of all, our country has chosen a path that we feel certain will be full of hardship and pain.

We agree to meet in a few hours to go through his resignation speech.

Admiralty House seems far too far away for a short sleep, so I settle for the green sofa in the office just off the Cabinet room instead. I am too tired to compute everything. When I wake a few hours later, I am at first not sure where I am, or why. And then it all comes back. The referendum result. David's decision to resign. *This is the end game.* I am too disorientated to feel emotional, probably because I am in a state of shock from which I will not fully emerge for some time.

I check the time. It's just after six. The children won't be up yet.

I have a sinking feeling as I imagine their worried faces as they wake to the news. They have never known anything but a life with me working for David. I will ring them later. I have a quick shower and get dressed. I am on autopilot, trying to focus on the things that need to be done today rather than thinking of the future.

No. 10 is eerily silent. Stunned colleagues emerge and hug in the corridors, tiptoeing around 'the House' like they are at a funeral service. We meet in the den as agreed, to go through the speech we have been dodging for years, but finally is to have its day. Once the speech is signed off, David goes up to the flat to change. In the background, we hear the news bulletins on rotation: 'Britain votes to leave the EU'. It seems like we have woken up in a different world.

My phone shows a text. It's Samantha's team. She is planning to join David outside; Lino, her hairdresser, has been summoned. I go upstairs to check she is in one piece. Samantha is valiantly trying to keep it together. Lino wields his brush as a soldier sharpens his sword for the final battle, all the while sniffling into the hair-dryer. I give her a hug. 'Go out there, do Dave proud, as you always do,' I say.

Downstairs, Liz is issuing instructions – there's no question of us standing outside No. 11 for the statement, as is customary for arrivals and departures of prime ministers. This is not David's farewell. Instead, the team gather in our office, along with politicals from Nos. 10 and 11 and the private office. And Lino. We watch David stride out of the door, live on television.

'I am very proud and very honoured to have been Prime Minister of this country for six years . . . I have also always believed that we have to confront big decisions – not duck them . . . the British people have made a very clear decision to take a different path, and as such I think the country requires fresh leadership to take it in this direction.'

Now that I hear his words and see his face struggling with emotion – standing down from the job he always wanted, fought so hard to get for his party, was the honour of his life to do – the tears start trickling down my cheek. Minutes later he walks back inside to rapturous applause. He thanks us for being on this incredible journey with him – voice breaking towards the end – then walks into his office and shuts the door behind him.

'What happens now?' someone asks.

'We go for coffee,' I say, leading our stunned political team out the back gate, over the road, to the café by the lake in St James's Park, which I had discovered with my daughter. Together we sip our lattes and see in this morning which marks the beginning of the end of the Cameron era.

32

FALLOUT

We haven't left Downing Street yet. David is still prime minister until the Conservative Party has chosen their next leader.

Conservative leadership competitions are notoriously unpredictable things and it is difficult to see how this is going to be finished this side of the summer. So, a September date is eventually settled on, which gives David the summer at Downing Street, and a final G20, in China.

My time is now given to planning sessions for the final months of David's premiership. I see our team one by one to talk about what they want to do next and how I might help. Many are venturing into the unknown after years working in politics. I also find myself in the audience of a live soap opera: the Tory leadership competition. George takes soundings about his chances and is advised not to stand. It is difficult for him. He gave the campaign everything he had and sacrificed his immediate political future in doing so. It's like there has been a political tsunami, changing the landscape overnight. (Worse still is that, in the end, the party chooses to rally round a status quo candidate who supported Remain – which in other circumstances would likely have been him.)

Boris and Michael emerge after the referendum to thank their supporters and effectively launch their campaign for joint leadership of the party. They have a strong case, having successfully run and won a campaign for Britain to leave the EU – and toppled a prime minister in the process. And it makes perfect sense that the people who have campaigned so passionately for Brexit should be the ones who are tasked with making it work. There is real momentum round the duo. Michael, the political intellectual, and Boris, the popular showman. They seem a good fit.

Sarah Vine writes in her weekly *Daily Mail* column: 'given Michael's high-profile role in the Leave campaign, that means he – we – are now charged with implementing the instructions of seventeen million people. And that is an awesome responsibility.' She is certainly right. Leave do have a responsibility to the people who voted for them. But it is the use of the world 'we' which attracts most attention. 'We' meaning presumably herself and her husband, Michael Gove.

Amidst the pain of defeat, the personal disloyalty of a broken friendship weighs heavily in the flat upstairs. The idea of Michael running No. 10 alongside Boris disturbs. Having wielded the knife, and with the blood fresh on the carpet, the aforementioned 'we' now seem to be busy measuring up the curtains. However, the prospect of a Boris premiership is not straightforward either. We remain suspicious of his motives. To win the crown fighting for a cause he may not have entirely believed in seems the ultimate false victory.

Theresa May also throws her hat in the ring. Her bid is followed by others. Stephen Crabb stands on a joint ticket with Sajid Javid, championing 'blue-collar conservatism'. Andrea Leadsom for the three Bs – Brussels, banks, and babies. And there are the usual suspects, like Liam Fox, who can't resist a leadership competition.

Gavin Williamson bounces into the afternoon meeting and announces he is going to help Theresa. 'I'm doing this for David,' he says. We are all greatly supportive – especially David, who really wants Theresa to win. She certainly needs all the help she can get to rally the MPs round her. Though respectful, they have not greatly warmed to her over the years. Gavin is off. We wish him well.

Claire, one of the private secretaries, comes in to talk to me about the 'dog bowls'. This is light relief in all the pandemonium. We have been wracking our brains to think of a suitable present for David to give the Queen for her ninetieth birthday. Some suggest a brooch, but surely the Queen has a million brooches. It's got to be something different, and personal, and preferably made in David's constituency. Then it comes to me: Emma Bridgewater and her husband Matthew Rice live locally and could make a set of bespoke mugs. 'Brilliant,' says David. 'Only not mugs – dog bowls.'

Each bowl is personally designed for each of Her Majesty's four dogs – two corgis and two dorgis (Claire and I go online to check out what a dorgi actually is) – illustrated with scenes of Balmoral. We set them out on the table. Here is something to smile about.

I AM IN THE car with George on the way to the memorial of a close friend's father. It is a day before the list of candidates for the leadership closes. George says he is not sure that Michael won't decide at last minute to stand on his own. Michael's allies are egging him on. To be his own man. The certainty of the Boris–Gove axis seems to be crumbling.

The next morning, we do indeed hear that there may be another, last-minute entry. We settle into a morning of political voyeurism in David's study, television on. There are a few hours before nominations close. Then the news breaks: Michael *is* to stand on his own. Yelps from the den. Later that morning, Boris – who was due to formally launch his own leadership bid alongside his ally, Michael – stands alone, in front of an audience of press and supportive MPs, and announces he will pull out of the race.

Michael's support is whittled away and he falls out of the second ballot. Now the two politicians who won the campaign for Britain to leave the European Union have devoured each other in political acrimony, just at the time when they should have risen to the occasion to do their best for the seventeen million voters who put their trust in them.

It saddens me that Michael, whose political credibility was built up around intellect, loyalty, and decency, became an arch-assassin. It was a role that never suited him, and still doesn't. Nevertheless, it is part of history. His head was turned by petty political games. Not just blowing up a few good men, but himself in the process. At least for a while.

And now it is Theresa May versus Andrea Leadsom. A picture of Leadsom's supporters compared to those of Theresa May is telling. Andrea's supporters are for the most part hard-line Brexiters, many of whom consistently voted against us in government. It is a case of them rallying round the only Brexit candidate left standing, in opposition to May and the mainstream of the party.

On Wednesday David heads off to the palace, dog bowls in hand.

By Friday I feel a sense of calm for the first time in days. The leadership election is in its second phase; we have a summer ahead of us in Downing Street. For the first time since the referendum result, I feel I have time to reflect and make plans. Ed, whose heart is in foreign affairs, is again eyeing up a career in the Foreign Office. Everyone is relieved for the reprieve save David, who is dying to leave so he can rebuild in private. Before we head off for the weekend, he wants to meet so we can make a contingency plan – just in case there is not a full-blown leadership election. I don't think that's going to happen, but we discuss it anyway. It would take two days, three maximum, to get out. After PMQs would be best. Like Blair.

On Monday morning, I drive into work. I find my car place on the Mall is blocked. I make a quick call to security and get the go-ahead to park my car in the L-shaped road at the back of No. 10 instead. I am hoping for a peaceful start to the week. David is on a visit. George is in New York. After the morning meeting, the Chief Whip, Mark Harper, pulls me to one side. 'Be warned,' he says, 'things may move faster than you think.' I sense he is up to something.

A few hours later, Jeremy Heywood appears in an agitated state. He has heard Andrea Leadsom is about to withdraw from the leadership competition. I ask Gavin to come round as soon as he can. Another few texts and it looks like Jeremy is right. I call

David: 'Prepare yourself.' A few minutes later, Andrea announces her decision to stand down from the race. Theresa is declared leader of the Conservatives and Prime Minister in waiting. David offers a fulsome congratulations. He calls me from the car: 'Press the button on Plan B. I want to be out by Wednesday. After PMQs.'

Only weeks ago we had been imagining three more years in Downing Street. Then, after the referendum, we thought we had three months. Now we have three days. Ed and I call our team together in the Cabinet room. This is the fourth of this sort of meeting we have had in as many days. Everyone is in a state of shock. Colleagues are crying in their offices. I try to see everyone to discuss their plans for the future, and do what I can to help. Again. I feel particularly protective of some of the younger ones, many of whom came to work for David pretty much straight out of university. They have had a gilded beginning to their careers, from which it is likely to take some time to recover. I make a list of some whom our successors might want to consider keeping, which I pass to Gavin, who I hope will be the next Chief Whip. He is an excellent choice. We are delighted for him.

David wants to have dinner with Ed and me in the flat. Samantha is presenting her new clothing line to key sellers the next day. It is bad timing – or maybe not. It is good to be busy, and looking forward. Over a takeaway curry and a lot of wine, we talk about old times. Of all we have achieved together. The hard-fought battles. The people we fought them with. The fun and the disasters, the victories and regrets.

Tuesday is our last full day in Downing Street. At David's last Cabinet we want to keep things relatively short, for everyone's sakes. Theresa has asked to say a few words. I take my place behind David, as usual. He begins, thanking colleagues for all he has achieved with their support over the six years in government. Restoring our economic strength. Creating over two million more jobs. Reforming welfare and education. Keeping our promise to the poorest in the world. Allowing those who love each other to marry, whatever their sexuality. Trying, as always, to build a stronger society.

I look over at Theresa, sitting, slightly taller, in her usual place across the table from David. She is gracious and professional in her tribute. George then makes the tribute on behalf of the Cabinet, praising David's leadership – not just over the six years in government, but over eleven years as party leader. We end the meeting there. David is close to tears as it is.

After Cabinet, David offers to show Theresa around the flat. I find her in the Cabinet Room and congratulate her on her victory. I am genuinely pleased for her. A sensible, strong woman seems the perfect choice to replace David. She is all smiles, giddy as a schoolgirl – the first time I have really seen a glimmer of what the younger Theresa May might have been.

We meet in the den to sketch out the next twenty-four hours. There will be a last PMQs, followed by a statement, and then off to Buckingham Palace to take his leave of the Queen. We are working on scripts. We don't want to put a foot wrong. The officials are busy working on the transition.

Helen, who manages the house side of No. 10, comes into the private office to say goodbye. She is clutching the samples of the new curtains we have chosen for the Cabinet room – a daring dark emerald in place of the dull reproduction originally on offer. 'Can I have the official go ahead?' she asks. 'I can't,' I say. 'It's up to Theresa now.' But they don't want to have to start all over again with a new regime. So, I sign off the curtains. It is the last thing I clear at No. 10. I ask Helen to send me a picture when they are fitted, if indeed they ever will be. I do not plan to return any time soon to find out.

Late afternoon, David comes down with a few bottles of champagne to share with the private office. These are the best of the civil service, all good men and women who have served David well and know that, in a day, their duty will be to a new Prime Minister. It is tough.

The No. 10 and No. 11 political teams gather in the early evening on the terrace. Andy Parsons is there taking pictures. Isabel Spearman, Gabby, and I sneak outside for a selfie in front of the door, asking Gary Gibbon to wait two minutes before he broadcasts into the evening news.

That night we have planned a farewell dinner. It starts with the core team and grows. A few of David and Samantha's family. Some close friends. The Feldmans. A few MPs who have been with us right from the start: Hugo Swire, Greg Barker, Olive Dowden, Gavin Williamson. For once, the state dining room warms with the intensity of the moment. It falls first to George (again) to pay tribute to his friend and ally. And then Samantha and I decide it's time for the women to speak. She, first – of her pride in her husband. Then me, on behalf of the team – 'We would like to thank you for the privilege of the last six years' (for some) 'or eleven years' (for others).

We sit out on the terrace of No. 10 – glass of wine in hand, reminiscing until the early hours, looking out over the rose garden and beyond, to the parade ground, whose clock counts down the last hours of our time running the country.

Tomorrow it will be someone else's turn. But our friendship will remain.

WEDNESDAY, 13 JULY. I am up early, and too much on edge to mind my hangover and lack of sleep. We have a busy day ahead. Our first task is to prepare David for his final PMQs. As usual, we start with a meeting in the den, but there is little of the traditional prep at this gathering. This is David's farewell to the Commons, which must be delivered through a series of staccato answers.

I take my place in the box. David is at his best – funny, self-effacing, but serious too. ('I really do love Larry – I promise,' he says, holding up a picture of the mouser sitting on his lap.) Samantha and the children are watching from the gallery. He concludes: 'I will miss the roar of the crowd, I will miss the barbs from the opposition, but I will be willing you on.

'I was the future once.'

And as he gets up to leave, the Tory MPs stand and clap. Some of the Labour MPs follow suit.

I fear I will be crying all day at this rate.

Back in No. 10, we have a few hours until we have to leave. Liz has planned it all meticulously, as usual. David will make his final statement outside with his family at his side. Then off, to say farewell to the Queen.

I have spent so much time helping to coordinate everyone else's exit that I still have a lot to do to sort out my own. Pack my things. Write my thank-you letters, say my goodbyes to friends and colleagues, make a quick visit up to the flat to see Samantha and the children, who are hopping around in their smart outfits. I write a 'good luck letter' to my successors – Nick Timothy and Fi Cunningham. David writes his to Theresa.

When I am finished, I wander down the now rather empty corridor to find George. We all have gone through his options a thousand times. He does not feel ready to leave politics – for now. So, he has chosen to wait, to see what Theresa might offer him. I know one day he will serve his country again; he has so much to give. But I am not convinced they will reach out to him this time. We worry about leaving him to await his fate, upstairs in his flat, as the conquering army takes hold downstairs. But I feel sure that Mrs May is a decent woman who will behave well. She is a parson's daughter after all.

The time rushes by. I find myself in the den with David, Samantha, and Ed. Liz comes to the door. It's time. 'I need Ed and Kate to go ahead,' she says. While we have been talking, No. 10 has silently gathered to say goodbye in the traditional way. Ed and I find ourselves 'clapped out' as we are swept along the corridor by our colleagues – a dress rehearsal for the Camerons. It is the most touching, memorable goodbye of my life. I cannot think about it even now without a sense of humble pride and welling emotion.

We are directed to the No. 11 door where the rest of our team is waiting. And together we walk out to the street to listen to David's statement.

David wishes Theresa well. He wishes success for 'this great country that I love so very much'. He pays a personal tribute to Samantha and the family, and tells the assembled crowd that being Prime Minister has been 'the greatest honour of my life'. He pulls his family round him for a group hug. Nancy's chin is wobbling. Elwen looks determined. Flo relinquishes her hold on the railing in favour of playing to the crowd. Just before he gets in the car he turns to us all and waves. We wave back.

And that's it. David leaves for the Palace and we leave No. 10. The corridors are empty now. Our former colleagues return to their desks to prepare for a new Prime Minister. This is a place that I have loved like a second home, but it is now no longer our No. 10. Gabby and I find each other.

We walk down the stairs, along the corridor, past the cops, out the door. We get into my car – squeezed in between two huge removal trucks – and drive out the back gate of No. 10, into the rest of our lives.

AFTERWORD

CAFÉ LISBOA, 14 JULY 2016

It is a warm summer morning. My children and I set off for a short walk up the road.

David is waiting for us with Nancy, his eldest daughter, at a Portuguese café he is fond of. A few minutes later we are joined by George. We sit outside, sipping our coffees, the children eating *pastéis de nata* (the house speciality). Yesterday, George Osborne was Chancellor of the Exchequer, David Cameron was Prime Minister, and I was his deputy chief of staff. Today we are unemployed.

Just over a year ago, we were enjoying an unexpected victory with the prospect of five more years in power, and all the promise it offered. For David, that Holy Grail was in sight – a dignified exit at his time of choosing.

Instead, the referendum brought to a head a debate that has raged in the Conservative Party, and the country, for years – our relationship with Europe and vision for Britain's standing in the world. The idea that we could have contained an anger which was growing across the country and never renewed a mandate which was becoming increasingly tattered seems hopeful, at best.

But we have nevertheless failed. Failed in our mission to persuade the people of our country that a British future in Europe is the right path.

As we sip our coffees in the morning sun, we know we have paid the price for that failure, and yet the full impact of the defeat has not yet sunk in, either for us or for the nation. We are at a point halfway between immediate acceptance and the full realisation of what it all actually means. This is to come, day by day, as the ramifications cascade around us.

My children have been brought up with 'Project Cameron'. 'The good news,' I tell them, 'is you don't have to stand up for the government at school anymore.'

I need to think about what's next. I find myself wondering if my best days are behind me. But then the words spoken by Richard Chartres, the Bishop of London, at Thatcher's funeral come back to me: 'What, in the end, makes our lives seem valuable after the storm and stress has passed away and there is a great calm? . . . Have I found joy within myself, or am I still looking for it in externals outside myself?'

And I decide: my best days are not behind me; I shall not let them be. If they were, what a sad, shallow person that would make me. That is not to say I won't miss No. 10. But as I reflect further, I decide it's not the power that I will miss. It was a huge honour to be part of the team running the country. I had my time and now it is someone else's. Power for too long, in the same hands, is corrosive and detaching. There is a time to say your goodbyes and move on.

The people are a different story – I will miss them terribly. For eleven years, but especially for the six I spent in No. 10, other than the most important job of being a mum, my life and those of the people around me was devoted to one thing – supporting the Prime Minister in his endeavour to do his best for the country. That was it. No conflicted objectives. No internal politics. The solidarity of our purpose of this magnitude will be hard to replace.

Not all the friendships have lasted the course. I think back to the early days of Sunday night pizzas in the Camerons' house in west London, to the faces who looked at me across the kitchen table, and contemplate painful rifts that may never heal. This saddens me. Friendship and loyalty, political belief and personal ambition – they don't always go together in lockstep. You can say, it's just politics, silly. But politicians are humans too. They get their feelings hurt, just like anyone else.

THE BREXIT FOG CLOUDS the months and years after our departure. The sense of fury, division and blame engulfs the country. And, along with the chaos, weighs heavily on us all. I mull it over with a friend and former colleague over a drink. We call it mutual therapy.

'Let's admit it,' says my friend, a few drinks on, 'the referendum might well have been inevitable . . .' The question is, should *we* have dodged it? Left it to someone else to face the music?

But that wasn't the Cameron way. David didn't dodge. He tried to grapple and resolve. Yes, he could have left it to another leader, but he would have thought that dishonourable and poor leadership. He chose to tackle the issue and try to take the growing poison out of public life because he thought the British people deserved a choice, and that our best chance of winning was off the back of a clear victory at the ballot box, with a strong economy and the support of most of Parliament. He had a touching faith in the country he governed, and confidence in his ability to lead it in the direction he believed to be right.

But I certainly do not reproach people for their anger. We took the decision, and we cannot duck our part of the blame.

And there are things we could have done better, or differently. We should have made the case for Britain in Europe more strongly and for longer. Perhaps we should have recognised the difficulties of pivoting off the back of a negotiation straight into a campaign. We should not have set targets on immigration that we could never meet against the background of a weak Eurozone whose army of jobseekers were drawn to Britain's strong economy as an irresistible magnet. Perhaps we could have done more to encourage a grown-up debate about the good that immigration brings and the need to control it – since both can be true.

Perhaps we, and other leaders before us, should never have allowed the mandate to fray in the first place, by allowing the British people to have a say, like others did, on some of the EU's treaties. Had Britain said no to Lisbon, it might never had said no to Europe.

It remains my personal view that the result, which we fought so hard to avoid, set our country on the wrong track. That we will be poorer and less safe as a result. That we are wasting time and energy which could be spent addressing more pertinent problems. That this path will entail yet more sacrifice from the very people who deserve so much better.

At heart, I am an optimist and a patriot. I have no doubt that the divisions and hostility of this time will pass. That a future generation of leaders will emerge to do our amazing country proud. And that the Cameron government will be remembered for its huge achievements. Forming the first coalition since the Second World War, and coming together to bring our country back from the brink of economic disaster. Protecting future generations by bringing sound finance back to governance. Pioneering reforms in education and welfare. Championing equality with gay marriage. Standing by the world's poor. And most of all, presiding over a time of tolerance, decency, and discourse in public life.

For months after we leave Downing Street, I awaken most mornings with a sense of loss, as if after a bereavement. I work through my days feeling disorientated. But now, climbing slowly and sometimes painfully out of the ditch, I turn to other things. Step by step I am starting to pull a new life together.

With my new life comes a sense of liberty. I am master of my day; I can freely give voice to my own opinions. I am no longer subject to the will of every twist and turn and responsibility of government, or available to the Switch 24/7, one eye on the phone and half a mind on a story. Over time, I feel a renewed sense of balance in my life. Most importantly, I am now better able to focus on my two wonderful children. And on my new work. I have friends and family to see, and a book to write.

After the storm, life goes on.

ACKNOWLEDGEMENTS

I am fortunate to be supported by so many friends, some of whom have helped me with the writing of this book. I want to thank Niall Ferguson, Alice Thomson, Tom Bradby, Gabby Bertin, Simone Finn, Kate Rock, Hugh Powell, Anthony Seldon, Andrew Goodfellow, Camilla Cavendish, Jess Cunniffe and Ed Llewellyn. I am especially grateful to George Osborne whose support and advice has been so invaluable.

I want to thank David Cameron for his friendship over thirty years and for the privilege of working for him, and Samantha for her wonderful friendship and support.

To Andrew and Gabby Feldman, and Alan and Jane Parker who are always there for me and my family.

I count myself extremely lucky to have worked alongside some of the brightest and best people I have known in David's No. 10 and George's No. 11 – for the battles we won and lost and the lifelong friendships we formed.

I write in fond memory of two former colleagues and friends, Jeremy Heywood and Chris Martin, both outstanding public servants, both of whom we have so sadly lost to cancer.

For the Ant-shaped hole left by the loss of Anthony Gordon Lennox, who supported me throughout this decade of my life and who I miss so much. And to my beautiful goddaughter Allegra, who died so tragically two weeks after her sixteenth birthday in 2015, whose memory will never leave us.

I would also like to thank my sisters Mel and Meredith, who are always there for me, and especially to Mel, who won her battle with cancer during this time with quiet, determined dignity. And also my parents, who have done so much for me, most of all in giving us sisters one another.

To my children, who I could not be more proud of and who I adore – thank you for your endless support and for putting up with it all.

To my wonderful agent at AM Heath, Zoe King, who has made this all possible, and to my two amazing editors at HarperCollins, Kate Fox and Liz Marvin.

INDEX